The Memoirs of
Baron N. Wrangel

FROM SERFDOM TO BOLSHEVISM

The Memoirs
of Baron N. Wrangel
1847-1920

Translated by
BRIAN *and* BEATRIX LUNN

HASKELL HOUSE PUBLISHERS Ltd.
Publishers of Scarce Scholarly Books
NEW YORK, N. Y. 10012
1971

First Published 1927

HASKELL HOUSE PUBLISHERS Ltd.
Publishers of Scarce Scholarly Books
280 LAFAYETTE STREET
NEW YORK, N. Y. 10012

Library of Congress Catalog Card Number: 76-154043

Standard Book Number 8383-1262-4

Printed in the United States of America

Contents

From Serfdom to Bolshevism.

CHAPTER I

1847-1859

As I have never interested myself in questions of genealogy I do not know whether it be a fact that my name is, as the experts state, one of the oldest known to students of genealogy. It is certainly mentioned in 12th century documents.

One of my ancestors, the son of Count Charles Gustavus Wrangel, the Swedish Field Marshal who distinguished himself in the Thirty Years' War, took service under the Czar and settled permanently in Russia. And, as one of my female ancestors, who was the granddaughter of the Commander-in-Chief Hannibal, known as Peter the Great's Moor, and from whom the poet Pushkin was descended, was a member of the Greek Church, her descendants naturally also became members of the Orthodox Church. Since that time the Luhde Tournis Luhdenhoff branch of the Wrangels have regarded themselves as Russian, quite as Russian indeed as those arch-Russians, the Rurikovitch family who, like ourselves, are descended from a Russian who was no Russian at all.

My father, true to the family tradition, took up the profession of soldiering. He became Colonel of the Imperial Guards, and having been severely wounded in a

fight against the Turks, left the service, to retire to one of
his properties in the neighbourhood of St. Petersburg.

But as he was intelligent and exceptionally energetic,
the life of a simple country gentleman soon began to pall.
He built factories in the Ural, acquired gold mining
properties in Siberia, in fact tried his hand at most things.
Finally he was elected Marshal of the Nobility, an office
which at that time, when serfdom was still in force, was no
sinecure. As marshal he was a benevolent despot. According to his contemporaries, his kind acts were as numerous
as the beatings which he dealt out to those who were too
much inclined to take bribes.

To his children he was a comparative stranger, but we
were terrified of him. We only saw him at meals ; he
spent the rest of his time in his private rooms which none
of us dared to enter save at his command.

A masterful, violent nature, he either could not or
would not control his temper, and was an object of terror
to us and to his servants. However, he had a good heart.
But at the period when he lived, harshness had become a
moral principle. To shew benevolence was to be weak,
to be cruel was to be strong.

The Emperor Nicholas I ruled his country like a gamekeeper. Under his administration of the empire, based
as it was upon a system of flogging, imprisonment and
exile to Siberia, the great could indulge their caprices
with impunity, and my father, like most men, was cast
in the mould of his period. He carefully concealed his
feelings under a mask of harshness.

He was certainly brutal ; he was also compassionate in
his own way. He could feel pity only for physical ills, and
probably did not even suspect the existence of other

suffering. At this period children, the poor and the weak, and still more the serfs, were scarcely considered to possess a soul. This was the exclusive monopoly of the great, and of beautiful women—and of these only if they belonged to society. My father therefore saw to it that his children were surrounded with luxury, well fed and clad, that his employées were decently paid, and that his serfs were not in want. He was generous in alleviating such physical suffering as he came across, but remained indifferent to suffering that he did not understand.

One day my sister, who in spite of her youth took charge of the household after my mother's death, begged my father to allow one of his valets to marry a girl with whom she said he was desperately in love, instead of the girl who had been allotted to him. I shall never forget my father's outburst of prodigious mirth on hearing this. He nearly choked himself with laughing.

"The creature in love! How delicious—a valet suffering the darts of Cupid! Such a unique specimen must be allowed to marry his lady love. To complete the farce I'll have them taken to the altar in state in my carriage. Great souls must be treated according to their deserts."

On another occasion my father made a present of a woman who had belonged to my mother to one of our aunts. The woman's son, a lad of about ten, stayed with us. Some time afterwards my aunt asked my father to take his present back.

"Why, don't you want her any more?" he asked.

"The poor creature is wretched at being separated from her child."

"How dare she? . . . I've never really gone into

these things . . . it's quite possible after all that these people have a soul just like ourselves. Keep the woman —I'll give you her son."

It is difficult for people of to-day to visualise the horrors of serfdom. The serf was a chattel that could be dealt with by the owner just as he pleased. He was given away, separated from his children, beaten as much and as often as his master chose. The latter had the right to exile him to Siberia, to shut him up in a madhouse, and had, if not the legal right, at least the opportunity to cause his death with impunity under the whip. And not a few lords abused their power.

But the serf was not the only slave. In reality, if not in fact, the masters were also slaves. Every man, whoever he might be, was dependent on someone more powerful than himself who could with impunity make him wretched, and over him again there was someone still mightier. The lord, it is true, lived in comfort, and the serfs in squalor, but that was all. They were all slaves, one as much as the other.

One day, at a state banquet at which I was present, an aide-de-camp of the Emperor, with the rank of General, ordered one of the guests, a rich and independent man of fashion whom he had never seen before, to leave the table. An opinion expressed by this gentleman had unfortunately happened to displease his excellency, and the rich and independent man obeyed.

I was born, brought up, and I lived among those in power. But my wet-nurse was a slave. So was Niania,[1] who took the place of my mother. My playmates were serfs. I have seen both oppressors and oppressed at

[1] Niania, children's nurse.

close quarters, and I can aver that the inhuman régime of bondage corrupted and depraved one as much as the other.

I was only four years old when my mother died in Dresden. Judging by her portraits she must have been very beautiful, and according to those who knew her, she was goodness itself. I can only remember her vaguely. Small children generally retain certain details only—not the whole impression. Thus I can see myself seated on a lady's knee, who I now understand was my mother. She wore a blue dress trimmed with red, and her hair was in ringlets ; but I cannot see her face. We are bowling along in the park in a dog-cart—I would recognise the spot even now. A groom in doeskin breeches and top-boots gallops behind us. My father is driving, but I do not remember that—I have been told so.

On the other hand, my mother's last departure for the town in which she was to die, remains engraved on my memory to the last detail. Her " dormeuse "—so the carriages in which a bed could be put were called—harnessed with six horses, stops in front of the steps. My mother and my elder sisters get into it . . and we quickly race across the garden towards the road the carriage will take after having circled the park. Mama, seeing us, stops the carriage, and Niania holds us up in turn to the window. My mother weeps and strains us to her breast and then turning to my nurse says, " I entrust them to you," and sobbing she seizes the old slave's hand and covers it with kisses.

Later, there we are, big and little, governesses and servants, all of us clothed in black—just like crows !

B

That amuses us and makes us laugh. And we do not understand why the ladies who come to see us and bring us pretty toys say, " Poor little things."

We were a large family. There were four brothers, three sisters, two governesses (one French and the other German), my brother George's tutor, and Niania. Two aunts, my father's sisters, lived with us besides ; Aunt Ida, who was nicknamed Chipie, and Aunt Jeanne. The former, who looked like a badly stuffed giraffe, was intriguing, shrewish and spiteful. Everybody hated her, but she had my father's ear, and he was all attention as far as she was concerned.

Aunt Jeanne, on the other hand, was a kind soul, simple-minded and good-hearted. Brought up when the Emperor Paul was still alive, at the " Convent of Smolny for daughters of the nobility," she retained the traditions of that period. Through fear of being thought " shameless," she never spoke to young men, and would blush and cast down her eyes when replying to gentlemen of ripe years. She usually kept to her own apartments, and preferred playing with her pugs and listening to the song of her canaries to taking part in conversation in the drawing-room. The amount of sweets she was able to devour was unbelievable. Even to watch her was enough to give one indigestion.

Our great delight was to ask her the time. The answer was invariably the same. " Thank God, I have never been compelled to learn that. For such things I have my women." And she would ring for her maid.

" Tell me what time it is by this watch."

The house was run—as far as social matters and education were concerned—by my sister Vera, who was barely twenty ; while a majestic major-domo, who looked more like an ambassador of His Brittanic Majesty than a serf, was Minister of the Interior and Finances.

My father reigned, but did not govern. Like Jupiter, he only interfered in the affairs of mortals in moments of crisis. But when he did interfere it was no laughing matter, and everybody, from cellar to attic, trembled in his shoes. Niania alone was unimpressed by his thunderings. She too was an Olympian.

The delicious old creature ! Good, sweet, patient, she was the embodiment of devotion. She belonged to the classic type of nurses of whom our great poets have sung ; but she was something even nobler. Generally the manners of these good souls are servile. Our Niania, however, was hardly less than a lady. She had no knotted handkerchief on her head, such as was worn not only by the common people, but even by millionaire merchants' wives ; nor did she cross her arms on her breast as a mark of deference. She wore an attractive bonnet with silk ribbons, and her gestures were simple but dignified. She was shrivelled and wrinkled like a baked apple ; but her fine clear eyes and beautiful white hair made her seem young and fresh. In short, she was, or at any rate we thought her charming. And we worshipped her.

The family was divided into two clans, the elder and the younger.

The elder ones were proud, rich, all powerful, fearing none but Jupiter. They had fine rooms where they could run about and play without fear of colliding with the furniture ; they lived in style and despised us and punished us.

The youngsters were weak and oppressed, with only a little room as their domain; they were kept running errands and had sweets to eat only on the rare occasions when they were given a few.

They were teased and were accused of lying when they were not telling lies, but were only saying things which seemed true to them even if they may not have been, and they were unhappy.

They had none to defend them against the iniquity of their elders. Their mother was dead—and their father?— He was himself an object of fear. Niania, it is true, used to take their part. But what could she do? She would attack the enemy with spirit, but instead of giving battle the miscreants, who had all been brought up by her and all adored her as we did, would hug her, pull her about and make her waltz, and in the end she had to flee to get off with her life.

Besides, the clan of the little ones was so limited; the elders were so numerous. There were only four of us little ones—no, only three. My small sister, whom every-one called Bunny, Niania and I. My brother George had ceased to be one of us two months ago. He now had a private tutor, wore a coat, and treated us as a negligible quantity. He became a kind of cross between the elders and the juniors, a neutral, who, like all neutrals, tried to curry favour with the strong. The two clans carried on a constant warfare. The little ones sought to extend their territory; they were particularly anxious to get a close view of the manners and customs of their neighbours in order to introduce them at home, as Peter the Great had done. But more often it was the elders who were the aggressors. They would treat the youngsters as vassals and make fun of them ; then, of course, honour had to be satisfied.

In Town in the winter we used to live in a huge house— childhood has its own proportions for estimating size— not one room of which was comfortable in the true sense of the word.   There were suites of rooms, large and small, sumptuous but inhospitable.   Heavy, impressive, clumsy gilt furniture of West Indian wood stood along the walls. Sphinxes and chimeras supported tables whose marble surfaces were cold to the touch.   There were large porcelain vases of Imperial Chinese design, Empire bronzes depict- ing classic scenes, marble jars, mirrors reaching to the ceiling, crude canvasses poorly painted but in the grand manner, portraits of emperors and of ancestors.

Such was the room used by the elders, or to be exact by my sisters. My father, my brother Alexander who was in the diplomatic service, and George and his tutor were on the ground floor.   Michael, who was in the Horse Guards, lived in barracks.

We children had only one little room, looking out on a narrow yard whose only ornament was a huge rubbish pit.

I do not want to suggest that we were housed in this way through ill-will or hostility. By no means. It was quite the general custom to give the worst room to the children. Hygiene was still unknown, and such action had the disciplinary motive of inculcating habits of frugality at an early age. Besides in those days comfort was not a prime consideration ; there was a barrack room flavour about the whole household. Decorations were introduced to emphasize one's personal rank rather than to give pleasure.

Like everything else, our retreat had its points. It was separated only by a wall from the ballroom. And when there was dancing we heard the music and even the steps of the dancers. Later on, thanks to George's ingenuity, we could even see their legs, for my brother had managed to drill a hole in the wall.

We could thus have a dance of our own. Niania would bring us fruits, sweets, refreshments, and later on some supper from the buffet, and we used to dance until morning.

Michael used to tease us most, but we liked him best. God had made him to be worshipped, and everybody, especially women, adored him. My father himself was proud of him and gave in to all his whims. He was handsome and witty and led a gay life; but was a devil for work when he took a thing up, so that nothing seemed impossible to him. He always achieved his desires. And he had a really extraordinary talent for music. The famous Rubinstein said that he played " like a young god."

He naturally thought the universe had been created for his personal pleasure. When he was in the mood he used to play with us quite nicely ; but when he thought it funnier to tease us and make us cry he did not hesitate to do so. In fine, we were just like clever little dogs to him, whose reason for existence is to amuse their master. When he came home, if he did not find the elders in, he used to burst into our domain.

" Hullo kids !"

" Back again, you wretch," Niania used to say. " Are you going to bully the children again ?"

" Not at all, my dear Niania."

" I know you. But let me tell you, if you try it on I'll throw you out."

And then the fun would begin. Michael made us drill, and we marched past to the drum, presented arms, galloped across the Champ de Mars. Then he taught us songs, which were certainly very amusing but would scandalise the governess and get us punished—why, we shall never know. Then he would start pinching our cheeks, pulling our noses and in the end, without meaning any harm, he would make us furious and reduce us to tears.

One day Niania, who had gone away for a moment, came back to find us dancing and bawling like little devils. Michael had made us drink champagne and we were drunk.

On this occasion Niania did not confine herself to scolding. She turned Michael out and went to complain to my father.

I learnt by chance what happened. Bunny and I were lying under the sofa when my sister Vera came into the room. Niania told her what had happened.

" And you bothered father about such a trifle ?"

" Trifles indeed ! Nice trifles," scolded the old woman.

" What did father say ?"

" Oh your father ! Where his dear Michael is concerned what do you think he would say ?   He laughed."

" That was all ?"

" When I told him that kind of thing must be stopped, he interrupted me. ' Very well,' he said, ' Put your brats to bed and let them sleep it off.' "

But that was not the end of this memorable incident. Next day we came down to bid my father good morning.

In the ordinary way we used to find him at his writing table. Bunny used to drop him her most graceful curtsey, and I would make a respectful bow. Without stopping work he used to give us his hand to kiss. Another curtsey and we hurried back to our room, glad to get the business over.

That morning he did not hold out his hand, but looked at us with a terrible expression.

" You ruffians," he said. " You dare get drunk. I'll shew you. Niania, send for the birch. You shall be whipped."

" Your Michael and not they should be whipped."

" Shut up, you old fool, and do what I tell you."

Niania did not budge.

" Well ? I'm waiting . . . take care ! Are you going to obey me ?"

" I shall not obey you."

My father jumped. " How dare you ?"

" Their mother put them in my charge, I am responsible for them. Neither you nor anyone else shall touch them."

There was silence. And then a kindly smile passed over my father's face.

" Very well, you obstinate old mule ! Take the children for a walk."

And he stroked our hair and said, " Poor little devils."

When anyone fell sick we were immediately hurried off to my mother's uncle, General Mauderstierna, Commandant of the Fortress, the Russian bastille, to avoid infection. My great uncle, who was kindness itself, adored children and especially us. So the Fortress, the very name of which inspired terror, was a place of joy for us. The Commandant's big ship, manned by twenty-

four sailors, came to fetch us, and landed us at the foot
of the grim Fortress. We passed through the huge gate, a
kind of tunnel pierced in the thick walls, and we were
seized with a feeling of cold and terror. But inside the
walls there was nothing gloomy. Opposite the entrance
was the white church with its gilded spire which contained
the tombs of the Czars, and on the left lay the Commandant's house, surrounded by a huge garden. But this
green and smiling garden was enclosed, and one could
only catch glimpses of it through the little peepholes which
pierced the walls here and there. According to our
nurse, it was there that the *Décembristes* had been imprisoned.

" Tell us, Niania, what were these *Décembristes ?* Brigands ?"

" No, children, they were great lords . . . generals."

" And why were they put in prison ? Were they
wicked ?"

Niania smiled and did not answer.

My great-uncle's house was cheerful, roomy, full of
sunlight, and furnished just like any other house. But
thanks to the village gossips, everything about it seemed
mysterious to us. One room in particular interested us.
It was a vast, unused apartment, full of old plumed
helmets, cuirasses and big swords. Our great-uncle shewed
us the uniform which he wore at the battle of the Moskva
where his jawbone was shot away by a bullet. After
lunch great-uncle always locked up this room himself
and put the key in his pocket. Then he would open it
again an hour or two later, so that we could admire its
treasures at our leisure.

" Great-uncle, give me your key ! I want a helmet to play with, please . . . ?"

" Later on, my dear."

" But I want it now."

" You can't have it. I want it myself."

" But why ? Why do you shut up this room ?"

" Why, that's obvious . . . so that no one can get it."

" Why don't you want anyone to go in ?"

" Well, because . . . because . . . because Croquemi-taine goes in there for his siesta after lunch."

" It's not true ! It's not true ! There's no such person as Croquemitaine. He was invented to frighten little children, you told me so yourself."

Great-uncle would open his eyes.

" I told you that ? Oh, come now what an idea ! No such person as Croquemitaine ! But I have seen him with my own eyes."

" Where, where have you seen him ?"

" Why, here, only last week. But run and play, my boy. I want my siesta, too."

And he was gone. I went to consult Niania, and she told me that my great-uncle had said that to get rid of me. My continual questions got on his nerves. Bunny, who was very well informed in these matters, and who never spoke thoughtlessly, also assured me that Croque-mitaine was a myth. But my great-uncle, who never lied, had seen him. Therefore he existed.

It was a cruel puzzle ! Come what may, I had to solve it. I cross-questioned my great-uncle in a truly magisterial manner.

" Perhaps it was someone else, not Croquemitaine, who went to sleep in this room ?"

" No, it was really he. He can't be mistaken."

" How did you know him ?"

" By everything about him ; his appearance, his age."

" Is he old then ?"

" Very old."

" Older than you ?"

" I should think so. I'm not so very old."

" Much older ?"

" Oh, yes. Besides, he has quite a different face."

" What is his face like ?"

" Dreadful, you have only to look at him to know that it can't be anybody else."

" How can he be seen ?"

" Ah, that's a difficult question."

" Can you go near him ?"

" It's very dangerous. Invariably . . . but anyway, I believe it's impossible."

" But how did you manage it ?"

This was a ticklish question, but the witness did not falter.

" How did I manage it ? What a strange question ! But that's quite easy !"

" If it's easy, tell me."

" I looked through the keyhole."

" You . . . you looked through the keyhole ! Is it all right to do that ?"

" All right ? No, you must never do it."

" But then why did you do it ? A grown-up man . . . aren't you ashamed of yourself ?"

" Now listen. When it's not done out of curiosity, but for a scientific end . . . do you see . . . it's a different matter."

But I was no longer listening. I had made up my mind.

And I spent my whole time with my eye to the keyhole. But there was nothing to be seen, and I made a heroic resolve.

One day the moment lunch was finished I tiptoed into the mysterious room and hid myself under an old sofa.

But I gradually became seized with panic. These ogres had such a sharp sense of smell! And the fate which awaited me made me shiver. I would have fled, but the key turned in the lock. I was a prisoner. And I lay quiet, more dead than alive, praying to God not to let the ogre devour me.

But nobody came. Heaven had evidently heard my prayer, and had stopped Croquemitaine from coming for his siesta. I came out of my hiding-place and went over to the window.

It looked out on a tiny garden, enclosed like my great-uncle's and probably only separated from it by a dividing wall. There were a few trees, a bed of dahlias and a wooden seat. A big yellow cat with black markings was stalking a sparrow which was hopping about on the gravel. Would he catch it ? Wouldn't he ? And suddenly a little door opened. . . I nearly fell backwards. Croquemitaine appeared in the garden.

It was really he ; it was impossible to mistake him. He was much older than any man—quite, quite old, all warped and bent with age. Leaning on a stick, he moved along very slowly, his head shaking so much that it seemed about to fall off his neck, his eyes appearing to see nothing. He lowered himself on to the seat, placed his skeleton-like hands with their long emaciated fingers on his knees, and sat there motionless with his eyes lost in space.

I was not frightened. Croquemitaine was so unhappy and wretched that I began to cry out of pity.

Many years afterwards I learned who the poor old man was. Just before the Empress Catherine's death, quite a young man whose name nobody knew was imprisoned in the Fortress. The letter authorising his imprisonment simply stated that " the unknown " was to remain a prisoner during Her Majesty's pleasure. He was treated with consideration and lacked for nothing. The expense of his maintenance was defrayed from the Emperor's private purse. Three reigns, and more than sixty years had gone by since then. Great-uncle had repeatedly spoken of the wretched man to the Emperor, but the answer was always the same. " There is no use talking about it. It is impossible."

At Easter and at Christmas we were taken to the " balaganes," a people's fête in the Admiralty square. On this particular day my father would, according to the local custom, take the place of the footman beside the coachman.

These " balaganes," survivals from the time of Peter the Great, are like many other things, forgotten now. The traditions of the past are not kept up in Russia.

There were tents, wooden booths, menageries, acrobats, harlequins, colombines, pierrots, giants with fur shakos ; and moujiks with red noses and false beards down to their knees and bottles of vodka in their hands, shouting ribaldries which made the men guffaw and the girls blush. The acrobats climbed to enormous heights, the merry-go-rounds whirled, the music played and a huge crowd shouted and sang, making an infernal din. Cossacks with whips (nagaïka) in their hands, kept order.

An endless procession of carriages moved round the outer ring. Streams of court carriages with four horses preceded by lancers and followed by grooms on horseback in scarlet and gold liveries and three cornered hats, would carry girls from the schools for "daughters of the nobility." Then came the gentlemen's carriages drawn by thorough-bred horses, and vehicles from the remotest corners of the provinces, with horses to match. Other carriages moved round in an outer circle at a slow pace. There was the grand-duchess Hélène with her high stepping horses, the other grand-duchesses, and the Emperor's son. And suddenly a cheer rends the air. A little " droshky " drawn by a superb dappled grey horse of the famous Orlov breed passes at a smart trot. It is the Emperor ! Tall, majestic, he is as handsome as Apollo and holds himself as stiff as a Prussian corporal.

On Palm Sunday we went with Niania to the fair of the same name which is held in front of the " Gostinny Dvor."

All sorts of toys and trifles were sold here : wooden horses that looked like an unknown breed of poodle, whistles that didn't whistle, tambourines that burst if they were played on.

The novelties of the day were rabbits whose heads wagged, Turks with gold turbans made of ginger bread, and little demons in bottles, who would caper when you pressed the button. True, these toys were dreadfully expensive. For instance, for two kopeks, about the equivalent of a farthing, you could only buy three Turks. But we were rich and did not mind, and we had to have them at all costs.

We would mix with the crowd at the risk of being crushed ; Niania elbowing her way through, cajoling and threatening, and we would finally emerge quite happily, bearing our trophies.

But alas, happiness does not last. Our elders were delighted with our purchases, and would set the rabbits' heads going and make the demons dance, and then crack ! and they wouldn't work any more. Michael, affirming that as a soldier he was bound to exterminate all infidels, would break off the Turk's head and eat it.

We would bellow and our elders would call us cry-babies and send us back to our room.

Thus ended all our pleasures.

Occasionally we were taken to children's balls. I loathed these balls, but there it was. It was necessary from the earliest age to become accustomed to society and good manners.

Our necks were washed till the skin nearly came off, our nails were manicured, the hairdresser came to curl our hair, we were scented, and lemon-coloured gloves were bought for us.

" Now," says Niania, " stay quiet a moment. I am going to fetch the new suit and shoes which your sister Vera has ordered for you."

She comes back furious. My sister has forgotten to give the order. What is to be done ? My old party suit has got too short for me, and the shoes are in a deplorable state. A consultation is held with the grown-ups. Aunt Chipie decides that " it's all a fuss about nothing." And in spite of my protests, off we go.

At the ball I try to hide my feet for fear of shewing my

shoes. The little girls say nothing, but the boys point at them in a teasing way.

" You *have* got smart shoes on," says one of them. " Did they come from Paris ?"

Aunt Marie, who is very fond of me, is distressed to see me rigged out like this.

" But my dear," she says to my sister, " just look at your brother."

My sister blushes.

" Aunt, it was I who gave orders that he should be dressed in that awful suit. That child is simply eaten up with vanity. He must learn not to think so much of trifles."

" You are always right," says Aunt Marie.

That infuriates me. She tells a lie and she is told that she is right. We return home, and I pass the night in tears.

The injustice of humanity revolts me. We are punished when we have not lied, and the real liars are believed. These grown-ups are all horrid. There are only three fair people in the world, Niania, Bunny and I.

I was only eight years old when the Crimean War broke out. But certain details with reference to this period are engraved on my memory.

Our grand-parents (I do not speak only of my own) spoke, thought, and wrote nothing but French. Their whole culture came from France, and besides, the mental outlook of the Russians and the French is similar. Neither of them have the ability to concentrate on details, like the Germans, but they tend rather to seek a broad grasp of the whole. Their horizon is wider than that of other nations. It is their good quality and perhaps also their failing. Consequently the upper classes looked upon France as their second country.

The Emperor Nicholas I, who was very German, both in intelligence and sympathy, looking on France as the source of the liberal ideas of which he was the sworn enemy, had done everything to alienate the sympathies of his subjects from this " degenerate and noxious " people. He had failed in this object. But as the Czar had drilled his people to take their cue from him, one was careful not to express one's own opinions. Besides. it was rather annoying to see the France whom we loved so well marching against us. Our pride was wounded.

The war was spoken of as a piece of foolishness on the part of a friend, as a temporary aberration from which he would presently recover. It was madness for them to set themselves up against us, who were invincible. And we sneered at the fickleness of the French, without really believing in it. The theatre of war was so remote from the capital that it was hard to realise that the war was in progress. At the same time one made bandages to show one's patriotism ; the women wore brooches in the shape of little gold bayonets and the men wore overcoats that had a military cut.

Lint bandages were made everywhere. It became a positive rage, and people met together for it, as we do nowadays for bridge. Even the children were admitted to the drawing-room to swell the number of available hands, and while we worked, one of the party read the war bulletins. As a rule they did not vary. " The losses amongst the allies have been immense. We have only had two men wounded and one killed."

c

" And anyway," said Michael, " that's the same one
that was killed yesterday."

We no longer saw anything of my father. He was
overwhelmed with work. The nobility were raising regiments of " opoltchentsi," a kind of militia, at their own
expense. Each landed proprietor gave a certain number of
serfs and equipped them out of his own pocket. The
equipment was the serious business. There was nothing
much in sacrificing a few men, for a serf only cost about a
hundred roubles. But what ought one to give them in the
way of clothes ? The Emperor was very particular about
that. He insisted that the strength of an army lay entirely
in the drilling of the troops, and in the cut and colour of
their uniform. Anything else was of secondary importance. It was not for nothing that the Grand-Duke Con-
stantine, the Emperor's brother, declared that war was
detrimental to the troops, as it got them out of the habit
of doing manœuvres properly.

Eventually, after much delay and argument, uniforms
were found. The tunic and trousers were grey with a red
stripe, and the helmets of the same colour bore a cross
with the inscription : " For God, the Czar and our
Country."

My father, glad to have finished with the business,
ordered me a copy of this uniform. And thus attired, very
proud to be a militiaman too, I went with my nurse to
swagger in the Summer Garden, where all the people of
fashion walked.

The ground had become soaked by the thaw, and as
was usual in spring, a narrow pathway of planks had been
laid down along the roads, and at a turning of one of the
paths, we saw the Emperor, tall and majestic, wearing an

ordinary soldier's cloak, coming towards us. We hastily got off the footpath to give him room, and I stood at attention, having been well drilled by Michael.

The Emperor, seeing the trooper's uniform, stopped.

" A militiaman ?"

" Quite right, your Imperial Majesty."

In accordance with an army order, a soldier's answer had to resound like a thunder clap, so I puffed for all I was worth.

" Don't puff like that, little frog, you'll burst," said the Emperor.

" Glad to do so in your Imperial Majesty's service."

The Emperor seemed to smile. He was said to be fond of children, though that did not prevent their being beaten to a jelly in the schools.

" Whose son are you ? "

I told him my father's name.

" I know him well. Give him my regards."

" Glad to do so in the service of your Imperial Majesty."

" Tell him he's to make a good soldier of you. Give you a good taste of the stick. Smack, smack. That does little rascals good."

" Quite so, Your Imperial Majesty."

The Emperor went on his way. Even in jest, Nicholas I remained true to his principles of administration.

A little while afterwards the Emperor died. It was rumoured that he foresaw the catastrophe of the Crimea and, unwilling to survive such a blow to his prestige, poisoned himself.

My uncle took me to the Fortress church where his body lay in state so that I might kneel before his mortal remains. Although the public was not admitted at that time, sentries, generals, aides-de-camp and chamberlains, as rigid as statues, watched over the corpse. The Emperor's face was almost black. It was the first dead body I had seen, and for a long time I thought that the faces of the dead were all like that.

The death of Nicholas I was the salvation of Russia, but everyone pretended to be broken-hearted. Yet one day I heard a gentleman say that on the whole his death. .

" Hush !" said one of my uncles, horrified. " Take care ! If you are heard, it's all up with you."

Thirty years afterwards, when I was talking to the Grand-Duke Nicholas, the Grand-Duke Michael' son, and a well-known historian, I recalled this incident.

" It's hardly surprising," said the Grand-Duke. " The Emperor had succeeded in so terrifying his subjects that even now, after an interval of three reigns, my father (his son) trembles at the thought of incurring his displeasure."

We spent the summer in the country, at our beloved Terpilitzy, which was a veritable earthly paradise for us little ones. Everything was delightful there, and our room not the least so. The sun poured into it, and the windows were almost overgorwn with lilac. We were allowed to play and run about wherever we liked ; and the whole house, with the exception of my father's rooms, was at our disposal. It was not in the least like our town house, for everything there was for comfort rather than for show. And how charming my mother's apartments were, which were kept as they were when she lived in them. There were sofas covered with flowered silk, little stands surmounted with bronze sculptures, tables that one almost longed to stroke, innumerable queer little odds and ends to please the eye, and masses of flowers. Among the pictures were miniatures, and the portraits of my grandparents. He was bronzed, almost brown, and wore 18th century dress—a white coat with the *cordon* of the Order of St. Vladimir ; she had powdered hair and wore the slightly simpering smile of the ladies of that period. Another canvas depicted our whole family, including Niania. I was the only one absent, for it had been painted before I was born. It was a very quaint portrait. My father and brothers, almost suffocated by their neckties, and with their arms encased in sleeves too tight for them, looked more like comic puppets than real human beings.

There was nothing alarming even in my father's study. It contained engravings, and etchings by one of our serfs, our great friend Black Peter. This was an exceptionally gifted youth of about twenty, who combined the functions of servant and artist. He drew without having ever been taught, spoke French and German, was an excellent actor and a perfect shot—in short, he possessed all the accomplishments, but could neither read nor write. And this was only because he had not thought it worth while to learn. He continued to live with us after the emancipation of the serfs, although in what capacity it would have been hard to say. He had no job and did just what he liked. He was one of those useless people whom one cannot do without.

Those were indeed happy times ! We harnessed or saddled our ponies, which were our very own, without asking leave of the grown-ups, and galloped in the park. We embarked on great voyages of exploration with the village children—we were the explorers and they were the native porters. The remote parts of the park, where ancient trees grew, were inhabited by Red Indians and cannibals, and herds of lions and elephants. These countries were only known by hearsay, for no European had ever ventured into them.

And it was we, and not the grown-ups, who followed the example of Christopher Columbus !

At other times we would go mushroom-gathering in the real forest in great parties which included the grown-ups, neighbours, and keepers armed with guns in case of encountering bears or wolves. Then there was haymaking ! We were sometimes allowed to bring in the hay, and we were hoisted up on the cart and given the reins to hold. Really and truly ! The driver walked by the horse's head, but it was we who drove.

We had garden plots of our own, and we grew vegetables there on a large scale, in the American method. But ill-luck dogged our efforts—nothing would ever come up. The only thing that disappointed us was that George would not have anything to do with us, and even that did not worry us very much—" all the worse for him." It is true that he had plenty to do. He spent his whole time from morning till night training a Newfoundland to become a sporting dog, and trying to fit a wooden trigger to his gun in place of the one which was missing.

What excitement there was when the performing bears arrived ! The whole village, old and young, would turn out to see the fun. The programme was always the same, but the spectators not difficult to please.

One of the bear-leaders put his head into a sack decorated with two horns—he was supposed to be a goat and capered round the bear, making facetious remarks, and so the entertainment would begin. The bear would

shew how the village children steal peas from their neighbours' gardens, how the women go to work in the fields,
and how they go to the fair. He would shew them kicking
and limping and pretending to be ill when they were
going to work, but they would hurry along to the fair,
strutting and swinging their hips, making the most of
their charms.

Then came scenes from private life. The bear would
shew the young women making themselves pretty, their
flirtations with the men, how they danced, how they
quarrelled with their husbands ; and the show would end
up with a fight with the goat. That was all. The gentry
would give the bear-leaders a few roubles, and bread and
milk would be brought for the bear, and then—goodbye !

Another sight, but this time a sad one, was the departure
of the recruits.

The landowner was bound to provide a certain number
of men, the choice of which rested entirely with him. The
period of service was twenty-five years, and the military
system was terrible. More was demanded of a man than
he could possibly do. They were beaten and treated like
dogs, and many died under the lash. The method was to
kill three if necessary, in order to train one man.

The people themselves looked on the conscript as a man
condemned to death, and on his departure as the equivalent of a funeral. As soon as the choice was made, the man
chosen by his master was immediately handcuffed, imprisoned and guarded to prevent his committing suicide.
The whole village gathered about his prison, and he would
be given spirits to console him.

" The drunken man," says a proverb, " forgets his
misfortune." And the conscripts, maddened with drink,

would sing, shriek, and weep in the most heartbreaking way. Wives, mothers and children would do likewise. It was terrible. But such is the human heart that all sights, and particularly the visible suffering of others, will draw the crowd. Old and young would run to see.

We, poor innocents, were unable to understand the dramas which we witnessed, until much later. Children are more impressionable than thoughtful, and it is beyond their understanding to grasp the real meaning of things.

At the same time I often wonder how it is that we small children did understand many things which escaped our elders, whose intelligence was, nevertheless, riper than our own. Perhaps it was simply that they were hardened to them.

Sometimes our precocity got us into trouble.

One day we were sitting quietly on the terrace listening to the reading aloud of *Uncle Tom's Cabin*, a book which was then in fashion. My sisters could not get over the horrors of slavery, and wept tears at the sad fate of poor Uncle Tom.

" I cannot conceive," said one of them, " how such atrocities can be tolerated. Slavery is horrible."

" But," said Bunny in her shrill little voice, " we have slaves too."

" What nonsense ! Where did you get such an idea ?"

" But they are flogged just like Uncle Tom," I put in.

" Hold your tongue. You children are stupid. Where have you ever seen any slaves ?"

" Jean and Alexis were bought."

" That's quite different," said my sister. " Father bought them because they were unhappy with their master."

" But at any rate their master sold them."

" He was poor and had to do so."

" Pardon me," said the governess. " Let me endeavour to explain to them the difference between serfs and slaves ; they are obviously confusing the two. Slaves, my dear children, are poor negroes torn from their native country and from their families, and so you can understand that they are naturally very wretched. Serfs are people of the same religion and race as their masters, living in their own country and among their own people, only they are attached to the soil. Do you understand now ?"

" But they are sold and beaten. Why, only yesterday a coachman was flogged."

·" In any case, that's no concern of yours," said Chipie. " And besides, if the steward punished him, he probably deserved it."

" It wasn't the steward, it was father."

" What, you dare to criticize your father ! We shall see about that." And she rose. " I shall tell him of this and then. . ."

" Oh, come, Aunt Chipie," intervened my eldest sister. " We musn't bother Papa."

" But these children are so disrespectful."

" It is true," said my sister, " that they poke their noses into everything. Leave the room at once ! If you can't understand what is read to you, there's no use in your staying here."

" But. . . ."

" But me no buts ! Do what you're told !"

And we never heard any more of the story which interested us so much.

How unjust these grown-ups are ! Oh no ! We had no slaves as in America—only serfs attached to the soil ! We could have made plenty of answers to that, which the grown-ups were quite as well aware of as ourselves, but they did not want to hear them.

One of our neighbours was Count Visapur, the last of his name. His grandfather, either an Indian or an Afghan —I am not sure which—had come to St. Petersburg in the reign of Catherine II to pay homage to his Empress. He died there and his son, the father of the man of whom I am speaking, was brought up in the cadet corps. The Empress pensioned him, and her son Paul conferred on him the title of Count. This gentleman, whom I had often seen at neighbours' houses, did not visit us, as my father would not receive him. He was a hideously ugly man getting on in years, but very elegant and polite, and always dressed in a blue frock coat with gold buttons, and white trousers.

One day after his death we went to see his estate, which my father was thinking of buying. Instead of one big house he had six or seven fairly roomy small ones, each built in a different style. According to his steward, each had contained a harem of women recruited from the wives and daughters of his serfs. They were all dressed to match their surroundings—in Chinese costume in the Chinese house, in Spanish dress in another house, and so on. The Count lived first in one house, then in another.

These houses were surrounded by a beautiful garden containing flower beds, canals with gondolas floating on them, artificial pools and statues. However the statues were no longer there and only their pedestals were to be seen. The Count's old steward explained their absence by telling us that they were working in the fields. In the dead proprietor's time the statues were living men and women, stripped naked and painted white. They had to stay motionless in their poses for hours at a time, when the Count was sailing in his gondola or walking in the garden. He even showed us the torture house—a torture chamber would not have been enough. It contained everything— whips, the boot—I cannot remember them all now. Being neither an executioner nor a victim, the names of these things do not interest me.

The Count's death was quite as fantastic as his mode of life. One day when he was strolling past a group representing Hercules and Venus, the two statues jumped down from their pedestal ; Venus threw sand in his eyes, and Hercules broke his neck with his club.

They were tried and condemned to the knout. Venus died under it and Hercules was sent to Siberia.

Another of our neighbours, a M. Rontzoff, Count Vorontzoff's natural son (in the 18th century the father gave his bastards his own name with the first syllable omitted) was also reputed to be cruel to his people. My father had many grounds of complaint against him, but as he had no actual evidences of illegal abuses, he could do nothing in his capacity as marshal. But my father never stopped at his house, which he had to pass on his way to the town.

One day as we were passing through his village, one of our axles broke. M. Rontzoff hurried to us as soon as he heard of the accident, and we were his guests for some hours. We at once noticed the way in which the servants walked about on the balls of their feet, and my father made surreptitious enquiries about it. He learned that to prevent his serfs from running away, as many had already done, M. Rontzoff had had the soles of their feet burned and horsehair inserted in them.

M. Rontzoff was put under surveillance.

It is certainly true that these two landowners were exceptional and worse than the majority. By way of contrast I must mention an odd character who was considered to be very humane. He was a freethinker, the encyclopædia was his bible, and Voltaire was his god. He chose his epitaph during his own lifetime : " God, if there is one, take my soul, if there is one."

He was a good man, well-informed but fussy and pedantic. He insisted on efficient service, and was very exacting in this respect. On principle he was against corporal punishment. His theory was to work on the feelings of the culprits, without wounding their dignity. For instance, if there was too much salt in the soup he would send for the cook and make him swallow the entire contents of the soup-tureen, which had been intended for twenty guests. The place was full of servants going about with a red tongue labelled " liar " stuck to their jaws, or wearing donkeys' ears. His valet, a grandfather aged eighty, for months had to wear a cap inscribed " lazy and stupid." The poor old man became ill with chagrin.

It was in the country that we drew up our political programme, which was as follows :

Article I. When we are grown-up we shall be famous like Napoleon, or the man who discovered steam.

Article II. All our serfs will be emancipated, and we shall never treat them, or our children, unjustly.

Article III. We shall keep lots of horses and dogs.

Article IV. I shall have a double-barrelled gun like Alexander.

Bunny would have liked to modify the programme, but she did not insist upon it. Instead of being celebrated, she would rather have had twins, a boy and a girl. If that was not feasible, she would have been satisfied with a nice little monkey, or a very tiny little white elephant. He musn't be too big as she wanted him to live in our room and not in the stable. In the interests of truth I ought to add that our programme was never realised. Like all the programmes of political parties in Russia, it was impracticable. Practice and theory are not the same thing.

The year 1859 was disastrous for me, and even now, after sixty-five years, I remember it with sorrow. It is quite wrong to think that children cannot suffer like grown men, except in the way of physical pain. It began with my separation from Bunny, whom I loved better than myself. She passed out of Niania's care and was handed over to governesses. Niania, to whom I was also devoted, moved down to the ground floor and I was left alone. My father had decided to send me to the *Lycée Impérial* as a boarder, and I had to work for the spring examinations.

Up to this time my education had been completely neglected. I knew nothing—or practically nothing. Anything I did know was by the grace of God. I could read and write fairly well in French, not too badly in German, but certainly anything but well in Russian. I had devoured all the French books in our library, which no one ever used, and had a vague idea of French history, culled from the works of Alexandre Dumas, Sir Walter Scott,

Voltaire and other historians of that type. Niania was entrusted with my religious instruction, and as she did not even know how to read, her ideas on theology were hardly those of the Church Fathers. She thought God was just like the Czar, except that one lived in heaven and the other on earth. He was the most powerful of all beings and inclined to be stern rather than merciful. At any rate she always spoke of his severity and never of his goodness.

" He'll teach you to behave yourself ! He doesn't forgive people ! He is pitiless when He is offended !"

She would shrug her shoulders when she heard anyone invoking the help of God,

" Take my word for it, my dear, He won't listen to you. Rely on yourself instead of on God, and you're not so likely to be disappointed."

But she believed firmly in divine justice.

" I am going to light a candle to God," said some old woman to her.

" You ought to be ashamed of yourself. Do you think that God is like the *tchinovniks* (state servants) to be bribed with a bottle of wine ? It's no use trying to grease His palm."

The saints were of negligible importance in her eyes.

" Oh, they don't amount to much. I suppose you think that the moment God deigns to speak to them, they have the power to help you ? Rubbish ! You can give up any idea of such a thing. After all, the baron speaks to his servants, but does that make them powerful ?"

And that was the entire extent of my scientific stock-in-trade.

But my unhappiness was derived from other causes. I remained in sole possession of our room after Bunny and

Niania had departed, and as I now had more space than
I needed, according to Chipie, she moved in all her trunks
and boxes. In the end there was no table at which I could
work. I appealed to the house-steward to give me one.
He said that there was not one to spare, and that he could
not buy one without reference to my father.

"A writing table?" said my father. "What nonsense.
Any table will do for him to write at. That's quite good
enough for what he's got to do."

And that was the end of that. But where was I to work?
It was easy enough when my tutors were there. My eldest
brother worked at the Foreign Office for part of the day,
and I would take them to his room.

But where could I do my preparation? I installed
myself in the dining-room with my books and papers.

"It's time to lay the table, sir," said the butler.
"Would you mind clearing it?"

"But I've got to work."

"You can work in your room."

"I haven't got a table."

"I'm very sorry, but I can't help that"

I went on writing.

"I shall have to go to your father, sir."

I would hastily collect my things and move into a
drawing-room. Chipie would catch sight of me as she was
passing.

"What are you doing here? This is not the place for
you. You'll ruin that table. Look, there's an inkstain
already!"

"That's not a stain. It's a vein in the marble. You
might take the trouble to look before blaming me."

"You would teach me manners, would you?"

" But. . . ."

" Hold your tongue and clear out."

" But I haven't got a table."

" All right. I shall go to your father this time."

I could have hit her . . . but I would collect my books and try another place . . . only to be turned out again. My lessons would not be ready.

" It is disgraceful," my tutor would say.

" But I don't know where to write, sir."

" You won't do your work and then you lie about it."

" But, sir."

" Be quiet. No table ? In a house like this !"

And it was the same every day. I used to settle first in one room and then in another, but I was always turned out. My masters were cross with me and so were the grown-ups. I spent my days on the look-out for danger, and my nights in tears. The one thing that revolted me more than anything else was injustice. It was their fault, not mine, that I had nowhere to work, and it was I who had to suffer for it. I hated them all.

I hated them, and the worst of it was that I could not hide it, and seeing my hatred made them angrier with me than ever.

One day, when I was if possible more miserable than usual, Michael came into my room. He disliked scenes, but he was kindhearted, and probably guessed that I was unhappy.

" Are you working ?"

Realising that tears were very near, I did not answer, but only nodded my head.

" Well, I won't disturb you. Cheer up, all boys have to go through it."

He turned on his heel, but he stopped at the door.

" I'll try and fix up something for you." And he went out.

My friend Black Peter, who was second valet to my father, told me that Michael really had spoken about me, but my father had answered that he was very much displeased at my conduct. Everyone complained of me—I would not work and was rude to my aunt.

" I am not going to interfere yet," said my father, " but he had better take care that I am not forced to do so. I'll teach him how to behave."

" He is thin and off colour," said Michael.

" Well, let him go riding. Nothing like it. See to it, will you ?"

And to my great delight I went off to the riding-school three times a week. But that did not help me to get a table, and my unhappiness continued.

To crown my misfortunes my second sister got engaged. At that time it was not the custom to allow engaged couples to be alone together. A warder, just as in prison, had to be in attendance at all interviews. But where was one to be found ? Aunt Jeanne would not do it, and they would not have Aunt Chipie. My eldest sister was not to be thought of. It was considered indecent that a young girl should see lovers flirting. The governesses had two days off each and went to give lessons in the town, and the one who was left had to look after Bunny. Fortunately Chipie had an idea.

" It's quite simple—Nicholas spends his whole time wandering from one room to another with nothing to do."

And I was chosen to look after the morals of the future bride and bridegroom. The happy fiancé, with the inevita-

D

ble bouquet in his hand, would appear regularly at three o'clock, at the very moment when my masters left. My sister would be covered with confusion and astonishment on seeing the bouquet

" What a surprise !" she would say. " What a lovely bouquet ! But really, I beg of you not to bring me any more."

The fortunate man would smile tolerantly, stroking his moustache. By degrees everyone would discreetly efface themselves.

" What luck ! At last we are alone !" and then it would begin.

The two turtledoves would coo gently. She would dart coy glances at him, blush, cast down her eyes, and begin to stuff herself with sweets. He would play the gallant, twirl his moustache and light a cigarette. They were deliriously happy, I daresay, but how about me? Oh, how bored I was !

By way of distraction I would admire the Mother of the Gracchi in gilt bronze, who, heedless of the ticking of the clock on which she was seated, made her sons swear that they were ready to die for their country. I would gaze on the Emperor Nicholas in his red uniform and blue riband, putting on his glove. He had been trying to do so for many years, but did not seem likely to succeed.

I would look about the room, every detail of which I knew by heart. Prometheus bound was always twisted with agony ; two Romans who were not the Gracchi were also taking an oath under some trees which bore candles instead of leaves. Then I would admire myself in the glass, and decide that I was quite nice-looking, though I had forgotten to brush my hair. Eventually, feeling sleep

stealing on me, I would stretch my legs, scratch my neck
and begin to study the Romans again. Oh, those Rom . .
. . tick-tock . . . their country . . . tick-tock . . . and
I would fall asleep.

What a lovely dream ! I am happy, absolutely happy.
I have my own corner where I can work in comfort. The
bad times are over. I am sitting comfortably on the roof
of our house, writing on the chimney-stack ! Chipie lies
at my feet, bound, like Prometheus. The Gracchi drop
their swords ; the Emperor Nicholas picks them up and
hands his glove to my father, who blushes and eats some
sweets . . . I feel myself suffocating, wake up and begin
to sneeze. Michael, seeing me asleep, has pushed a roll of
paper up my nose.

The result is that three hours are lost and I have done
no work. My tutor warns me that he is getting tired of it
and is going to complain to my father next time.

This will be to-morrow, as I find it impossible to work
again to-day, and the following would take place ; the
tutor would complain, and Black Peter would tell me the
details of the interview, for he always kept me supplied
with any information that might be useful to me. At my
tutor's first words my father, who hated prolonged discussions of this kind, would interrupt by saying :

" All right, we'll whip him."

But the master would protest and begin a long disserta-
tion on the principles of teaching.

" It has been proved that such antiquated methods do
more harm than good," he would say, and so on and so
on.

" Quite, quite," my father would reply. " Teaching is
your special subject, I know nothing about it. If you say

so, you must be right. All right, we'll follow your method. Good morning."

Then he would send for Chipie and my eldest sister.

"The tutor says that we must use moral persuasion with Nicholas. You are a sensible and practical woman, my dear sister, and you, my child, are a mother to him. See what can be done. I have other things to think about. I rely on you."

So they, or rather Chipie, to be precise, proceeded to reform my bad character according to modern ideas of dealing with children.

You might have thought that her first idea would be to give me a table ; but not at all, it was to forbid Niania to see me. In this she failed. My nurse stated quietly that she would continue to come as often as before. My aunt could do nothing with the dear old creature. Then Bunny was forbidden to talk to me and the governesses were told to see that she obeyed.

I was never to see Bunny again, Bunny, whom I loved more than life itself. I nearly died of grief. Then she had another idea. I was to have no more riding : instead, she took me to church twice a day, and I had to buy candles at my own expense to induce the Lord to have pity on my soul and give me a new one.

Bunny was lost to me. Michael had left for the Caucasus. Only Niania remained. I loved her dearly, but she was not able to understand. When she was with me I was happy, but I had nothing to say to her. I was alone in the world and indescribably unhappy. In the mornings I was driven from room to room, then I had to suffer the reproaches of my tutor and the harsh nagging of Chipie. My worst sufferings were at meal-times. I would sit nervously on my chair, not daring to raise my eyes for fear of meeting Bunny's. I was constantly in fear of Chipie's reproaches or an outburst of temper from my father ; I could hardly eat or drink. My father had lately been in a very bad humour. In the middle of dinner he gave the butler a box on the ear, and everyone, including the major-domo, trembled when they spoke to him. I, the culprit in chief, trembled more than the others.

But by now I was able to conceal my feelings and to control myself. I met Chipie's attacks with placid smiles, and that exasperated her. That was my way of taking revenge. From being a pleasant, affectionate child I was being converted into an evil and malevolent fiend.

One night, when I was unable to get to sleep (I had suffered from insomnia for some time), I heard footsteps in the passage. This surprised me. My elder sisters were at a dance, Bunny and the governesses had been asleep for some time, and my father and my brother never came upstairs at that hour. It seemed to me all the more curious as the steps were heavy and suggested that a burden was being carried. I opened my door slightly. It was Black Peter and another man carrying Sophie, who was pale, limp—perhaps dead. Her mother walked behind her with a little parcel covered with a linen cloth. Sophie was my sisters' principal ladies' maid ; in the country she slept in a room between their dressing-room and my father's. Everybody in the house was fond of the girl and even my father used sometimes to speak to her. She was gentle and kind and remarkably beautiful. I was upset by what I had seen ; typhus was raging in the city and she must have caught the infection.

Next morning I wanted to ask Black Peter about

Sophie's illness but he failed to come to my room, as he usually did.

I asked an old servant to send him to me.

" He is hunting," the latter replied.

" Where ?"

He replied with a proverb : " He who knows everything soon grows old. You would do better, batuishka[1], to get on with your lessons. There is thunder in the air. Be careful."

Niania came in. She seemed to be furious.

" Niania, do you know, Sophie . . ."

" Be quiet."

" Has she got typhus ?"

" What if she has got typhus ? Neither you nor I are doctors. Whether it is typhus or anything else has nothing to do with us. If you start chattering you'll only get yourself disliked. Not a word about this, you understand. Will you promise ?"

At that moment Black Peter came in. Niania rushed to meet him.

We always laughed when Niania whispered. It was no use, she might just as well not have been whispering at all.

" Well ?"

" She died on the way to hospital."

" What about the child ?"

" It's at the Foundling Hospital. The masters . . ."

" Hush. It is not for us to criticise them."

She went out and slammed the door.

I wanted to know more, but Peter, who was always ready to joke, was not to be moved either. He spoke to me with a gravity which was new to me.

" Be silent as the grave. Neither you nor I know any-

[1]batuishka: commonly rendered "little father."

thing. It's as much as our lives are worth. You know my devotion to you and I am not a scaremonger."

Suddenly I understood.

The day was spent as usual. One would have thought that nothing had happened. It made me quite ill, and I loathed my father.

The next day, when I was watching over the engaged couple, my father came into the drawing-room. He was followed by a servant carrying a lot of parcels. My father was fond of shopping and loved to display his purchases at once. On this day he appeared to be in high good humour, but on seeing me his face darkened.

" Idling as usual. Why are you here ?"

" He is carrying out Vera's instructions," said my sister.

" That's another matter. Bring me some scissors, quickly."

" You will find a pair on my dressing-table," said my sister.

I ran off, but the scissors were not on the dressing-table. At last I found them ; when I came back I saw that my father was annoyed at having been kept waiting.

" Idiot ! I believe you do it on purpose."

I was disgusted at his injustice, but naturally I did not dare to say anything.

He proceeded to unpack the parcels, displaying their contents.

" They're all for you," he said to my sister. " This comes from Paris and that comes from London. How do you like them ? That's a jolly bracelet, isn't it ? Do you like this hat and the shawl ?"

He took pleasure in the things himself and indeed they

were charming. My sister was in the seventh heaven. My father's temper had changed ; he was laughing and joking ; I couldn't understand it. Was it possible that he had forgotten ?

My disgust increased in proportion to his good humour. I felt a wave of indignation nearly choking me and I found it difficult to conceal my feelings.

My father, noticing my distress, put his hand on my shoulder and smiled.

" Do you like these things too ?"

" No."

I saw that he was on the point of losing his temper, but he restrained himself. Then, turning to my sister, he said :

" We have made a pretty mess here. That's enough for to-day. We must clear it all up. Call a maid," he said to me.

I was just starting off, but I suddenly remembered the girl who had been carried away yesterday and the thing that had been wrapped in a cloth. Instead of obeying him, I went up to my father and looked him straight in the eyes.

" Well, did you hear what I said ? Call a maid."

Quite quietly, though my heart seemed ready to burst, it was beating so hard, I asked him :

" Which maid ? Sophie ? She died in childbirth and the child is at the Foundling Hospital."

My father stepped back, coloured, then went pale, raised his hand and struck me full in the face.

" I, I . . ."

He could not speak and he left the room.

When I had recovered from the shock my first feeling

was : " I am going to fall." I gathered all my strength together and, straddling like a drunkard to keep my balance, with only one idea in my mind, to prevent myself falling, went almost subconsciously to my room. " Well, I have got here," I thought, and I collapsed on to a trunk. " Where am I?" I wondered. I had lost all idea of time and place.

Then I came to. Quite coolly and without hurry, fully conscious of what I was doing, I went to the cupboard where I kept my exercise-books, took one, looked for a blank page and was going to pull it out, but it tore—it was the last page. I looked through the other books and at last found a blank page, which I tore out. In my best handwriting, taking care to make the up-strokes thin and the down-strokes thick, I wrote :

" To Bunny and Niania only, but not to those who are unjust and wicked. I love you and I despise them."

Then I read it over, altered a " j " which looked like an " l," put the letter on my pillow, fastened it on with a pin and threw myself out of the window.

A sharp stab of pain . . . then I remembered nothing.

A light shone in the darkness. A shadow bent over me : " Would you like something to drink ?" Where had I heard that voice ? Memory began to return and I regained consciousness. I was in my own room. A night-light was burning under a green screen ; Bunny, leaning over a chair, with her head on my bed, was sleeping and holding my hand. Niania's eyes were fixed on me. I tried to smile, and I gently stroked my sister's hair.

" Let the poor darling sleep," said Niania. " Many a night she's been sitting up nursing you."

Then I lost consciousness again.

When I came to myself Bunny was standing in front of my bed weeping.

" She's weeping for joy," said Niania. " I told her that you had recognised her."

I was a long time hovering between life and death, sometimes unconscious and at other times lucid. As in a dream, I used to see our old doctor feel my pulse, a dark man with a beard whom I did not know put leeches on my head ; and Black Peter brought me food. Bunny and Niania were always by me.

Then one day the door opened and Chipie came into the room with an unctuous expression. I shouted out :

" Niania, Niania ! Tell her to go away."

" Go away," said the old woman. " The doctor ordered absolute rest. Please go away."

Chipie shrugged her shoulders and, with a resigned look gave me her blessing and went.

" Horrid old wretch," scolded Niania. I laughed.

" He's laughing, he's laughing already," shouted Bunny, and she began dancing round the room. Niania wept for joy.

" Yes, he'll get better now," she said.

Then my father came in. As I didn't want to see him I pretended to be asleep.

" They say he is delirious again," he said.

" You'll wake him, he's gone to sleep," said Niania.

" We must send for the doctor."

" Quite unnecessary. He is out of danger, but please go away, he must be left alone."

" This room is hopeless. He must be taken somewhere else."

" Hush ! You'll wake him."

My father sighed and went out on tiptoe.

As the doctor had said that I must not be crossed my father had given orders that all my wishes were to be carried out, whatever they were.

I had three requests to make : that Bunny should stay with me during my illness, that when I got up I should be given a table to work at and that neither my father nor Chipie should come into the room. I don't know how Niania managed this delicate mission, but my wishes were carried out.

Then the doctor allowed me to go for short drives, but only at a slow trot. Black Peter was always on the box instead of the footman. That was Niania's wish ; in all matters affecting me the decision lay absolutely with her.

One day Bunny told me that my brother, Alexander, was going to get married. One of his fiancée's brothers was grown up and a groom of the bedchamber to the Empress ; the other brother was about my age and at school in Geneva.

" The gentleman with whom he is boarding—his name is David—is very kind and very just, remarkably just . . ." She blushed.

" You have been told to ask me whether I should not like to go there ?"

" Yes, but no one wants to force you."

" Would you come with me, Bunny ?"

She sighed. " I should very much like to, but it's impossible. Sasha is getting married and one day Vera will get married too. Who is there to stay with poor father ?"

" Are you fond of him ?"

She began to cry. " I am so frightened of him. . . But I'm sorry for him. He's getting old."

I asked to be sent to Switzerland. It was decided that Henselt, [1] who was going there, should take me with him.

I had not seen my father again since his visit. He had frequently asked whether he could speak to me, but Niania always found an excuse for putting him off. Then he had left for Moscow, where he had business.

On the eve of my departure for Switzerland, as I was coming down the main staircase to go and see Niania, I met him. He had just arrived and was going up to the first floor. We both stopped spontaneously. We were only a few steps apart and as he was below me our heads were almost on a level.

" You're off to-morrow, aren't you ? "

" Yes, father."

" Have you packed ? "

" Yes, father."

" Have you nothing to say to me ? Have you everything you want ? "

" Yes, father."

A shadow passed over his face, but he remained impassive. I realised that he was unhappy. I was moved almost to tears and would liked to have thrown my arms round his neck . . . but the memory of the past came over me. I lived over again my own sufferings and those of so many others. His caprices, his outbursts of temper and his brutality—they all came back to me. No, I could neither forget nor forgive.

I looked at him coldly.

[1] Adolphe Henselt, a famous musician.

He too understood what was passing through my
mind. For a moment—an eternity—we stood thus, as
though petrified, seeking to plumb one another's souls
with our looks.

" Yes," said my father, " goodbye, my child."

" Goodbye, father."

And, still impassive, he went on up the stairs. I made
way for him respectfully. He passed me without a glance ;
and I went down without looking round.

CHAPTER II.

1860-1864

I CAN hardly imagine anything more melancholy or decayed than a village of serfs in the north of Russia. A grey sky covered with still greyer clouds. On the horizon the inky black outline of a pine forest. Low, dilapidated log cabins, blackened with age and covered with rotten thatch. A half dug pond. Barefooted men wearing coarse canvas shirts and trousers, who bend almost double as you pass. Dirty, underfed cattle ; dogs that look like skeletons.

After this there was something dreamlike about my journey across Europe. Well-cultivated fields under a bright blue sky ; little white, red-tiled houses smiling in the sun, green trees, gardens full of flowers, hedges in bloom ; clean chubby children, sleek well-fed cattle.

I wondered why all seemed so happy here and so wretched at home.

Monsieur David was waiting for me at the station at Geneva ; Henselt handed me over to him and continued his journey.

David was hideous. He looked like a white negro. He had thick red lips and fuzzy hair ; in fact a face for the gallows.

" My house is rather a long way from here," said David " but if you are not too tired we may as well walk. It will save a cab. I never take one. We've got a turkey for dinner to-day. My mother gave it to me for my birthday. Hullo ! there's Marmillot.   An odd fellow but good-hearted."

He spoke to me as to a friend from whom one has parted the day before.   That put me at my ease, and the house too had an air of simple friendliness. My room was small and simply furnished, but it lacked nothing.   I particularly noticed a writing table.

Madame was nice looking and very simply dressed ; she seemed kind and gentle. A small boy and two little girls gazed at me as though I were an ogre about to devour them.

I smiled at them. Fifi, the smallest, gave a tiny smile in return, then very seriously she came up to me slowly and held out her hand. I kissed her ; but seeing her mother look astonished I felt embarrassed.

" I beg your pardon, Madame ! Perhaps that's not allowed ?"

" Not at all. You are one of the family now. What surprises me is Fifi's courage. She is so shy. Fifi, you're not frightened of this gentleman, are you—his name is Nicholas——?"

By way of answer the little girl put her arm round my neck and leant her cheek against mine.

I found it hard to restrain my tears.

" Come, come !" said David. " I hope that we shall all be friends soon."

The other boarders came up and David introduced us. They consisted of two English boys, Harry and Charley, who were older than I: they both grinned and said simul-taneously, " How do you do ?" They nearly crushed the bones in my hand as they shook it. There was a young Turk with eyes like a gazelle's who wore a large diamond ring on his forefinger, and a lad with prominent cheek-bones whom I recognised at a glance as a fellow country-man. He was my future sister-in-law's brother.

" You know him, don't you ?" said David.

" No, sir."

" Why, you must ! He comes from St. Petersburg."

" St. Petersburg is a very big city, sir,"

" No matter. So is Geneva, but people always know each other slightly here. Well, now we're all here. Let's sit down. Aha ! boys, we are having turkey to-day. My mother sent it me from the country."

And we sat down.

" Do you drink red or white wine, Nicholas ?"

" I used not to have it at all at home, sir."

" Oh, I know. You Russians never drink anything but vodka at dinner. But I'm afraid you can't have that here. It's not the custom, and besides it's unwholesome. You must be satisfied with the thin wine of the country."

The idea that we drank spirits at meals seemed so funny to me that I burst out laughing. I would never have dared to be so disrespectful at home. I was already becoming a republican.

My new life started from the next day. I went to school in the morning and when my work was done I could go for a walk wherever I chose. On Sundays and holidays we went for excursions to the mountains, or went riding or sailing. David allowed us complete liberty, and never interfered unless it was absolutely necessary.

He was neither clever nor particularly learned, but he had been born and brought up in a free country where for centuries men had been respected, whatever their origin or age ; where everyone was equal in the eyes of the law. And his personality was coloured by the general standard of civilisation in the country. We were soon friends. He trusted me completely and I hid nothing from him. My masters were satisfied with my progress at school, while at home I was liked by David and the children adored me. I was happy, for I no longer disliked anyone but loved the whole of humanity.

Time passed ; three years slipped away and the child became an adolescent. I often found myself thinking of my country, of the Russia which in the dimness of my childish memories seemed so delightful yet terrible to me.

I was aware that the country was now becoming enlightened. Serfdom had been abolished, and Alexander II was doing great things. I dreamed of doing my share in the work of this great reformer, of living for the good of my country. The illusions of childhood gave way to the illusions of youth. Childhood was merely the past.

It is generally assumed that youth and love go together, and that to speak of one's youth without mentioning one's first-love affairs is absurd. That may be, but when one is sixty-five years old, as I am, one likes to have one's ideas clear, and to know what one is talking about. Definitions of what is called " love " are so different ! Thousands of books have been written on the subject and yet we get no nearer the truth. However, I suppose I must conform, irrelevant to my theme though it may be.

My first love was a young English girl (Americans were not yet invented), pretty, as all English girls are—when they do not happen to be ugly. The British never do any-

E

thing by halves, and their daughters are either hideous or charming.

Her name was Mary . . . or Emmy . . . or it may have been Alice—I cannot remember now, and in any case it does not matter. She did not really appeal to me more than any other girl, but she arrived, just at the psychological moment, when I was ready to fall in love. That is how things generally happen. Besides, she was my best friend Harry's sister, so that it was all very natural. It was a friendly duty.

I need hardly say that I never spoke of my love to Kitty. A young girl is sacred ! And besides I was afraid of injuring her in some way . . . women are such fragile creatures ! Too burning a love might have made her consumptive, like Héloïse or " La Dame aux Camélias." Such things, alas, happened only too often, according to the books. In those prehistoric times we were still old-fashioned. Young men and women did not slap each other on the back then.

I opened my heart to Harry, however, having first made him swear never to betray my secret.

He looked favourably on my suit, and it was understood that until I was of age the matter should remain a secret between us. But where love is concerned these wretched women have a nose keener than that of a bloodhound. They can pick out by instinct from a thousand others, the poor fool who is ready to sacrifice his life to them—and Sophy understood. On the eve of her departure, she sent me a lock of hair in a pink envelope, inscribed " for ever." Six months afterwards she married a Scotsman, and I have never seen her since.

If this story is not to your taste, I can tell you another

one. I have a whole stock of first loves to offer. But I warn you this will be the last, for the subject is far too stale.

One day when I was in the riding school, a lady, followed by a group of men, appeared in the gallery. She had rather a full figure, deep, black, languorous, Oriental eyes, and hair with tawny glints in it. She was distinction itself.

The men who were with her were also distinguished-looking, with the exception of one who was rather too handsome, too well-built and too well-dressed for a man of breeding.

I was completely bowled over. I saw that she was aware of it, and she watched me for a moment and seemed to smile.

After this encounter she filled my thoughts completely, and I could neither eat nor drink. One morning I was walking along the lake on my way to Ferney. The heat was terrific and I went into the garden of a little café to have a glass of beer. Suddenly I saw them at a table, the lady and the " too handsome " man. I already knew who they were—she was a Russian lady of high rank, the wife of an important Court official, and he was a celebrity of the hour.

She stopped me in the hall.

" You're Russian, aren't you," she said. " You are so like a friend of mine, Baron Michael, that I had to speak to you."

" He is my brother, Madame."

" I thought so. Sit down and let us talk about him."

But it was not a success. I was confused, while she was thinking of something else.

Her companion seemed annoyed, and drank glass after glass of wine and chewed his cigar.

"I suppose you're drawing comparisons," he said in an undertone with a sneer.

She blushed.

"Oh, well, a bon-bon is quite pleasant after a square meal." And she rose. "It is time to go back."

She turned to me, saying: "I am staying at the Hotel des Bergues. I am always at home in the evening. We can talk about Russia. Do come and see me."

"Don't forget," said the man with his ugly smile. "The Countess is quite alone in the evening. I am busy at the theatre."

I went there the next day. I found her with her hat on, just going out.

"How unfortunate! One of my relations is passing through Geneva and I must meet her at the station."

And she suddenly raised her head, gazed into my eyes, while her lips found mine. I became wildly excited.

"No, no! Go away now! Come to-morrow." And she vanished.

I spent the night re-living the moment and the day in counting the hours. I wasn't seventeen. You may be sure I was punctual next day. She was sitting in an armchair reading. She received me as though nothing had happened; but I could see from a scarcely perceptible twitching of the lips that she was disturbed.

There was a knock at the door.

"What a nuisance! Come in."

It was David.

"Please excuse me, madam, but a relative of this

young man, who is my pupil, is seriously ill and wants to
see him."

" You'd better hurry," said the Countess, " and when
you write to your sisters remember me to them."

We went home in silence.

" Nicholas," said David the next day, " I've noticed the
state you've been in during the last few days, and this
kind of thing is bound to end in a catastrophe. So I had
to intervene. You see, my dear fellow, a man who is not
chaste is absolutely done for."

The remarkable thing is that the good fellow firmly
believed what he said.

And now I have done with this subject. Let us pass to
other matters.

By the last year of my time at Geneva I was a fully
fledged young man ; and for the first time I was treated
accordingly. I was introduced to some very interesting
people. Alexandre Dumas and Princess Metternich made
the most vivid impression on me. It would be foolish to
try to add to all that has been said of the former. A good
deal has been said about the Princess too, but she was
generally only known superficially and such knowledge
was unfair to her. Many years later I had the honour of
enjoying her friendship and had the opportunity to appreciate this extraordinary woman at her true worth. She
was the strangest and most complex being imaginable.

Those manners of the gutter which were adopted by
society during the Second Empire, not only in Paris but
in all our capitals, were first made fashionable by her.
She was the darling of Paris and worshipped in Vienna.
When she appeared in the Prater everybody would sing
the popular catch :

S'gibt nur a Kaiser Stad,
S'gibt nur a Wien,
S'gibt nur a Wiener Mad,
Metternich Paulin. [1]

She was red-haired and rather ugly, but charming ; a
great lady to her fingertips, but a good sort ; sensitive,
discriminating and well read ; she was well versed in
political questions and could give sound advice on serious
problems ; in her odd way she would make the wisest,
most profound and most comic remarks ; she did her
utmost to seem like a cocotte, or rather the great cocottes
made prodigious efforts to copy the Princess. But they
were useless. There was only one person in the world in
the least like that extraordinary woman, and that was
Pauline Metternich herself.

I was introduced to her and she kept me to lunch.
During the meal she said some quite shocking things,
which to her great joy and that of the other guests made
me blush ; she made epigrams worthy of Chamfort and
made wise and profound remarks which provided food for
thought. It was a real display of fireworks, a mixture of
wisdom and folly. Then we went for a stroll. As we were
going along the rue du Rhone she remembered that she
had a note to leave. I knew where the person lived and
offered to show her the way. The others waited for us
downstairs. The stairs were dark, winding and slippery.
They were not easy to go up, and still less easy to come
down, and we were rather a long time.

[1] There's only one Imperial City,
There's only one Vienna,
There's only one Vienna lass,
Paulin Metternich.

"Well, you have been a long time ; we can guess what you've been up to," said one lady.

"You're wrong," said the Princess. "Why, this innocent did not even make an attempt on my honour. It's disgusting. I might be an old hag."

"My natural respect. . ."

"Respect indeed ! Let me tell you, young man, you must shew respect to women in public—that is essential—and drop it when you are alone with them. Mere politeness requires that you should."

I called on her next day and, finding her alone, I thought it my duty to be polite. She was indignant and her indignation was perfectly genuine.

"But I am only carrying out your instructions, Princess. You gave me the idea."

She laughed. "Gave you the idea ! Why, my dear sir, I only say that kind of thing for the benefit of my women friends and not for my own. You may be sure that if I had meant it I should not have had to say so. Anyhow I'm rather like a clock winder ; I set the works going but I don't work myself."

I was more interested in my fellow countrymen than in anybody else I met at Geneva. About 1863 Geneva was over-run by them. The Russia of Nicholas I was a prison from which it was impossible to escape without His Majesty's personal permission ; so that the Russians whom we met in Europe in his time belonged exclusively to the ruling class ; they were the legendary "boyars" whose riches, luxury and grand manner made such a sensation.

When Nicholas died the frontier was thrown open to

all, and, especially after the troubles in Poland, Europe was introduced to a type of Russian very different to that to which it was accustomed. The Nihilists were the most striking. Their menfolk had hair down to the shoulder, while the women's hair was cropped short, but whatever sex they belonged to they were as a matter of principle always slovenly, dirty and unkempt. The inference was that one could not bother about one's appearance when there were more important matters to see to. Their mission was to preach a new gospel to humanity, though it was new only to them, this " new gospel " being as old as the hills to everyone else—I am speaking only of civilised people. It consisted partly of doctrines which had long been generally admitted and were considered to be dangerous only in Russia, and partly of paradoxes which were out of date and almost forgotten. These prophets were generally ignorant, though they had a great idea of themselves. You had to applaud everything they said. They regarded those who did not agree with them as congenital idiots—and they did not scruple to tell them so.

The Nihilist was a caricature of the " intellectual," which was also a recent type. Up to this time there had been no middle class in Russia ; it was only just in the process of formation. Two of these intellectuals were engaged to give me lessons; Monsieur Andrezev in Russian literature, and Monsieur Daniloff in Russian history.

One gathered that Monsieur Daniloff had had to leave Russia for political reasons. He had been too advanced for the régime of Alexander II, that reactionary tyrant who had been unable to keep up with the times.

' But it was he who abolished serfdom."

"A wonderful achievement. It should have been abolished centuries ago. He should not have stopped at that, he ought to have made the serfs the equals of their lords."

"What about the new law courts?"

"The judges aren't all elected, but nominated by the Government. It's disgusting."

"He abolished the thirty years military service and corporal punishment."

"He ought to have paid off the whole army. War is an iniquity. He abolished corporal punishment, you say. Why, my dear sir, all punishment should be abolished. The so-called criminal is merely the victim of a society that is badly organised."

He had an answer ready for every point I raised.

His knowledge of history was rudimentary—if that— apart from revolutions. He held that revolutions alone were the vehicles of progress.

Being good-looking and a good talker, he was soon popular in the Russian colony and had a host of pupils. He made money, went to the theatre and to fashionable restaurants and in the end ran away with one of his pupils, the daughter of a wealthy Moscow business man, taking her mother's diamonds with him. Why shouldn't he?— Proudhon had demonstrated that property is theft.

Thirty years later I saw Monsieur, or rather to give him the title he had acquired, His Excellency Daniloff. He was one of the most influential members of the ultra reactionary party and held an important post. I reminded him of his former beliefs. He replied in Latin, as was appropriate for a supporter of classicism : " *Tempora mutantur nos et mutamur in illis.*" He was a smart fellow.

Andrezev was plain, poorly dressed and diffident.   He lived in an attic and sometimes went without his dinner. But he was an honest fellow who would have suffered martyrdom for the cause.   He did his utmost to make a convert of me.   But he did not succeed.   Even at seventeen I was too mature for that.   So was Fifi, who was only six. As I have said, a country's civilisation colours the outlook of the young as well as of the old.   Nevertheless, in spite of the difference in our opinions, we became friends.

I have several times since met people of these two types. The Daniloffs turn their convictions to account, become the leaders of political parties and often achieve their ends.   The Andrezevs are dupes and foot the bill.

The day before a holiday, Andrezev, very much excited, came to tell me a great piece of news.   Bakunin, the great Bakunin, was in Geneva.   He was to address a meeting at Carouge in the evening.

We went to the meeting.   The room was packed.   French emigrants, Italian emigrants, Russian emigrants—the discontented of every country under the sun were there.   I had the honour of being introduced to the great man before the meeting.   He kindly consented to say a few words to me and I perceived that great revolutionaries are as subject to petty vanity as grocers.   Then he went on to the platform.

What he said was neither very intelligent nor very logical—but the eloquence with which he said it ; what enthusiasm he inspired !   It was impossible to resist him and to remain unmoved.   The man was a born revolutionary.   I am sure that if he had succeeded in making himself president of a republic he would immediately have set about his own overthrow. He carried his audience away with him. All the Russians left the meeting with him. As we passed an eating-house Bakunin paused.

" Let's have something to eat."

There was some hesitation. Most of them were poor devils without enough money to pay for a meal. Bakunin saw what was the matter.

" Of course I'll pay. No false shame, my friends. I've been through it myself. It is more disgraceful to be rich than to be poor."

We went in.

" What will you have, gentlemen ?"

With the diffidence of the needy, one ordered a half portion of cheese, another a small black pudding. But our generous host protested.

" No, no ! We must have a feast to-day."

And he ordered the best dishes available.

Then raising his glass he shouted : " Down with the tyrants ! Long live the revolution !"

And we clicked glasses again and again. It was dawn when he asked for the bill. He took out his pocketbook, searched in it and burst out laughing.

" Citizens ! The state exchequer is lacking in funds and must levy an internal loan. All contributions will be repaid to-morrow in gold or silver, according to taste." And everyone gave whatever they had.

Nobody was repaid. Bakunin, in the manner of the truly great, forgot this trifle.

Eventually I took my degree. I was going back to Russia to spend some months there before entering the University of Berlin, where I wished to complete my studies. I felt very sad at leaving the place where I had been so happy, and yet I looked forward to being happier

still in the place to which I was returning. I had said
good-bye to my friends and my trunks were packed.

On the eve of my departure I met Bakunin.

" Would you take charge of a small parcel for a friend of
mine ?" he asked.

" Certainly."'

" The only thing is, you'll have to smuggle it past the
customs."

" I can do that legally. I have been promised an official
permit."

" Excellent."

I was just about to start for the station when I saw
Andrezev. I was astonished, as we had already said good-
bye.

" Haven't you a parcel that you're taking for Bakunin?"

" Yes."

" He has asked me to bring it back to him. He has
changed his mind."

I handed it over.

I learned later that Andrezev had lied to me. It was a
bundle of pamphlets and Andrezev was anxious to save me
from getting into difficulties, as indeed he probably did.
Another quite young man, called Diakoff or Diakonoff—
I cannot remember exactly—was less fortunate than I.
He was caught with a parcel on him at the frontier, and
exiled to Siberia.

The train whistled . . . a last goodbye . . . and the
delightful days at Geneva were also a thing of the past.

CHAPTER III

1864-1867

In order to understand what happened in the empire of the Czars from the time of Alexander II until Russia's collapse, which we are now witnessing, we must go back a little. History is not a series of isolated and independent phases, but a continuity. Each phase is the outcome of the past and one of the determining causes of the future.

It is generally accepted that Peter the Great changed the face of Russia and transformed a barbarous country into a civilised nation. But this is open to question. Russia possessed a certain culture long before the time of Peter the Great, a culture, it is true, that was Byzantine rather than European. Peter created a regular army and a navy, brought his people into touch with Europe and introduced certain industries. Apart from that he was an anarchist rather than a reformer. He destroyed the old order without setting up anything in its place. The new Russians, turned by him into Europeans, or rather into European clothes, so that they wore suits instead of cafe-tans and three cornered hats instead of fur caps, remained what they were, Orientals. Only the upper classes left the ways which had hitherto been those of the whole nation, to follow the European tradition. The people remained where they were, and a gulf was formed between the upper and lower class which nothing has succeeded in bridging since.

We then had the comedy of " Russia changed into Europe." During the eighteenth century it was performed by lords dressed up as Dutchmen by Peter, as painted marquises and free-thinkers by the empresses, and as German corporals by Paul, Alexander I and Nicholas I. The people, that is the greater part of the nation, took no part in the show. They stayed outside the theatre. The play was not being acted for them but for the pleasure of the actors themselves, and especially to dazzle Europe. And sometimes it was so well acted that the world was taken in and mistook the sham for the reality.

But play-acting is not life, it is merely an imitation. Progress is not achieved by Imperial decree, and does not depend on the goodwill of a genius or on the whim of a comedian.

Progress is the outcome of the needs and aspirations of the nation itself, of society in the mass. Evolution towards a better state of things is the result of a struggle which is generally almost imperceptible, but occasionally violent, between the privileged classes and those less favourably placed. Where this struggle has not taken place, progress is impossible.

In Europe the struggle between feudal lords and their serfs gave rise to the establishment of the commoners, the bourgeoisie. And the bourgeoisie became the principal lever of progress.

In Russia, the bourgeoisie did not exist before the time of Alexander II. There was the privileged class—the nobility, and the peasants—either serfs or freed-men. Between these two classes there was nothing. The nobility

already possessed all the rights which they needed and
were satisfied. Kept fast under the yoke of absolutism as
they were, they solicited favours but did not attempt to
demand political rights. A few of them had done so, but
their fate had restrained the others from following their
example.

The peasants were an inert mass, large in numbers but
powerless, resigned to their lot and convinced that God
had ordained things so. Politically they did not count.
The elements essential to progress were missing.

The commoners only came into being after the emancipation of the serfs.

The commoners were known as the Intelligentzia, a
designation which they themselves adopted. They
differed in many respects from the bourgeoisie of Europe.
In the Western countries the bourgeoisie possessed a
culture which was already old ; they had had time to
develop and were ripe for the part which history had
assigned to them. Our Intelligentzia was merely the
product of vague aspirations which for centuries had never
materialised. The bourgeoisie had a definite objective—
the " Intelligentzia " had none. They were tending in
some direction, but the question was, where ? And this
was a question that they themselves were unable to answer
clearly.

As yet immature, and without balance, they nevertheless possessed the ardour of youth, and were impatient to
play a part. They threw themselves into the fray and
from the beginning took the wrong course. Instead of
ranging themselves on the side of Alexander II, the great
reformer, they set themselves up against him, and instead
of becoming the lever of progress as they wished to do,

and in the nature of things ought to have done, they became a check upon it.

As is invariably the case after a war that has turned out badly, Russian society after the Crimean campaign was hostile, though merely passively so, to the government. The majority of the nobility could not forgive the Emperor for the abolition of serfdom, and the old serfs were discontented too. They had hoped to be given all the lands belonging to the lords and had only received a minute portion as their share. And while they bore the yoke of the tyrant, Nicholas I, without a murmur, everything which emanated from his humane and liberal successor was condemned by them. This opposition was headed by the Intelligentzia. And Alexander II, finding the path such a thorny one, stopped midway. Disgusted with his own work, he began to disbelieve in it himself, and, what is worse, ended by spoiling it. Finally, harried on all sides like a wild beast, terrified by endless outrages, he no longer bothered about anything but his personal safety, left the power of action in the hands of men who abused it, and degenerated into the mere shadow of a sovereign.

Yet at the time I was glad to get back from Switzerland to the new Russia of which I had dreamed so much. For one thing, it was no longer a case of travelling by stage-coach, on bad roads when the horses were never there, and one could never get anything to eat, but was eaten oneself by bugs. A railway now connected the capital with Germany. We rolled along in a Pullman which was more comfortable than the European railway carriages.

It is true that the villages we passed through were more dismal and wretched than ever, but the men looked different to me. The moujik no longer bowed to the ground at each passer-by. The people no longer had the sleepy look of people who do not live but merely vegetate. And St. Petersburg, too, was no longer the same as when I was a child.

The town itself had changed very little, but the atmosphere was quite different. The soldiers were no longer like wooden soldiers, they no longer walked like automatons, but like living beings. The artisans had given up their striped dressing-gowns, and were dressed like everyone else. Ladies walked alone, without their escort of tall gold-laced lackeys. There were no more drunken and filthy " budotchniks " with their useless and ridiculous halberds, but policemen, who were less fierce-looking but more useful. Blows were no longer exchanged in the street, but people went about talking, laughing and smoking. The streets looked more or less like those of Europe.

But on the other hand the capital had lost its peculiar character. There were no more itinerant pedlars, Tartars in cafetans, moujiks in their red blouses, women swathed in innumerable kerchiefs, and Italians carrying whole shops full of plaster statuettes on their heads, all musically crying their wares in different tones. Gone were the queer crudely coloured shop signs which were so grotesque but amusing ; a negro smoking a cigar nearly as big as himself—a blood-coloured fountain gushing from an old man's arms. And the tailors' advertisements—a group of children, boys and girls, and underneath them the inscription : " Made here to order "—they were gone too !

F

My own people no longer lived in their former town house, but occupied a flat in an apartment house. It was old Tania, Sophie's mother, who opened the door to me. Everyone was in the country and she was left in charge. The flat was quite unlike our old home, with its cold and majestic vestibules. It was a pleasant apartment and looked hospitable and cosy. The awful pictures of classical subjects were gone, but I was quite touched to find Nicholas I still putting on his glove, and the Gracchi still with their hands raised to heaven, swearing to die for their country.

Tania told me what had become of our old servants. Big Jean had taken to drink, and others, including Paul, Pierre and Nicholas had gone the same way. Alexander and Jean and his brothers changed masters almost daily—sometimes they went of their own accord, sometimes they were dismissed. The women were still worse off. " I shouldn't like to tell you their profession," said the old woman.

" How sad it all is. They were such nice people."

She sighed. " Liberty, batiushka, has turned their heads."

" But liberty raises men, Tania, it doesn't make drunkards of them."

" That may be true of wise men, but not of ignorant creatures like us."

I started for Terpilitzy the next day. What a journey it was, with its delicious memories. The fields that stretched as far as the eye could reach, the ancient forests that I had seen so many times in my childhood. How often I had played in these gardens, so silent and deserted now.

But how changed everything was. The manor houses had a decayed air which denoted only too unmistakably their owners' absence. The pretty ponds were overgrown with weeds, the hedges were neglected.

The household was still asleep when I arrived. As my carriage drew up to the entrance, the door opened and a strange servant appeared and informed me that the baron was at Yamburg, and asked me to wait until the ladies were up.

Then Niania appeared at a window. She did not recognise me at first, but when I shouted, just as I used to do as a child, " Niania, dear Niania !" she ran up and threw her arms round my neck.

Later, a pretty and graceful young girl came out, laughing and crying at the same time. Could it be possible ? It was Bunny ! Then came my eldest sister, Aunt Jeanne, followed by her pugs, and the old servants who had stayed with us. But only the old ones were there, all the younger ones had gone for good. Black Peter was out hunting.

The whole day was spent in talking about the past, in questions, and in cries of astonishment. My eldest sister complimented me on having changed for the better.

" You must admit that you were rather a dreadful little boy."

Bunny and I exchanged a smile, and I agreed.

The next day Bunny begged me to go and meet my father, who was due back that day. He was at Yamburg, attending quarter sessions, of which he was chairman.

This journey too was full of memories and, alas, of disillusion ! Again there were beautiful forests, but spoiled by wanton cutting down of trees, fine properties falling in ruins, villages more wretched than ever. But to judge by the number of drunkards that I met, the men were happier than before.

My coachman—an old friend of mine who had taught me to ride when I was four years old—was a great talker.

" They say, batiushka, that you saw some fine sights abroad. Do you see such a fearful lot of drunkards there as you do here ? "

" Very few. Why are there so many here ? "

" Oh, it's simple enough. At one time, the peasants thought that a good harvest depended on the dampness of the soil, now they think it depends on the dampness of the throat, so they keep moistening it. But it's not much good, to judge by their fields."

" The landowners' fields don't look much better."

" Who would be bothered to look after them ? "

" Their owners of course."

" The landlords ? They've got something else to do now. They've gone abroad to drink waters to improve their digestions, and to see the Paris women walking naked about the streets. Neither landlords nor peasants care about the land now."

" Hello, a new road."

" Yes, but I'd rather bring you by a by-road. We'll come back this evening by this new road. I wouldn't like to be in the Ispravnik's[1] shoes to-night. My word, no ! He's in charge of the work, and he's had his palm greased so often that the contractor has no money left to buy gravel.

" And why do you think this evening—"

---

[1] Ispravnik—a little lower in rank than the under-sheriff. At this time the Ispravnik was still elected by the nobles.

" Why, because the old barine's¹ coming this way to-
night for the first time.   Oho !   After your father's
blessing, the Ispravnik will become orthodox again.
The baron knows how to bring heathens back to the fold."

I found my father in his office.   The sessions were over
and he was signing papers handed to him by his secretary.
He also did not recognise me at first.

" Oh, it's you."   And he gave me his hand to kiss.
" Just a moment while I sign these, and we'll have dinner,
and then start back.   You must be famishing.   How
amazingly like Michael you are."

He said all this as though we had parted only yesterday.
The past was forgotten.

We dined at the club, rather a primitive place, but we
got an excellent dinner.   The conversation turned on the
memorable sitting of the St. Petersburg zemstvo at which
the speeches of Deputies Platonov and Kruse were loudly
applauded.   The meeting was dissolved by the Emperor's
order, and all the deputies were accused of high treason.
The next day the sitting of the Imperial Council could not
take place, as a number of their members, and amongst
them the Governor-General of St. Petersburg, Prince
Suvorov, were among the accused.

The order was withdrawn.

" They can do what they like," said a man near me,
" we'll soon get what we want."

" What's that ?" asked my father.

" Why, the Parliamentary system, as in England.
Only with a more liberal constitution.   The English system
is a bit antiquated."

" I have not studied the English Constitution," said my

¹Barine—master, lord.

father. " I was educated in a cadet corps, so what can you expect ? I know less than you do, so I cannot say whether it is antiquated or not. But last time I was abroad I saw a machine at Manchester which worked so well that I bought one. However, it was impossible to find men here capable of working it, and in the end they destroyed it."

" We shall find them," said my neighbour.

" Oh, yes," said my father, " as many fine talkers as you like. We have enough and to spare of those—and men with theories too. But theories and speeches won't make anything work. For instance, we have been looking for months for someone to replace our dead friend, and nobody will fill the vacant post, and the country is suffering in consequence. Come, gentlemen, one of you must sacrifice yourselves."

There was silence—and then, one after the other, they all disappeared. My father sighed.

" It's always like that. They want the devil and all, and when they've got it they don't know what to do with it. Come along, the carriage is here."

I had not seen my father since the abolition of serfdom, and I was interested to see how he was taking things. I expected to see a man who had lost his bearings, and who found it difficult to adapt himself to the new order of things which was so different from the old. I knew that he was most enthusiastic about the reforms undertaken by the Emperor, but I was quite unaware of how the new state of things had affected him. He was no longer the same man. He seemed to have thawed ; he talked, laughed and behaved almost heartily.

We talked of the day's sitting.

" You remember old Count Jean ?" asked my father.

" Yes, of course. He must be pretty old now."

" Poor fellow. We put him under arrest to-day."

" What for ?"

" He boxed his valet's ears. An insult is punished by a fine—a blow followed by an arrest. That's the law. Perhaps it's a bit severe, since we've been accustomed to striking people all our lives. But it must be put a stop to, and it's all the worse for those who won't understand that."

There was a jolt, and then another one. We were on the new road of which my father was so proud. It had been due to his initiative that it had been constructed. And as the zemstvo had not the money for it, it had come out of his pocket. The Ispravnik followed us in a troika[1]

Another bump !

" Coachman, stop !" shouted my father.

The carriage stopped.

The Ispravnik tumbled out of his vehicle, and ran up, with his hand to his hat, as discipline demanded.

" Wait," said my father. " I'm coming back in a moment." And he got out of the carriage.

The coachman turned to me.

" Look out ! The baptism's just going to take place."

My father strode along, stopping every few moments and tapping the road with his stick, and then walking on and gesticulating.

" Look out !" repeated the coachman.

My father went on with his performance, the official kept on explaining, and picking up bits of gravel which he shewed to my father.

And suddenly—I could hardly believe my eyes—my

[1] Troika—A carriage drawn by three horses.

father raised his stick and a rain of blows descended on the Ispravnik's back.

" That's the way," cried the coachman, laughing. " He's a good Christian again now."

My father got back into the carriage.

" Drive on !"

The carriage went on for a bit.

" Stop, coachman !"

We stopped again.

The Ispravnik tumbled out of his carriage once more and ran up, but this time he halted prudently at a respectful distance.

" Please come here. Nearer ! Nearer ! Damn it all, nearer than that !"

The man turned pale but obeyed.

" Now, sir," said my father, " you know that blows are prohibited by the new laws. You can't even thrash a man who takes bribes. So you're at liberty to lodge a complaint."

" Your Excellency. . ."

" Please hold your tongue when I am speaking. You can make a complaint. Rest assured that I shall not attempt to exonerate myself, and I trust that the judges, who I believe to be fair minded, will find me guilty. Good day, sir. Drive on, coachman."

The carriage went on.

" The scoundrel !" said my father. " And yet he's energetic and intelligent—an excellent tchinovnik (State servant) on the whole. When he drops the habit of taking bribes he'll be perfect. Bribe-taking, just like beating, was one of the customs of the country, you know, an   one always returns to one's old habits. Yes, indeed, we're a pretty pair."

The next day when I went into my father's study, I stopped in astonishment. He was indeed a changed man. A little creature like a Chinese idol sat on his shoulders and was banging him on the head, probably mistaking it for a tambourine. My father seemed to be perfectly happy.

" But he'll stun you !" And I offered to take the baby.

" Leave him alone ! Aren't they delightful, these little darlings ? I've always had a soft spot for small children. Only I never suspected it before. The régime of serfdom stifled all feeling in us."

" Where did you come across the little creature ?"

" Why, he's my grandson, Loulou. Don't you know that your sister Nasha arrived this evening ?"

That day we went round the estate.

" I've made some reforms too," said my father. " I've only got twelve carriage horses in the stables now, and five saddle horses ; one for myself, two for your sisters, and two for visitors. It's quite enough. Nobody comes to the country any more. The kennels are done away with, the hot-houses are shut up, and there are only eight gardeners left. Manners change with the times. You've got to put a check on your fancies nowadays."

" What is that new building ?"

" Oh, that ? That's an error of judgment. It's a school which I gave them. But they won't send their children there. According to them, education is all right for the rich ; the poor don't need it. They don't yet know what's good for them."

" It will come eventually."

" Perhaps so. But they won't find fools like me ready to give things to them, and the Government won't do so either. They've already got the notion that there's danger in education. But I hope I'm wrong. One sees the blackest side of things as one gets old."

The village which was so clean formerly (there wasn't its equal in the whole district) was just like all the others now. The beautiful birches along the sides of the roads had been cut down, the little gardens were gone, the thatched roofs which had been so well kept formerly, now looked like bundles of straw from the stable litter. My father sighed.

" I no longer have any say in this. It belongs to them and they are their own masters."

A group of peasants approached with their caps in their hands.

" Well, lazybones, have you got your hay in yet ?"

The peasants scratched their ears—the Russian's method of answering when he doesn't wish to say yes or no.

" If you had been working instead of spending yesterday and the day before in getting drunk on the excuse that your neighbours were having a holiday . . . there's no doubt about it, I didn't beat you often enough in the old days !"

The moujiks laughed. " But, batiushka, that wasn't what was the matter."

" It seems it was. You'll end by dying of hunger."

" Oh, but you would come to our help. If we have no bread you'll give it to us. You are our father. . ."

" Indeed I won't. You ought to be ashamed of

yourselves. You won't even look after your own welfare any more."

" That's true," said one of them. " Since we were set free we have been lost. Completely lost."

" I know you," said my father, " I've only got to look at you to see what a fox you are. Now look here, Serge, do you also think that liberty is useless to you ?"

" It all depends. For the idle, yes ; but for the industrious, no. His lot is much better than that of the serf."

My father clapped him on the shoulder.

" Well said. I was glad to see your new barn. You're a man. But why didn't you rebuild your stable at the same time ? It's falling to pieces."

" I haven't got the wood. In time. . ."

" I'll give you the wood. Call in at my steward's. But on one condition, and that is, when you are mayor of the village—and you will be—give these lazy dogs a good beating." And the peasants laughed.

" This man Serge seems a good fellow," I said, when the moujiks had gone.

" Good fellow ? No, he's a ruffian like the others. As treacherous as the devil. But he's a man that works and doesn't drink, and that's the kind we need in Russia. A beautiful soul is of no use in itself, my dear boy. You can have a beautiful soul and be worthless, and *vice versa*. Now, look at this fellow who's coming up. That man's worth his weight in gold."

A little springless cart, such as the pedlars use, came along at a trot, drawn by a well-fed, well-groomed horse. It was driven by an old man with a white beard, wearing a cafetan.

" Good-day, Jean Petrovitch," my father called out to him.

The old man stopped his pony, handed his reins to an urchin beside him, got down, and holding his hat in his hands as a sign of respect, approached with the dignity of an Oriental.

" I give good-day to your Excellency Georges Egorovitch. I give good-day to the young barine."

My father held out his hand to him. I could not remember him.

" What good wind brings you this way ?"

" I'm on a tour of inspection."

" How is the bridge getting on ?"

" Slowly—but quite well. But I've insisted on their changing three defective girders. The bridge will be all right. But the road ! It's an absolute disgrace."

" I know, I know," said my father. " I've seen it ; but it will be put right."

" Do you think so ?"

" We've already had a talk with the Ispravnik."

The old man smiled imperceptibly.

" If you've talked to him, it will be done."

" Oh, yes," said my father. " The Ispravnik is a very intelligent man. A hint is enough for him. It will be re-made. How are things with you ?"

" Oh, not bad."

" Thanks to yourself. The others don't do anything."

" Petr Petrovitch is in very poor health. . ."

" His health's all right when it comes to enjoying himself. He'll have to be replaced at the next election. But where are the men to be found ? If we had one or two more like you it would be all right."

" And if we had men like your Excellency at the head of affairs, it would be splendid. But if I stay here talking to you I shall be late. Please excuse me."

My father gave him his hand, and he went. I asked who he was.

" A simple moujik, formerly a serf. Now he is a member of the Uprava. He's really the only one who has any business to be there. Yes, indeed . . . There's enough material among the Russian people to achieve anything. But . . . we still lack men. Among the nobility, yes . . . there are a few here and there. But on the whole they've had their day. The people . . . they're still children."

" What about the Intelligentzia ? "

" They're an absolute curse ! They're demoralising the country with their extreme theories, which the people cannot understand. They have more knowledge than many of ourselves, they're more active and perhaps mean well, but they have no patience and look on evolution with horror. Revolution is a fixed idea with them. To them, revolution is not a means but an end. Oh, don't let us talk about them, it makes me ill. The devil take them. The poor Emperor ! He thinks only of his people's welfare."

I stayed in Russia until the autumn, and then I went to Berlin.

These months which I spent in the new Russia gave me an impression which I cannot describe. A new era had begun. Serfdom, which is an obstacle to all progress, no longer existed, but its abolition had not yet had the results which one was entitled to expect.

Neither the lords nor the former serfs could keep pace with the new order. The former, accustomed to forced labour which cost them nothing, thought themselves ruined, let their land go to the devil, turned everything they could into money by cutting down their woods wholesale, and by selling their property to speculators who did not buy with the intention of working the estate, but held it in the hope of a rise in land value.

The serfs, trained in obedience, and as yet incapable of looking after themselves, used their liberty to have a good time and to drink as much as they could hold. Meanwhile, agriculture and the land fell into decay.

The Russia of the past had vanished, and that of the future was yet to come.

CHAPTER IV

1867–1872

AFTER graduating as a Doctor of Philosophy, I went, before I returned to Russia, to say good-bye to the famous Professor Pirogov, who also lived in Berlin. He asked me what career I intended to adopt. I said that I was going to take up work under the Ministry of the Interior.

" For what reason ?"

" Why, to serve my country."

He laughed. " My dear fellow, how innocent you are ! Be careful never to say what you said out loud or you'll be made fun of. Government servants are of no use to anyone but themselves."

I asked the advice of my brother Michael, who was already a general, and on the Staff, and had just been made governor of a district in Poland.

" So you're going to be a quill-driver ?" he said. " It's the stupidest of all jobs. There's only one possible career in Russia—the Army. Once you are a general you can become what you like—an archbishop, if you feel inclined to. It's absurd, but there it is."

" That's all going to change."

" Let us hope so. But meanwhile, it's the only advice I can give you. I've never been a tchinovnik myself, but I'll introduce you to my deputy—an insipid fellow, but a tchinovnik to his finger-tips. He'll tell you where to make a start."

The man of whom my brother spoke so irreverently was M. Goremykin, who became President of the Ministerial Council under Nicholas II, and who was celebrated for his ineptitude and lack of *savoir faire*.

I met him at dinner at Michael's house on the same day. Prince Stcherbatov, Governor of Kalisz, who was on the Staff with my brother, was also dining there. M. Goremykin gave me all the necessary details, but the more he talked, the less I knew what I ought to do.

" What a set they are !" said the Prince when my adviser had gone. " If you ask a tchinovnik the time, he'll tell you how time was first measured, how watches are made, and will give a lengthy description of the various ways of constructing them—but never, never will he tell you the time ! You want a job, do you ? Well, come to me as *attaché* to the special mission. The post is just vacant."

" And what would my duties consist of, Prince ?"

" How shall I put it ?" said the Prince. "A governor, especially in Poland, is like a castaway on a desert island. It's not exactly deserted but it's the same thing. If the governor comes into too close contact with the natives, he gets eaten by them in the end. So Robinson Crusoe needs a faithful Man Friday to act as a go-between, between him and the savages. You would be Man Friday, and there you are."

To be brief, I accepted.

Poland had been quiet for some years then, but the state of siege still continued. It must be admitted that the policy of the Russian Government in Poland was neither wise nor practicable. It tried to arrive, by means of force and violence, at a result which could only have been achieved by justice and a wise administration. Instead of winning the country over, our methods exasperated it.

The Viceroy of the former Kingdom of Poland was Marshall Count Berg, a shrewd fellow as sly as an old fox, with the manners of the eighteenth century. He was a perfect diplomat, and knew better than anyone else what could be done to reconcile Poland to Russian rule. But he had the ultra-Russian chauvinists of Moscow against him, and he hedged, seeking to maintain a policy of conciliation but abandoning it whenever he felt it dangerous to his career.

My Robinson Crusoe, Prince Stcherbatov was also a man of parts, but he was without balance, and allowed himself to be guided by his whims rather than by his common sense. He was without principles, or rather boasted of having only one : " to have no principles." When he managed to reach a certain position he never knew how to maintain it and generally ended by getting into some scrape from which influence alone would rescue him, still alive although somewhat battered.

He was a good fellow, though difficult to get on with. He was always ready with a joke, and easy to live with until a time arrived when one had definitely had enough of him. The Poles loathed him and he returned their feeling with interest. He considered it a point of honour never to make any advances to them, and this made Count Berg beside himself with fury. In consequence there were continual passages at arms between the Viceroy and the Prince.

G

After each altercation, Stcherbatov would be meekness itself for a few days—and then he would begin again.

One day when I was in the room where the Prince usually held interviews, an old lady came to ask for a permit to leave the country in order to go and see her son who was ill in Paris. I gave orders for the necessary papers to be got ready and was bringing them to the Prince to sign, when he came into the room.

"What can I do for Madame?" This was said in Russian.

"I came to beg your Highness," said the lady in French, "to be so gracious as to give me permission to leave Poland."

"First of all," answered the Governor in the same language, "I am not your Highness, but simply Prince. Secondly, I am never gracious. Thirdly, I only listen to Russian."

He bowed and went out.

The poor lady was ready to weep. I told her that there had probably been a misunderstanding, asked her to wait a moment, and went in to the Prince.

He was immovable.

"These dirty Poles think that they can win me over with flattery, do they? She knew perfectly well that I wasn't a Highness. And to dare speak to me in French and not Russian! What impudence!"

"First of all," I said, "this lady has no means of knowing whether you are a Highness or not. Secondly, she doesn't know Russian. Thirdly, I believe she will get her passport all the same."

"We shall see about that."

"She'll go to Count Berg and he'll certainly grant it.

You have acted according to your convictions, and he'll
act according to his, and there you are !"

" No, hang it, I won't give the old brute that satisfaction. Give me the papers and may they choke her."

My duties as " attaché " to the special missions seemed
to consist in doing nothing. In the morning I read the
Prince the foreign newspapers, which abused him violently,
later we dined together, and in the evening played " bac "
or went to the theatre. Finally I got bored with it, and
as the Prince would not give me anything to do, I applied
to his chancellor. He had never been a tchinovnik either.
He was a clever man, a country neighbour of the Prince's
who had gaily run through his patrimony and had taken
service while he was waiting for an inheritance from an
aunt, who according to his calculations, was soon due
" to kick the bucket "—to use his own words.

" You want to work ?" he said. " How odd ! Don't
you know that a civil servant who works is a lost man ?
There are only two kinds of civil servants, you know.
There are the needy, who do the same job day after day,
and end by being good for nothing else. Then there are the
gentlemen, who don't do anything, but conserve their
mental faculties and in a few years become State Council-
lors, and who can get anything they want, if they know
how to go about it. You must choose."

" But I am here for special missions. . ."

" When we have any special missions you shall be given
them."

" But there are hardly ever any."

" The attaché for special missions is meant to be ornamental, not useful."

Soon after that I was sent on a special mission. I was

sent to the frontier to meet a Bishop who was on his rounds.

Then one day when the Princess, her husband and I were in his office, the chief of police arrived to make his daily report. Among other things he mentioned a scandal which had taken place in the evening at the theatre, which was owned by the State.

" Since the director's death, goodness knows what's been happening. May I beg you once more, Prince, to appoint. . . . ."

" Very well, very well," said the governor. " Thanks, that's all right."

" May I hope, Prince, that it will be done soon ?"

" Certainly, certainly," and he held out his hands. " Good-bye."

The chief of police saluted and went away.

" He is a tiresome fellow, always worrying me about a director for the theatre," said the Prince. " It's becoming an absolute bore."

" But why do you keep putting off making the appointment," asked the Princess. " He has been talking to you about it for months."

" I have promised the post to a man on whose behalf I was approached by a very influential personage."

" Well, why not nominate someone else while you are waiting ?"

" Now that's an idea. Baron, you can take his place. I appoint you."

" Oh, come !" said the Princess. " At his age—nobody will take him seriously."

" Won't they indeed, we'll see about that. I'll make these cursed Poles shake in their shoes in front of him."

And he immediately gave orders for the producer and his stage manager to come to him the next day. Then turning to me he said :

" I shall expect you sharp at ten o'clock. But put on your uniform. You look too young in mufti."

The next day he told me to await in the adjoining room, leaving the door ajar and summoned the two Poles.

At this time a governor was all powerful in Poland and the inhabitants were only too well aware of it. The Prince began to storm at them and the poor wretches were soon more dead than alive.

This soothed him.

" This time," he concluded, " I shall not be hard on you. But this is the end. You are going to have a director who . . . ." and he was off again.

According to him I was a man that even he could not trifle with, a man who had grown old in this kind of work, a man who . . . .

And, opening the door, he said, " Come in, Baron, if you please."

And instead of an ogre with white hair, there appeared a lad whose beard had hardly begun to grow.

" Baron I am going to give you *carte blanche*. You are at liberty to dismiss anyone. It will be forbidden for anyone to go behind the scenes who does not belong to the staff. I will shortly indicate other measures for you to take."

When the managers had gone he began to laugh.

" Did you see what a funk they were in ? Only your baby-face nearly ruined the whole scene !"

" And the measures . . ?"

" Give me a rest ! Just keep everyone away from the stage door, and be the only Sultan in the harem."

Then taking my arm, " Come and have lunch, you old polygamist."

Some days later, as I was leaving the room, he said :

" By the way, do you know that the Colonel of the Hussars is furious with you ? He complains that he can't go behind the scenes any more."

" And what did you say to him ?"

" I promised to speak to you about it."

" But, Prince, it was your own wish."

" Yes, yes, but try to fix this up. I don't want to have a row with him. He is an A.D.C. to the Emperor."

" If we make an exception for him, everyone . . . ."

" You're quite right. Let nobody in. Nobody. And don't mention it again."

The Colonel returned to the charge, and I refused to admit him. He appealed to the Prince and came back with a permit. I gave orders for him to be admitted, and asked the Prince to relieve me of my duties as director.

" But why ? I'm very pleased with you."

" The feeling is not reciprocated, Prince."

He laughed.

" You forget, my dear boy, that we're living in Russia, not Switzerland, and here we have to go with the herd."

" I don't see any need to, if one is a man and not a beast."

" Well said. You'll get the reputation of being a man of independent principles if you make replies like that. Only—I'm really fond of you and wish you well—they won't help you to get anywhere. One respects men of principle, but one avoids them."

" I don't want to get on at all costs, I want above all to serve my country."

He chuckled more than ever.

" Good lord, how young you are !"

" I don't see that age . . ."

" Oh, yes, I know, I know. ' The worth of a noble character is not measured by years !" It's a fine sounding line, but its absolutely ridiculous. If you have a noble character you ought to be a soldier and not a tchinovnik. A man of high character in the Civil Service is an absurdity."

I began to believe it myself after a time, but I was not yet certain about it, so I went on waiting for " special missions." At last, one night, I was woken up and summoned to the Prince's presence.

" A gendarme has been assassinated in the town of Kola," he told me. " A state of siege exists, the affair will be brought before a court-martial, and the enquiry will be held by the military authorities. But, as the murderer may be a civilian, a representative of the civil administration must be present. The man I had intended to send is ill and you will have to go instead. See that everything goes smoothly. The old ape (this was his usual name for the Viceroy) is anxious on this point and keeps bombarding me with telegrams. You must start at once. I give you forty-eight hours to settle the matter—Goodbye and a pleasant journey."

I did not delay, and I was on the spot in a few hours.

The accused, who had already been arrested, was a Pole who knew hardly a word of Russian. He obviously did not understand the questions which were put to him in Russian, and answered them at random. When the interrogation was at an end, I was handed the protocol to sign.

" I don't believe," I said, " that this man has understood our questions properly, and neither have I quite grasped his answers. It is essential that an interpreter should be sent for. It is impossible for me to sign his deposition like that, especially as he can't sign it himself, since he can't write."

" We have no interpreter at hand," said the officer of the police, " and anyway, I understand Polish more or less." And he signed the paper.

" But . . ."

" I understand your scruples, and theoretically you are quite right. But you can conscientiously rely on my experience. I am accustomed to this kind of affair. It would waste endless time to wait for an interpreter, and the Viceroy himself wishes the business settled as quickly as possible."

" But this man's life depends on it ! If he should be innocent. . ."

" You've only got to look at him to see that he's guilty."

" His looks aren't evidence."

" You insist then ?"

" Yes."

" It will mean delay."

" I'm sorry. It's impossible for me to sign otherwise."

" Very well. There's only one thing to be done. We must postpone it till to-morrow and get an interpreter."

And we parted.

I received a telegram from the Prince that night. The man whose place I had taken was better ; I was relieved of my mission and ordered back at once.

When I got to Kalisz, I made a detailed report to the Prince, but he interrupted me, saying :

" I know, I know. The officer of police told me about it. There's no doubt at all, my dear boy, you are still very young. Formalities have their uses, but they can be passed over at times. Come along, our partners are waiting for us to play baccarat."

Luck was against me that day and I lost rather a large sum. As the players were always the same, we had got into the habit of settling our accounts at the end of the month.

I had a bad night. The result of my first serious mission haunted me. Certainly the services I rendered to my country were not those of which I had dreamed. It might well be that the fault lay not so much in the career that I had chosen, as in the fact that my chief was not worthy of the post which had been entrusted to him.

I determined to talk it over with my brother Michael, and the next day, having obtained several days leave, I went to Warsaw, as I knew he was passing through there.

At the club I met General Frédérix, head of the royal police, who was a constant visitor at my father's house.

He spoke to me about my chief, and about Kalisz, which was going to the dogs, according to him.

" Your Prince," he said " is certainly not in the odour of sanctity as far as the Count is concerned. For instance, the other day another of my gendarmes was assassinated at Kola and the assassin, who was caught here at Warsaw, confessed his crime, which, by the way, was unnecessary as the victim's belongings were found on him. And here we have the Prince claiming to have found the guilty man who, he says, has made a complete confession. That seemed rather fishy to us, so the Viceroy sent one of the

Generals attached to his personal staff to get to the bottom of things."

I was on the point of telling him what I knew about this business, but I refrained. It would have looked like giving someone away.

When I got back to Kalisz the first person I met as I was getting out of the carriage was the Governor's chancellor. He gave me to understand that the Prince appeared to think that my indiscretions concerning the affair at Kola had got him into Count Berg's bad books. He also told me that the General, sent by the Marshal, had arrived the night before and that the Prince did not seem exactly pleased with his visit.

I went to the Palace and found him talking to the General, whom I did not know but whom I had often seen in the Countess Berg's drawing-rooms and to whom, so I have heard, the Count generally confided any delicate mission.

When I came in the Prince paid no attention to me. Then sharply breaking off his conversation he said :

" What do you want with me ?"

" My leave is up . . ."

" When a subordinate reports to his chief he should wear uniform."

I bowed and left the room.

Shortly afterwards one of the Prince's orderlies came to me.

" The Governor asks your Honour to come to him immediately."

" Just give me time to change and I'll come."

" He asks you to come in the suit you were wearing just now."

" Good. Tell the Prince that you found me changing my clothes. Now, in consequence of his order that I should come dressed as I was before, I shall have to change again and that obviously will take some time. You understand ? Now, repeat what I've just said. Excellent. You can go."

I took longer than was necessary over dressing. Then without hurrying, I went to the Governor.

When I came in the General gave me a friendly glance ; the Prince appeared furiously angry but trying to keep control over himself.

All the same he worked himself up as usual with the first words he uttered to me.

According to him, His Excellency Marshal Count Berg (he was talking of the old ape) was very dissatisfied with the juniors. They didn't work, there was a bad atmosphere about them, they even played games of chance, which was expressly forbidden, etc., etc. In short, if he was to be believed it was I who had set the bad example.

The General, taking advantage of a pause, diverted his attention.

" May I ask you to introduce me to this gentleman, Prince ; I have seen him several times at Warsaw and his brothers are friends of mine."

The Prince did so and then, as if nothing had happened, handed me his cigarette-case.

" Will you smoke ? Do sit down, won't you ?"

We began to talk of trivialities ; but I was also furious.

" By the way, while I remember it," as I took out my pocket-book, " I am still in your debt."

" In my debt ? You ?"

" Yes, of course. I haven't settled my last baccarat

debt, that game which is prohibited by law, but which is so popular in the best families."

And I handed him a bundle of notes.

The General wanted to laugh. But the Prince certainly had no such desire.

I handed in my resignation the same day, but we parted friends. The Prince was too light-minded to bear a grudge.

In the Czarist Empire, as we know, virtue is always rewarded. So that the signal services which I rendered my country at Kalisz were not forgotten. A month after I left Poland I was attached, again for special missions, to the staff, not of a simple governor of a Province, but to that of the Governor-General of the whole of Lithuania. I had got on. I was now almost a personage in provincial circles, if not in the capital itself.

This time the signs in my favour were propitious. My new chief, General Potapov, who was aide-de-camp to his Majesty, was the pleasantest man, or rather mannikin (he was no taller than a curassier's boot), whom one could meet. Cultured, witty and agreeable, he was completely devoid of feeling, a quality in a chief which is not to be despised. He was always even-tempered ; with such a chief there was no feeling of uncertainty, no unexpected moods to be bargained for.

If you got on with him, his liking for you lasted.

It is true he would never expand like a pelican opening its wings, but neither would he throw one over at the first opportunity, unless it really paid him to do so.

From the time of the Revolution in 1863, Lithuania

had been treated as a conquered country. It was in a state of siege and so subject to the caprices of martial law so that one could hardly realize that one was in Europe and not in Asia.

Potapov's predecessors, the fierce Muraviev and General Kaufman, who imitated him, had thrown the country into complete confusion. Potapov, on the other hand, came there with the best intentions and fully determined to put things straight. He set about his task with energy and gave us plenty to do. At last I had enough work to satisfy me.

Alas, it did not last long.

Potapov was before everything a courtier, and, observing that the wind was changing at court, he gradually began to change sides himself. And the reforms which he had inaugurated finally fizzled out.

He followed in the footsteps of the majority of Russian statesmen and no longer thought of anything but remaining in his master's favour. Eventually, with his nomination to the important post of Chief of Police of the Empire, he too obtained a sinecure.

I was no longer with him when this happened, but was living as a private individual at St. Petersburg, where I often visited him. In spite of our difference in age and position we remained intimate friends. One day I asked him what exactly his new functions were. He smiled that bantering, yet sad, smile which was peculiar to him.

" I have to poke my nose into everything and interfere with nothing. Between ourselves, I really have only one definite function ; and that is, to convey to the women on whom His Majesty's favour has rested the sums which he is pleased to grant them."

" And are there a great many of these ladies ?"

" A fair number."

" Society women ?"

" Very much so."

" And they accept the money ?"

" Accept it ! They extort it !"

Poor little man ! Some years afterwards, while he was with the Emperor in the Crimea, he suddenly went mad. The last time I saw him he was dressed in his splendid uniform covered with medals, with the ribbon of his Order across his chest ; astride a wooden rocking-horse and brandishing his sword he was charging a regiment of Turks in cardboard set out in battle array on a table.

I shall not dwell on my service in Lithuania. The Russia of this epoch had already become a stagnant morass, and to talk of a morass cannot be interesting to anyone except to the frogs that live in it. In any case I do not claim to be writing the history of my times, neither am I stupid enough to be writing an autobiography. I am not a man of note whose intimate life might be of interest to the public, and neither am I one of those good-for-nothing enemies or partisans of the old régime of absolutism, who to-day try to make people believe that they once played an important part in Russia.

Besides, when I began to write these random reminiscences, I had no intention of having them published. I wrote them simply and solely to occupy my spare time and to forget if possible the sad reality. Alone, old and infirm, ruined by the Revolution, and a refugee in Finland where I did not know a soul, the hours seemed like centuries to me. Then a friend had them translated into Finnish and Swedish and brought them to the notice of an editor. Some of them were published and had an unexpected success.

I am putting all this down in order to explain why these memoirs are written rather by fits and starts, why they are sometimes discursive and sometimes sketchy, why in fact they do not follow any rigid plan. I trust allowances will be made for me.

I stayed about two years at Vilna. The life there was pleasant and the people were charming. I retain the pleasantest memories of it. But the inevitable came to pass. I realised that, as things were, to be a tchinovnik and to serve one's country usefully were two things which were incompatible—so I resigned from the Civil Service. The sad realities of life had taken the place of the beautiful dreams of youth.

It was considered almost a duty by the nobility to serve the State, so that before deciding to leave the Service I was anxious to obtain my father's approval.

He did not make any objection.

" I quite understand," he said. " It's a wretched procession. What a pity you didn't go into the army instead of wasting years studying all these sciences which are more or less useless in Russia. I didn't try and dissuade you then because with you . . . well, because I made it a rule never to impose my wishes on you but to let you go your own way. By this time you might have been a Colonel already, or at least in command of a squadron."

A little while afterwards, as we were strolling along the quay of the Neva, as was then fashionable, we met the Emperor Alexander II. He recognised my father and stopped to say a few friendly words to him. Then, happening to notice myself, who was standing at a respectful distance, he asked who I was.

" My youngest son, Sire."

" But to let a fine fellow like that rot in the Civil Service is a sin ! He is made to be one of my Guardsmen."

And he went on his way.

" What regiment do you think of going into ?" asked my father.

" But he's decided that himself; the Horse-guards," I replied.

I did not hesitate for a moment. For one thing, there was no disobeying my father when he made suggestions in a certain way, and for another it was my reason alone and not my personal tastes which had led me to take up another career than that of the army. Our traditions were all military. Our family had produced five Field-Marshals, a number of Generals and officers of high rank—and atavism is a force that has to be reckoned with. The only thing that worried me was that I should have to start as an ensign, which, at my age, was almost ridiculous.

I also wondered whether, having been educated abroad and not in Russia, my degree gave me the right to become an officer, not after a period of two years but at the end of six months.

Happily my fears were unfounded. Count Shuvalov, Chief of Staff of the Guard, reassured me on this point.

" What an absurd idea," he said. " Why, of course, in six months . . . yes, certainly—in six months you will be promoted. In any case, I'll ask the chief of the section in order to set your mind at rest."

And he sent for him.

" Tell me, Colonel, what is the probationary period for people who have been to the University ?"

" Six months, General."

" It was a German, not a Russian, University," I said.

" It's all the same."

" There you are ! Thanks, Colonel," said the Count. " I have troubled you for nothing, but it's always best to be on the safe side."

But again I lost several months. My father died suddenly and as my brothers were away I had to deal with all matters referring to his estate.

The Horseguards and the " *chevaliers-gardes*," which in the eighteenth century formed a single regiment, had always been the two smartest corps of the Guard. Only the cream of the nobility served in them, and to be admitted to them was considered a favour. The late Emperor Nicholas I and his son Alexander II headed these regiments and generally wore their uniform, while most of the Grand Dukes were their officers.

They did me the honóur to admit me. Our uniform or, to be exact, our uniforms, for we had many of them, were splendid. We had a tight-fitting red tunic with gold braid for the Court balls, a green one with blue trousers for the town balls and a green military frockcoat for dinners and calls. Service dress consisted of a white cloth tunic with gold braid, top-boots coming up to the knees and a gold-plated cuirass and helmet ; on the crest of the helmet was an Imperial eagle with outstretched wings.

Mounted on splendid horses with flowing manes and tails, the men looked like an army of mounted giants. I forgot to say that both men and horses were huge.

H

In spite of my age and my philosophy, when I first saw myself dressed like this I was ready to follow the example of my new comrades, who were less modest than myself, and take myself, not for what I really was, but for a superior being, a demi-god, a hero of the Middle Ages. And, as can be imagined, my immediate circle looked on me differently too. Even my valet, whose services I had never made use of when dressing before, fussed about me in a possessive way, strapping me up and pulling me about. The first day I appeared in uniform my porter gave me a bow almost to the ground and my old coachman, a steady and sensible man, set off at a terrific pace as if the devil were after us. And the police sergeants, instead of taking him by the collar and laying information against him, stood at attention. Undoubtedly an officer in the Horseguards was a personage.

I was not an officer yet, but the majority of people took me for one and in any case at that time it came to more or less the same thing. The cadets of former times (later the name was only used for those belonging to schools) were not ordinary soldiers like the present-day volunteers. They were only private soldiers in the barrack square ; off parade they were the equals of officers. They dined in the officer's mess, they mixed with them in society, at the theatre, in the restaurants, at the cafés. There was nothing very terrible about being in the ranks under these conditions. One just had to subsidize the sergeant-major adequately and everything went smoothly.

The Colonel of the regiment, Count Grabbé, had been a comrade and intimate friend of my brother Michael ; most of the officers were friends of my childhood and the rest were relations of mine.

And as, in addition, I was a cheerful companion, a good rider and looked like a soldier they decided there and then that I was a man and not a miserable Philistine.

I, too, felt myself to be at home from the first. All my new brothers in arms were, without exception, well brought up, polite, correct and excellent fellows—or at any rate, if not, they appeared to be so—which comes to much the same thing in everyday life. Most of them were pleasant companions on the whole and some of them were even men of fine characters.

Nearly all of them made their way in the world. Of the thirty or so young men who were there when I entered the regiment at least half were taken afterwards into His Majesty's household troops, the rest occupied other important posts. How far they deserved their good fortune I do not care to say. But they belonged to the Horseguards and that was enough.

The following is a list of those I remember who belonged to His Imperial Majesty's Household Guards :

Aides-de-camp of the Emperor with the rank of General: Baron Meyendorf (attached to His Majesty's person), A. Strukov (Inspector General of the Imperial Cavalry), Count Frédérix (Minister of the Court), Count Benckendorf (Grand Marshal of the Court), Prince Vassiltchikov (Commandant of the Corps of the Guard), Baron Alexander Meyendorf (Commandant of His Majesty's personal escort), Prince Odoevsky (Commandant of the Imperial Palaces of Moscow), Prince M. Galitzin (Marshal of the Court of His Imperial Highness the Grand Duke Vladimir), Maximovitch (Assistant Minister of the Court), Novossiltzev (Commandant of a Cavalry Corps).

Aides-de-camp to His Majesty with the rank of Colonel :

Kladistchev, Prince A. Lvov, Prince E. Lvov, Baron C. Stakelberg.

In the spring we set off, headed by the band, for the camp of Krasnoe-Selo, where the Guards, both cavalry and infantry, stayed during the summer. The officers lived in little cottages which only contained two small rooms. I kept one for myself, in which there was hardly room to move, and gave the other, which was still smaller, to my old valet. Like everybody else, I only took my siesta there, and hardly ever slept there at night. The day was spent partly on horseback and partly in the mess, a vast barrack consisting of a single high hall which served as dining-room, library and reading-room all at once, the arrangement did not worry the readers, since the library consisted of various sporting journals, which somebody always lost the first day they arrived, and of the official gazette, which nobody ever read. As for other books, there were none. No, I am wrong. One of the officers possessed a novel by Paul de Kock, which everybody thought delightful. But it had already been read and re-read, and most of the pages were missing.

At dawn we were already in the saddle, and would come in about one o'clock in the afternoon dead tired, have a hasty lunch and go to sleep until dinner, which was a real Balthazar's feast, copiously washed down with champagne.

Our chef was the famous Dussaux himself.

In the evening we went to the theatre, or perhaps we went off to St. Petersburg, where we would have a good time, and we would only return to camp just in time to avoid being arrested.

An intellectual would probably find such an existence very distasteful, and in the long run I agree with him. But nevertheless a soldier's life has a charm which cannot be understood by those who have never taken part in it.

First of all, in a regiment one no longer feels one's self to be an isolated being, an atom lost in the vastness of the world, but part of a whole of a really tangible living body—a regiment, which in its turn is an atom, an inseparable part of a whole, of a larger and mightier whole—the army.

Formerly, before the system of compulsory military service had been adopted, before we had an " armed nation," to be in the army, whether as an officer or as a private soldier, was a calling, a career, often even a vocation. The soldier served twenty-five years, and the officer longer still. For then the army was everything. It was their world and there was nothing outside it. Soldiers and officers, with the aid of tradition, became beings apart whose thoughts and feelings were different from those of the rest of mankind.

To them to obey was not an enforced imposition, but something which came naturally. The flag was a tradition stronger than one's self, and to die, if it was necessary, came naturally too.

When compulsory service was introduced this was all changed. In peace time the soldier only stayed in the army for a limited period, just long enough to learn his drill, and too short a time to imbibe the military tradition and to feel himself to be a real soldier. The feeling of being a soldier only came to him in times of war, and then only when the officers know how to inculcate it in him. The officers themselves continued to serve for life, or for as long as they wished, and carried on the traditions of the flag and the military spirit—but they became the sole repository of these traditions.

Neither the government nor the people understood this.

After the Crimean disaster in 1855, the government treated the officers (I am only speaking of the officers of the line and not of the Guard) very brutally. They were badly paid, badly housed, and at the mercy of their superiors. They lived miserably from day to day without any prospect of promotion, and without any hope of a comfortable old age. They were looked down on by society and the intellectuals despised them as useless and worthless.

According to them the officer was an idler, a sponger who lived on the State, an ignorant fellow who brutalised the soldier and put harmful ideas into his head.

It is quite true that the officer had his faults. There are spots on the sun, but that does not prevent it from shining and giving light to the earth. The " intellectuals " only wished to see their faults, and deliberately shut their eyes to all their best and noblest qualities.

Great and noble qualities they certainly showed, wherever the flag called them. On the plains of Manchuria and of Eastern Prussia, in the heights of the Carpathians, in Galicia—wherever it was their duty to die.

And even to-day, in our suffering but unconquered Russia, treacherously stabbed in the back by her enemies, betrayed by her own children and forgotten by her allies, mocked by the intellectuals, the principal agents of Russian disaster, will fight on to defend the honour, if not the life of the country which gave him birth. And the standard-bearer of these men who are slandered by the Intelligentzia, is, I am proud to say, an officer of the regiment in which I once served as a common soldier, a guardsman—my own son.

I did not speak idly when I said " a common soldier," because, instead of being promoted to the rank of officer as I expected, I became a common soldier. But before I speak of this I must relate one or two incidents which agreeably interrupted not the boredom but the monotony of camp life.

One day the Grand Duke Vladimir told us on the quiet that he was coming to our mess unexpectedly the next day without our being supposed to know, and was bringing one of the German princes to dine with him. The Teuton had been boasting of the splendours of the mess of the Prussian officers in the German Emperor's Household Guard, a regiment that has the same uniform as ours ; the grand Duke proposed to take him down a peg or two by showing him how the Russian officers lived.

Great excitement ! The Prussian needn't worry himself. He would see what we could do !

We ordered a whole conservatory of hothouse flowers from St. Petersburg to turn our barn-like mess into an earthly paradise, and a troupe of gipsy singers—as for the wines and the dishes I shall not enumerate them, but they were all that could be desired. At the appointed time we were just about to sit down quietly to dinner when to our astonishment the Grand Duke appeared with the Prince.

We never dreamed of such an honour as this, and if their Imperial Highnesses would care to share our modest repast, we should be in heaven.

The Grand Duke, after a moment's hesitation, graciously accepted, and we all sat down.

The Princes did full justice to the meal, ate and drank their fill, said a few gracious words to the gipsy singer, pinched the pretty gipsy girls and then without saying a single word to the officers went away.

Really that was more than we could stand ! But our Colonel, Count Grabbé, put a stop to the chorus of indignation which was just breaking out.

" Gentlemen, do not forget that we are speaking of His Majesty's son. Besides, you may take it from me you won't lose anything by being patient."

We knew our Grabbé. The honour of the regiment was in good hands ; and we were silent.

It seems that the dinner wasn't bad, because some time afterwards the Princes announced that they would come again, but this time officially. Grabbé called for the chef. " We will have two dinners to-morrow," he said " one at ten o'clock which will be as good as usual, the other at seven. The seven o'clock dinner must be disgusting and quite uneatable."

" I must say that I have never tried to prepare a rotten dinner, but if you make a point of it we will do our best," said the chef.

" Do please, I am relying on you."

Dessaux as usual surpassed himself. You should have seen the Grand Duke's face. But he understood and was particularly gracious to every one that day.

It is true that the Grand Duke Vladimir had not the manners of a polished aristocrat. He was intelligent but ill-mannered. One day a lady who was talking to him addressed him as Monsieur instead of Monseigneur as was customary.

" My dear lady, I am generally addressed as Monseigneur."

" Oh! I beg your pardon, Monseigneur," said the lady; " I had entirely forgotten that you were not a monsieur."[1]

Bad fortune like good comes when it is least expected.

One fine day a new law on compulsory service, or a supplementary law, I don't quite remember, was announced and published. Ensigns were abolished. Their place was taken by volunteers who were to be treated in exactly the same way as private soldiers. They were no longer to wear epaulettes with broad gold braid which deceived the uninitiated into mistaking them for officers. They were forbidden to dine in mess, drive in a carriage or go to restaurants, or to sit down in the presence of a superior officer without his express permission. There was a volume of penalties and not a single privilege.

As always happened in Russia they had gone from one extreme to the other.

It is impossible for a person who did not live at that time to have even an approximate idea of the dog's life that we led as a result of this law.

There were not then as there are now rankers drawn from every class of society, but only ordinary private soldiers, moujiks straight from their villages. The simple soldier was regarded and treated by the public, including private persons, as an inferior and a rustic. The language used towards us was not merely uncivil, it was coarse. We were chivvied about, in fact we were déclassés. If we wanted to call on our friends we had to walk miles, if we wanted to dine we had to go to a restaurant with a private room and find our own cook. Even in society we were liable to insults of a most extraordinary type. One day a

[1] *i.e.*, a gentleman.

line officer who had just turned up from the provinces ordered the volunteer Prince Dolgoruky to fetch him a cab. The Prince, in duty bound, was obliged to do so.

A similar incident occurred to me. One day I was calling on Countess—— whose name I shall not give. You will remember her, she was my first love at Geneva. I was introduced to her again at St. Petersburg. I say again because the ungrateful creature had quite forgotten me. We soon became friends. She was a charming woman endowed with grace and tact beyond the ordinary and in spite of her numerous adventures she was very popular in society. One day I reminded her of our former meeting. She looked quite surprised. " So you were really in love with me ?"

" You were my first and only love."

She pondered a moment.

" What a pity the old man came in at such an awkward moment."

" We can still put that right, Countess."

" No, one should never make a lover of a friend. One loses too much by it. Lovers can be picked up at any time but real friends are difficult to find."

I went on talking. As we were sitting there in the drawing room an old general with a face like a bull dog came in. I got up and stood at attention. The bull dog, without paying the slightest attention to his subordinate sat down in an arm chair.

" But, General," said the Countess, " you ought to give the Baron permission to sit down."

" He can wait."

The Countess rose and took my arm. Then, smiling amiably at the old beast, she said, " Excuse me, General,

I shall be back in a few moments. I have got something important to say to this gentleman and I don't like standing up when I am talking."

We went into the next room and the general was left alone.

Fifteen minutes went by and we waited, curious to see what he would do. Eventually he went away. The Countess rang the bell.

" Please tell the concierge that I am never at home to the General."

Women were like that then.

Our colonel and also my former comrades made many attempts to alleviate our lot, but they could do nothing. Numbers of the ensigns in the Guards' regiments handed in their resignations. I held on in spite of everything. I had only a few weeks to go and then it would be over ; the convict would become an officer. But I was mistaken as it turned out. One fine day—I remember it even now— an army order arrived from the Ministry of War, to the effect that in accordance with the new laws members of foreign universities had no right to the privileges accorded to members of universities within the empire, and that therefore the volunteer Baron Wrangel could not become an officer until he had served for two years.

No, this was not good enough !

Fifteen days later I was an ordinary civilian, but I also enjoyed the rights of a private citizen again.

I made a final attempt to serve my country. I resolved to take up a diplomatic career, which was certainly not very logical. My aim was to be useful to my country, and who has ever seen a useful diplomat ? Fortunately for me and also for Russia probably, this enterprise of folly simply served to provide me with a story. My uncle, Alexandre Wrangel, aide-de-camp to His Majesty, the well-known hero of the Caucasus who had captured the Imam Shamil, mentioned me to the Chancellor who was an intimate friend of his, and the Prince, who had known me at one time, consented to take me on. I was asked to go and see him and make my personal request.

His Serene Highness, Prince Gorchakov, Vice-Chancellor and Minister of Foreign Affairs, was at this period at the height of his glory and self-satisfaction. The glory did not last, but his self-satisfaction lasted as long as he did, and I am inclined to think that even to-day in his heavenly abode he spends his time in self-admiration and a longing to preside at all costs at a world-conference of nations. Thanks to this self-love, in spite of his real intelligence, he had the knack of making himself ridiculous. He admired nobody but himself, talked of nobody but himself, and in spite of his age thought he was irresistible to women and posed as a Don Juan. They all made eyes at him, but laughed at him behind his back. They were not alone in their duplicity, for the men, excepting his principal secretary, all acted in the same way. The principal secretary, Baron Meyendorf, is worth a few remarks. He was the Prince's own nephew and he never lost an opportunity of trying to make him look ridiculous. It must be admitted that in this he was singularly successful, for he had a very biting wit and was not over scrupulous in attaining his object. His aim was, as you would hardly guess, to be dismissed by the Chancellor. The fact is that his uncle and chief had become a burden to him. But he could not withdraw his dutiful services from him of his own accord. He had promised his mother on her death bed that he would not leave him. And now he had found a way out of the difficulty—to get himself dismissed. One day they were dining with the beautiful Madame Yakunt- chikov. The Prince asked Meyendorf, who was leaving for Paris, whether he meant to see anyone when he was there.

" Certainly, Prince, I have several friends in the diplo- matic service. Have you any orders for me ?"

" No," said he shortly. " No, but say that you have seen the lion in his den and that he is seeing to the preserva- tion of the balance of power in Europe."

" Certainly your Highness, I shall not fail to tell them that I have seen the brute at home."

His Serene Highness pretended not to have heard but he meant to have his revenge.

" If you see Michael "—that was the name of the Prince's younger son—" by the way, I have often meant to ask you how much older he is than you."

" We are the same age, Prince."

" The same age ?" said the Prince, " well he has got well ahead of you, he is a chip of the old block. The same age, and he is a plenipotentiary, while you are only a secretary."

" I assure you, Prince, the fault is entirely mine, I wasted years in study and he never wasted an hour."

The avarice of the " Narcissus of the Ink Pot," as his nephew called the Chancellor, was proverbial. He spent whole days consulting his banker Frenkel, a well known Jew, about their means of increasing his fortune. Malevo- lent tongues said that Frenkel enabled him to make a good deal of money on the Bourse.

One morning, at the time when the Prince granted his audiences, I went to call on the lion in his den.

The Swiss porter told me that the Chancellor would not

see visitors that day, as he was expecting somebody with whom he had a special appointment, but if I came the next day I would be able to see him.

I was just going when another servant intervened and said, " May I ask your name ?"

" Baron Wrangel."

" Please sir, come upstairs. His Highness is expecting you."

" Are you certain ?"

" Absolutely. I was sent downstairs to see that there was no mistake."

I went up quite pleased with myself. I was certain that my uncle had succeeded in having this exception made in my favour. I told him the day before that I was going to see the Prince.

I certainly had an awakening as the door of the Minister's room opened and the Prince came out to meet me smiling and holding out his hand.

Then, suddenly stopping short he shouted, " What confounded impudence, daring to force my door when I am not seeing anybody !" Then he turned on his heel and left me quite crestfallen. The flunkey had confused Wrangel with Frenkel whom the Prince was expecting that day.

I thought it wiser to take no further steps in the matter. And I did well. The Prince never condescended to speak to me after that incident.

For years I had been living on my illusions, and now that I had finally to give up the idea of public service I felt myself at a loose end. A strong man, or even a man who is not strong but simply obstinate, having once chosen his path, follows it in spite of every obstacle. The question is whether it is weakness of character or common sense. I leave it to others to answer—I am incapable of doing so. If I make a mistake, I admit it at once.

I have walked in pleasant places which have brought me nothing but disillusion. I have floundered in the mud and dissipated my time and my money. I have been a man of the world, a judge, a globe trotter and a farmer. I have written books which have been stopped by the censor and plays which the censor has also had the kindness to stop.

Then one day in the depths of the country, as I was crossing a bridge in my carriage (I did not yet know that in my country bridges on country roads were made to deter people from using them) the bridge gave way and I fell into the water. Fortunately, or unfortunately as the case may be, I was fished out and had to stay there for several months in bed crippled with rheumatism.

I was quite alone, my only companion being my old servant who was senile. My only visitor was the doctor, who having lived in the provinces since prehistoric times had lost the faculty of thinking or talking. I suffered the agonies of martyrdom, but I look back upon that time with gratitude. I recovered, pulled myself together and came to understand the futility of things which formerly had seemed to me to be indispensable to my happiness.

I found out, among other things, that happiness is not outside us but within us, that life is beautiful in itself, and that what I lacked was peace of mind and moral balance.

It was after this that I went into business. Possibly I contributed somewhat to the industrial development of Russia. Certainly my sons have grown to be men more far-seeing and useful to their country than I.

CHAPTER V

1872-1895

THE opening years of Alexander's reign saw the beginning of renascence ; his last years saw the beginning of the agony which lasted until the final collapse of the Russian empire.

Absolutism and progress are principles that cannot be reconciled. And since history will neither re-establish the past nor permit things to go on unchanged indefinitely, the form of government was bound, once the first reforms had been instituted, to be converted from an absolute into a constitutional monarchy or else to go under.

Neither Alexander nor his successors understood this.

Alexander II was neither a man of genius nor of great personality. He was just a well-meaning person who wanted to see his people free and happy, but did not appreciate the extent of the task which he had undertaken.

Millions of men who, until quite recently had been mere chattels, dependent body and soul upon him who had bought them or acquired them by inheritance, had become free men. The face of Russia had been completely changed. Society needed to be reconstructed from top to bottom.

Reforms which had not been foreseen but which were called for by the force of circumstance were undertaken and carried into effect. But one reform constantly involved another and the men who were needed for them were not to be found. The nobility could only supply a comparatively small porportion of them, while the Intelligentzia was only just coming into being, and, as I have already said, took the wrong road from the first. They refused to ally themselves with the reformers, preferred revolution to evolution and assumed the leadership of the malcontents.

For lack of men worthy of the task things drifted to the bad. The opposition degenerated into terrorism and the emperor's life was constantly attempted.

The entourage of the Czar, which had always been hostile to the reforms, although in order to remain in favour they had played a double game and echoed his sentiments, made the most of these incidents and worked upon the emperor so as to make him see imaginary dangers everywhere. They discovered conspiracies which were really quite imaginary and succeeded in frightening him.

The poor man, reduced to a state of abject terror, disgusted with the ingratitude of his subjects, weary of a task which was beyond his strength, fell more and more under the influence of women, who relegated his authority to others, using him simply as a cat's paw, and induced him to vitiate the good works which he had carried through when he was still a man and an emperor. The poor emperor ! If he had carried his task through to its logical conclusion, he would have been a great sovereign, perhaps the greatest history has known.

The successors of Alexander II were even less suited than he to the role assigned to them by destiny.

His son, Alexander III, a man of vigour, though without any other qualities, decided, in spite of what was obvious,

I

to return to the past or at any rate to stop the reforms, forgetting that the work which had been started by his father had been left unfinished, and failing to realise that a transitional state of affairs cannot last indefinitely.

His grandson Nicholas II—but we have seen him at work, and it is unnecessary to speak about him.

Further progress was held up. The transitional state was made permanent. Evolution stopped. In its place we had the extremes of reaction and revolution. The country was divided into two camps. " We," consisting only of the government and its satellites, and " they," of the whole of the rest of Russia, millions of men.

" We " knew everything ; " we " could do no wrong, and could even defy the laws with impunity on the quiet.

" They " were suspect. What " they " said was stupid, what "they" did was harmful and what "they" thought was harmful. But " they " were a negligible quantity, riff-raff who did not count, whom it was only necessary to keep on the leash.

Nobody troubled about the nation. The nation was " they," and " we " were strong enough to make them obey.

On the other hand people pretended to be more concerned than ever with " Russia and her interests," but by this of course they meant their own interests, for which the autocracy was a sure shield.

The chief and only concern therefore was to watch over the safety of the sovereign and above all of the autocracy, to conserve it in its primitive form and if possible even to extend its power and exalt it into a divinity. And the more absolutism shook in its foundations, the more we tried to conserve it.

The natural results were not long in developing. " We " gradually lost any sense of shame ; " they " became more and more dissatisfied every day. Some of them made every effort to hasten the coming of the revolution, but others, from conviction or indifference, went back into their shells and retired from public life. The field was left free for intriguers for whom the country was simply a milch cow to be sucked dry.

According to " us " the policy which should especially contribute to the security and the glory of the absolutist system, and therefore conduce to the happiness of Russia was " Russification." All the subjects of the Empire, Tartars, Fins, Jews, Laps, Little Russians and Caucasians —I should never have time to mention them all, but either freely or forcibly all must be made identically of a pattern. They must be " Russified," speak nothing but Russian and join the Orthodox church if that could be managed. And the good work was set in hand.

We have seen the result. The first thing that these people did after the revolution was to separate themselves from Russia. This " Russification " sometimes took grotesque forms. One day, I was accompanying General Potapov, who did not approve of " Russification," but acquiesced in it, on a tour of inspection. We had dined with the governor of Grodno, the Prince Kropotkin, and were driving with a whole string of carriages with the general at the head, along a splendid road which had been specially made for the passage of His Excellency.

Suddenly the general's carriage upset. Potapov was unhurt, but his coachman was a pitiful sight. He completely lost his head. Probably thinking that he would be hanged he cried " Mercy ! Mercy ! Spare my life."

" There, there, don't get excited," said the general, " nobody wants to hurt you."

But the coachman went on, " I am Orthodox ; I am a cook and not a coachman. Yes, a cook I am, and I've never driven a horse."

" Poor devil," said Potapov, " he has gone off his head. He thinks he is a cook now."

" As a matter of fact, Your Excellency," said Kropotkin, " he is a cook."

" I beg your pardon, Prince, what did you say ?"

" I said, your Excellency, that he is in fact not a coachman but a cook."

" I am more at a loss than ever."

" He is Orthodox."

" I don't see how that prevents him from being a coachman and forces him to be a cook."

" The fact is, your Excellency, that it was impossible to find an Orthodox coachman to drive you in the whole town ; there were only Polish Catholics and naturally they were impossible."

" Now I see what you are driving at. You naturally thought it better that I should break my neck through an Orthodox cook than that I should be properly driven by a Catholic coachman."

To be a Jew was regarded as a crime, and to be a Pole as a misdemeanour. Even the aristocracies of the non-Russian nationalities were looked at askance, and were actually less tolerated than Russian " working men." They were subjected to every kind of humiliation, and were accused of felony if they showed any sign of resentment.

Autocrats, and their flunkeys the bureaucrats, are not satisfied with being obeyed. They want to be loved.

Since the Revolution of 1863 the Poles had lost their last remaining civil rights, and they were oppressed and considerably molested by pinpricks which were often more exasperating than blows. As far as they were concerned the government was out to maintain the *status quo*. No new vexatious measures were introduced. All that was necessary had already been done. But for dealing with the Jews and the schismatics of the Orthodox church we reverted to methods more worthy of Tamerlane than of an " enlightened " absolutism.

I say " enlightened," not because it was so, but because the Russian government in spite of all evidence to the contrary, prided itself on being enlightened.

Even in the time of Nicholas I the condition of the Jews was intolerable. They were compulsorily confined to certain provinces where they died of hunger and were treated as pariahs.

The reforms of Alexander II left things very much as they were, but the governments of his successors did everything in their power to make the lot of the Jews more terrible than ever. I quite admit that the Jews in Russia are a bane and exploit those of the population who are more ignorant than themselves. But the fault does not rest with the Jews, but with the government, who has confronted them with the alternative of dying of hunger or of exploiting by every means in their power the population of the districts to which they are confined. Faced with this alternative, even a race of demi-gods would probably choose to batten on their neighbours, rather than to die of inanition.

It is unnecessary for me to expatiate any further on this subject the persecution of the Jew. It has been sufficiently discussed in Europe. I would just like to state that the " pogroms " that is to say massacres, of the Jews on a large scale by the populace are a modern invention, to which we are indebted to the reigns of Alexander III and Nicholas II. They would not have been tolerated in the times of their predecessors. The government, such as it was, was at that time still a power which was able to impose its will upon the lowest strata of the population and to hold in check its servants and lackeys. It was not merely an authority more apparent than real, a shadow without a substance.

I was present at one of these horrible incidents. It took place at Rostov-on-the-Don, a large port and business city in the South of Russia. At this period, that is, if I am not mistaken, at the beginning of the reign of Nicholas II, " pogroms " were very popular. They had become a feature of Russian civilisation. The Liberal press suggested that the government itself fomented them. I doubt it. The " pogroms " occurred not because the authorities had an interest in them, but because the government was not sufficiently intelligent to anticipate them and was too feeble to control them. It was already the victim of a creeping paralysis and lacked the necessary vigour to deal with the situation. Pillage has an attraction for any populace and especially for the Russians. The people did not yet dare to plunder their landlords whom they believed to be tyrants, and while waiting till circumstances should be more favourable, they contented themselves with plundering the Jews whom they knew to be weak. Finding that they could do so with impunity they extended their activities.

I also doubt whether the cause of the " pogroms " was, as the government definitely stated, hatred of the people for the Jews. Hatred was the pretext rather than the cause. The Russian people had no hatred for the Jews nor for anyone else. They are a good-hearted folk, but like all savages they despise everybody excepting themselves, and especially those who are weaker than they.

In the year 188. . . I have forgotten the exact date, pogroms became more frequent than ever. They occurred in towns and villages where the proportion of the Jewish population was comparatively tiny. It was natural therefore that a pogrom should also be expected to occur at Rostoff. By way of anticipating it the Jews sent their merchandise out of the town—they consigned it first to one port and then to another, but the weeks went by and the expected pogrom did not take place. " If only this confounded pogrom would take place " an old Jew said to me, " we should at least have got it over." Anticipation of a misfortune is often more painful than the misfortune itself.

In the end confidence returned ; the wandering merchandise came back, and the market resumed its usual air of bustling activity.

But one fine day a peasant was dissatisfied with a herring he had bought from a Jewess and proceeded to villify the fish wife. She retorted and a dispute developed.

The passers by took sides and the street urchins ran about the streets shouting, " We are giving it to the Jews " ; the fat was in the fire.

In conformity with the requirements of tradition at that time, cushions and mattresses in the shops were first ripped open and the feathers blew about like snowflakes and covered the ground.

Then the booths were broken up and after that the small shops were plundered.   Finally, the large stores belonging to Russians and to strangers as well as to the Jews were plundered.   Only the Jews had a rougher time. That was a concession to the fashion of the day and to religious sentiment.   The public squares soon looked like a market place.   Respectable citizens bought rolls of stuff, trinkets, watches and clothes, anything they needed or had a fancy for, at ridiculous prices.   Everybody was laughing and chattering as though it were a public holiday.

" Are you not ashamed of yourself ?" I said to a worthy fellow whom I knew.

" My dear Sir," he replied, " if I didn't buy them somebody else would.   Why shouldn't I do as everybody else. It would be stupid to let such an opportunity slip."

Fortunately, in the evening, a regiment of Cossacks arrived at a gallop.   A few judicious blows of the " nagaika " and everything was over.

This " pogrom," though in other places it may have been different, was not a simple plundering of the Jews, but a rehearsal of the drama which was soon to be enacted throughout the whole country ; meantime it was being played under the name of " pogrom," later it would be enacted under the name of the " Grand Revolution." The name was different but the principle was the same. First they looted for the sake of loot and then they looted for an alleged principle, in the name of liberty and equality —even in the name of equity.

Before I finish with the Jews I must tell a story I heard during the war.   It is more eloquent than anything I

could say on the subject. A group of soldiers were conversing on the subject of the Emperor William.

" If I took him prisoner," said one, " I'd shoot him on
the spot."

" I wouldn't," said a Cossack, " I'd give him a good
whipping first."

" Whipping !" said a Mongol.   " Why that's good
enough for anybody. Before I shot him, I'd roast the
soles of his feet."

Then turning to a Jew he said, " Well, Moses, what
would you do to him ?"

" Oh ! I wouldn't be as gentle as you ! Only roast the
soles of his feet when he has made thousands and thousands of us Jews wretched ! Nothing of the kind. I'd toi-
ture him beyond the point of human endurance. I would
give him the kind of passport that they give to us and then
he would have what he deserves. "

The persecution of schismatics also began under the
reign of Nicholas II. M. Pobedonostzev, an orthodox
fanatic, who had got into power was merciless to them.
On the most casual denunciation they were seized, imprisoned and deported to Siberia.   Forty thousand
" Molokans " who had rendered eminent services to
Russia during the war of 1877 emigrated to Canada to
escape persecution.

I sometimes wonder how it was that these atrocities
could occur under a sovereign—a sovereign moreover who
was an autocrat and who was neither a savage nor
monster—whose bare word could have stopped it. In
order to understand this it is necessary to realise the
kind of man Nicholas II was. I should rather not have
discussed this, for when a man has been assassinated in a

particularly cowardly manner, one rather shrinks from saying much in his dispargament. But in a country which is subjected to a régime—absolutist régime—the personality of the sovereign plays such a decisive part that it is impossible in dealing with an epoch to make no mention of him.

It is difficult to describe the character of Nicholas II. What can one say of a nonentity—and that is what he was. He had no pronounced virtues or defects. He cared for nothing, clung to nothing, and to no person, not even as was for a long time believed, to his power. His abdication proved that. He allowed himself to be dismissed at a word without resistance, like a child that is sent to bed.

Polite and agreeable, he was charming to meet for the first time, but when one knew him better the charm wore off. He was wanting in firmness, but he was obstinate. He went back on his word as easily as he would give it. He instinctively feared men of worth and was attracted by nonentities. He would be delighted with a new-comer and would suddenly " sack " men who were most devoted to him. His chief fault was that he had not been born to occupy a throne and certainly not the throne of an autocrat. Had he been born in a lowly sphere, one imagines that he would not have been either above or below the average. He probably desired the good of his country. He is said to have done so, but the evil which he did to it is immeasurable.

At the beginning of his reign he allowed himself to be guided by M. Pobedonostzev, who alienated the affections of his country from him. And he was guided by others who were equally useless and less honourable and finally by his wife, a stupid and hysterical woman who ruined him and ruined Russia. Poor simpleton. To put him aside was a necessity ; to do so during the war was a piece of stupidity worthy of the Provisional Government. To kill him was a crime which nothing could excuse.

I have lived a little in every part of Russia. I have seen the peasant at close quarters, that primitive and complicated being who is both intelligent and stupid, both good-hearted and sullen, hard working and lazy, and who even to-day remains an insoluble riddle. He also, like the rest of Russia, has contributed largely to the ruin of his country. Though perhaps he will be called its saviour. I do not profess, as unfortunately some do who understand him least, to know his inmost soul. That would be difficult and almost impossible. He has been accustomed for centuries carefully to hide his feelings and every word that he utters is with reticence and has a double meaning, so that one cannot know, one can only divine his nature.

In many aspects it is detestable, in others likeable. One loves him for his impulsiveness and his patience, although it is true that it borders on inertia, but above all for his sense of fair play He is capable of doing you any conceivable villainy but, if you are just, he will never bear you a grudge even though you do him an injury.

One day, or rather one autumn evening, when I was a Justice of the Peace, I was coming home in a dog cart. Half way home, in the middle of a forest, the axle broke. I sent a man who was with me to the neighbouring village to get something to mend it while I remained alone to guard the carriage which was full of parcels which I was bringing back to the town.

It was a dark night and wet. I was wet through. The

place had a bad name. Escaped convicts were at large in the neighbourhood and several travellers had already been robbed. I was feeling anything but comfortable all alone in the forest.

After a while I heard a cart coming along the road. By the kind of noise it was making I knew it was a peasant cart going at walking pace. It was coming towards me and in order to avoid it running into me I shouted out.

" Who is that ?" came the reply.

" I have had an accident. My carriage is broken. I have sent to the village for help."

" You will have to wait a long time. The whole village is drunk Nobody will come."

Then, when he had ascertained the damage, he said, " I will get my axe. · Don't worry, I know how to use it."

He went back to his cart and then re-appeared holding his axe.

I got out my revolver and put it into my other coat pocket. Horse stealers are all more or less brigands and I had made up my mind to sell my life dearly.

He cut down a young tree and fixed it to the axle ; then he tied my carriage to his cart.

I wanted to stop him. " You musn't," I said, " you are going into the town and I am coming from it. We are going in opposite directions."

" It is no use, I tell you nobody will come. They are all drunk. Of course I'll go back with you."

" Go back forty versts ?"

" What are forty versts ? That's all right. It's not as though you were just anybody. Fortunately, one can recognise people It's settled ; it's done now, climb into my cart. But first I must wake my mate who is asleep. Hi there, pull yourself together."

" Let him sleep. I will walk behind. I am soaked to the skin It will do me good."

The moon came out and I saw his mate, a strong fellow with broad shoulders, rubbing his eyes. " Come on now, jump in," the horse thief said. There was nothing for it. I did as I was told and the cart moved on. Nobody said a word ; then suddenly the thief looked straight at me.

" Don't you recognise me ?"

" No "

" You were my judge. You sentenced me to prison."

" What for ?"

" Horse stealing, of course," he replied, " it is always the same thing."

" Ah, I see."

" I was sentenced for a whole year and during that time my family had nothing to eat. You ruined us completely."

" If a man steals   . ."

"   . . .And gets caught, he has to go to prison, that's quite natural, but I had not stolen—I swear I hadn't."

He crossed himself and caught the axe which was slipping off the bench.

Without taking it out of my pocket I cocked my revolver.

He went on emphatically.

" Stealing horses. Yes ! I have stolen horses, but not that time. I swear before God. It was another man who did it and it's me that was put in prison."

" If I punished you. . . ."

" But I don't bear you any ill will. Ah, you're a just man. It was the dirty witnesses who lied. Oh, yes you are a just man there is nothing to be said. You simply carry out the law."

He brought me home and absolutely refused to accept the money I offered him for his trouble.

" But no, you're just, you are. I didn't do it for the money. You are just. There is nothing to be said."

I had put an innocent man in gaol and ruined him, but he thought me just. Civilised people think differently when they lose their case.

While I am on the subject I may as well tell another story of robbers. It is also characteristic of the Russian people, and this incident too occurred in Lithuania. I was coming home on a fine summer's night which was light as they are in the north. I came through the same forest where I had met the horse thief. I was sleeping the sleep of the just and my trap suddenly stopped, when I woke up.

" Robbers," said my coachman, a boy, timid as a hare.

Two men on horseback carrying rifles blocked the road. One was some little distance off, standing at the head of my horse, and the other was coming up to the carriage.

I was not fully awake but instinctively took my revolver from my pocket and cocked it.

" Halt, or I'll fire," I said.

The man continued to come forward.

Quite unconsciously I began hurling the most violent abuse at him.

He stopped his horse.

" Animal ! dog !" A whole string of invectives. " How dare you hold up travellers, you robber. Who are you, idiot ?"

" Baron Ettingen's gamekeeper."

I mistrusted the baron. He was typical of the old

Kurland barons, who in their arrogant conceit thought they could do just as they pleased. The mention of his name infuriated me ; I gave it him hotter than ever.

" Tell your dirty baron that I'll break his neck the first chance I get, and be off unless you want to be killed like a mad dog. Be quick about it. I've had enough."

The men, quite bewildered, turned their horses and disappeared into the wood.

When I met the baron I complained of the extraordinary behaviour of his gamekeepers.

" My gamekeepers," he said in astonishment. " But the forest doesn't belong to me, it belongs to the state. I agree with your coachman in thinking they must be brigands ; they are supposed to be about."

It was the judges' duty to visit the prisons and see that no one was confined without a warrant. That kind of thing did happen. One day the governer asked me if I would care to see some escaped convicts who had just murdered a whole family. I immediately recognised one of them.

" It was you who held me up in the forest."

" I have never seen you in my life before." But I could see from his smile that he was lying.

A few months later I was standing near a train of convicts on their way to Siberia in a station near Moscow. One of them called to me. I stopped and saw the same man behind a barred window.

" Hulloa, you again," I said.

" Curious how one meets," he replied. " Who would have believed it, in the middle of Russia ?"

He seemed to be quite pleased to see somebody he knew.

" You were found guilty ?"

" I got it in the neck. Hard labour for life. It is all in

the day's work. You see I am an important person now, I travel in a reserved carriage free of charge, and like a great lord shall be kept at the expense of the State for the rest of my days. Only I have no pocket money for small luxuries—I have run through my fortune on women. You give me something."

I gave him a few roubles.

" May God reward you," he said, " only you might give me a little more. It is not enough. You owe me that. If you hadn't cursed me so hard you wouldn't be where you are now."

" Why didn't you kill me that time ?"

" You cursed me too hard. ' The devil take you,' I said, ' he must be a dangerous man. Better steer clear of him.' In fact we were glad to get rid of you so cheaply."

I naturally refrained from telling him I had been so terrifying simply because I hadn't properly woken up. It is always the same story. The people tremble before those whom they believe to be strong and do violence to the weak.

There is only one thing that can make the Russian peasant wild and bring him to lose his sense of justice. That is the land. His country, religion and family, these are all more or less indifferent to him. But he would assassinate his mother and father for another scrap of ground even if he did not know what to do with it.

The celebrated Asiatic explorer Przevalsky told me that when he was in Usuri, which is a fertile country three times as big as France, with a population of three hundred families, everybody when asked the reason for their poverty invariably replied : " We haven't enough land."

" But you have the right to take as much as you want."

" Yes ! but that is no use. There is not enough to go round."

One day in the province of Kharkov, where my property was, some peasants, neighbours of mine, chose me as arbitrator. It was a question of allotting some meadows to which each one claimed to have a right. They came to me with a map which I proceeded to examine. The property in question consisted of some land which I had bought the year before.

" But you have brought the wrong map, my friends, you have brought the map of my land."

" Yes, but it is going to belong to us."

" But I have no idea of selling it."

" We know that, but the Czar has ordered us to take it."

" What the devil put that into your heads ?"

" It was some students who told us about it. The imperial ukase on gold stamped paper has already come. They have seen it."

" Oh ! I see, Look here, you. Let me have that horse to-morrow that I was thinking of buying from you."

" Then you have decided to give me my price."

" Heavens, no."

" Why ?"

" You propose to take my property away from me, so I propose to take yours."

They began to laugh ; " that's good, but I paid the last farthing for my horse, batiushka."

" So have I for my land."

" That's not the same thing. The soil comes from God ; it belongs to the whole world."

" Then why does it belong to you and not to your neighbours ?"

K

Their only answer was to scratch their heads, and when a peasant scratches his head there is no use trying to get anything out of him.

The theory of " the soil belonging to the whole world " is, as I know, also a modern invention, contemporary with the Intelligentzia. No one had ever heard of it before. But the Intelligentzia were straining every nerve to teach it to the rural population. The students no longer paid any attention to their studies ; but they inundated the countryside, and " went among the people " as the phrase was, to awaken them to this fact.

And then Count Tolstoi, instead of writing his excellent books, took part in this mission and created a whole school of adepts who carried on the good work.

These much coveted lands now belong to everyone, with the exception of those who have a natural right to them. The only trouble now is that they are no longer cultivated and that millions of men are becoming cannibals.

There is no pleasure in receiving a visit from people of whom one has never heard. For this reason I am omitting from these Memoirs any mention of men who, although known to us, are either unknown or forgotten elsewhere. I am making an exception in favour of General Skobelev, whose name was at one time famous throughout Europe. Besides, he was the first man to work for an alliance between France and Russia.

As children, we could not bear each other. When we met it always ended in a fight. His superior airs irritated me and I always tried to take him down a peg or two.

It was only because he was taller than me and he generally came out top. That was but natural, as he was three years older than I.

One day he gave me a blow which made my nose bleed. When his mother asked me why it was bleeding, I said that it often happened without rhyme or reason. When she went away Michael struck an attitude which filled me with admiration. He behaved exactly like a hero of melodrama. He was majestic, noble and solemn. And in a grave voice he said :

" You are brave and generous ! Give me your sword ; mine was broken in the fight, and bend your knee. I am going to knight you ! "

Nothing could have pleased me more. At that time we were reading a story of the time of the Crusades and that was just how Richard Cœur-de-Lion talked. In place of a sword, which I did not possess, I handed him my ruler, and knowing the ritual knelt before him. And he said in a voice which sounded as if it were coming out of a cavern :

" In the name of God and our Lady of Amiens and Saint Michael, my patron saint, I make you a knight. Be noble and never waver."

And he touched me three times with his sword.

The words " never waver " fired me. " Oh no, I will never waver."

As a matter of fact I didn't really quite know what it meant. But that didn't matter ! It sounded fine.

He then gave me the knight's embrace.

The ceremony stirred me to the depths of my being.

" And now, my brother," said the knight Michael, " I am going to admit you to my secret. You are rather young, it is true, but I have confidence in you ; only you must swear that you will tell it to nobody."

" On my word of honour."

" Idiot ! you must say on the oath of a knight."

" Sorry. On the oath of a knight."

He unbuttoned his coat and showed me a white enamelled cross, which was fastened by a black and orange ribbon to the lining of his waistcoat.

" Do you know what that is ?"

" The cross of Saint George. Great Uncle and Uncle Alexandre have it.   Where did you get it from ?"

" I inherited it from my grandfather. When I am an officer I shall wear it on my uniform and not under my waistcoat."

" Oh rot. Anyone who chooses can't wear that. It is only given to heroes."

" I know that."

" You a hero ! You're just a silly boaster."

He boxed my ears.

Fifteen years afterwards I met him again in Warsaw ; he was then a lieutenant of the Hussars.

He was neither richer, handsomer or better dressed or of more distinguished family than the officers of his regiment ; he was not different from them in any way and had never been under fire ; and yet he was a hero in their eyes.

How had he become one ? I still ask myself that question.

He himself was not in the least surprised. He had not yet had any chance of becoming a hero, but that didn't matter. Sooner or later he would be one. Meanwhile he always wore his St. George's Cross on his vest though he no longer showed it to anyone.

When we were children we had been playmates but never real friends. Our tastes and characters were too different ; we had nothing in common. How it happened I don't know, but we became friends. And this friendship lasted till his death.

He passed through the military academy and afterwards went to fight in Turkestan.

One day he informed me of his marriage to the Princess Gagarin in Moscow.

One morning, about a fortnight afterwards, he burst into my room. " What are you doing this evening ?" he said. " I met a most amusing woman yesterday coming back from Moscow. A Paris cocotte. Her friend is great fun too. Why shouldn't the four of us have supper together this evening ?"

" What do you mean, my dear man, you've only been married a fortnight."

" That's all over, finished. My wife is charming but you know when all is said and done I am not the stuff of which husbands are made. Besides a soldier ought to remain celibate. It's impossible to be both soldier and husband. I have my work to do and marriage hampers me hand and foot. Napoleon left Josephine, whom he loved, for the same reason."

" You have been a bit late in discovering that."

" I have never thought of these things before. I had no time. Women you know just amuse men, nothing more. They do not hold me."

" With one exception, the Goddess of glory."

" She's a jade just like the others. She keeps me

languishing, but I shall win her in the end. It's just a question of time."

" I hope so for your sake. But meanwhile you have another one, your lawful wife."

" I have already told you she is an exception. I am really very lucky. Another woman would have made no end of fuss. She consented to our separation then and there."

He went back to Turkestan some days later.

From time to time his name was mentioned in the newspapers, and he was spoken of in the town and in society. One day, when I was going to Peterhoff on my return from France I saw in the distance a lady talking to a colonel, an aide-de-camp to the Emperor, whom I had never seen before. He was a Knight of the Order of Saint George and at this period His Majesty had no aide-de-camp who had this order.

The next day I saw him coming up to my house. It was Skobelev. The only difference was that he had let his beard grow. And pointing to his cross, " the same one that was on my vest," he said. " You ought to remember it. You got your ears well boxed on account of it."

" And colonel as well as his Majesty's aide-de-camp. You don't waste any time."

" I have come to enlist you. I am going back to Asia for I have been given a command. In one month, or say two, as the necessary preparations and the voyage will take a month, I shall complete the conquest of Samarkand. You shall be made an officer as soon as the town is taken. Come with me as a volunteer."

I consented.

" We are leaving in fifteen days."

But he went alone. It was then that the bridge gave way and I was confined to my bed, tortured with rheumatism.

I didn't see him until the end of the war in the East. He was a general by that time, and well in the limelight. His so-called friends discredited him in consequence and said all sorts of things about him. They did their work so well that His Majesty received him more than coldly. It was thought that his career was finally finished as indeed it probably was.

He did not get a command. But as he was attached to his Majesty's bodyguard he could not be prevented from going to the theatre of war, where the Emperor was going himself.

One day he showed me piles, mountains of his photographs. He appeared full face, in profile, quarter face, on foot and on horseback.

" Are these for your biography, great man ?"

" No, they are labels to put on chocolate, scent and soap boxes."

" Good heavens."

" Why not ? You must get people worked up. You can't do anything without a public. Glory is a strumpet. She requires it and you know that I mean to win her."

" Aren't you satisfied yet ?"

" Why, do you think that I shall be contented with having kissed the hem of her garment ? I want to possess her exclusively. Yes, all or nothing. This war will get my feet into the stirrups."

" And supposing they don't give you a command?"

He smiled. " You amuse me," he said, " it is not a question of ' if.' They are certain not to give me a command."

" And then?"

" And then I shall simply take the stirrup myself and get into the saddle. That's all."

He was as good as his word. When the Danube was forced he was present as a simple spectator, but the next day the whole army knew that the victory was due to him and nobody else. A few months later he was the idol of the soldiers. Then he became a hero, the legendary hero of Russia.

The photographs had played an important part in his popularity and Russia was flooded with them.

" You see, it wasn't so foolish and conceited of me," he said to me one day as he showed me some photographs in a shop window.

That was only the beginning.

" Have you already ordered the grey cloak, Bonaparte, that you are going to wear when you are Napoleon."

" Idiot, the white general—and that is what both his men and the enemy called him—has no need of a grey cloak. He needn't imitate the little corporal. Napoleon is the greatest man I know and even if I only come just second to him, I shall put up with that if necessary." Then after a moment of silence he added :

" I shall not fall on the field of battle. I may be wounded but I shall not be killed. I have been told that. Why, if it had been possible I should have been killed already."

" Do you believe in telling the future ?"

" Certainly I do, don't you ?"

" No."

" That is nonsense. You may have doubts about it, but to deny it is absurd."

"I shouldn't dream of denying the possibility, any more than I should of believing it. I simply don't know and I shall continue to doubt until the matter is proved."

"You sceptic, trying to find out the reason of things. And in the end you allow yourself to be taken in by words. I take things as they are, without asking for a reason. Explain, for instance, why each man has his destiny. Yet he certainly has. One man may be prudent, clever and far-seeing, to calculate everything beforehand, and still nothing will succeed with him. He walks on a beaten path and suddenly he gets into a morass and is drowned. Another may do the maddest things, hurl himself into the ocean, but things always turn out so that he escapes. Our destinies are written down for us once and for all. And the clairvoyants know how to decipher the book of destiny. That's all there is to it. And why not. Science has not yet said its last word. Only yesterday, electricity, hypnotism, were like old wives' tales. Yes, just like destiny, clairvoyants exist."

"Have you had your destiny foretold?"

"Twice! and on each occasion I was told exactly the same thing. The first time was in France. And the fortune teller was an old lady whom I met in the train. And the next time it was an old man at Samarand whom I met in central Asia. And I was told the same thing on both occasions. Isn't it odd?"

"What did they say?"

"It's a long story. The gist of it was, that I should go a long way, a very long way, and when I had almost got there, crack. I knew that without their telling me. One must die sometime or other. Only 'almost' is a very vague word. It worries me, 'almost.' Almost what?

That's what I should like to know. And that's what I have been thinking about."

I remember our last meeting as though it were yesterday ; and yet it was thirty years ago. It was at the house of a mutual friend, General Dmitri Doshturov, the last of the " preux chevaliers sans peur et sans reproches." He was the only man whom Skobelev took really seriously and respected and that is saying a good deal, because in his estimation almost all men were worthless.

There were seven of us at dinner. Our host, Count Vorontzov, the generals Tcherevin and Dragomirov, Skobelev, I and my former Robinson Crusoe who had just got into disgrace again and whom Vorontzov and Tcherevin, who were both all powerful with Alexandre III, were trying to help. They were wrong in doing so because there's a limit to everything. But Vorontzov could not bear to see a man in distress. He had to come to his assistance, even if it was against his better judgment. The dinner started merrily. Dragomirov, who although frankly fond of the bottle, was also a man of great wit, amused us with his sarcasms. In a few words he summed up the character of our friend Doshturov and the régime of the day.

Vorontzov was trying to persuade the master of the house to accept an appointment which he was being offered. But the latter would have none of it.

" Why don't you let him alone," said Dragomirov, " he knows he is no good for anything."

We protested. " Doshturov ? What a thing to say."

" But it is so. I don't deny his knowledge or his intrinsic worth or his capacity as a soldier, but. . . ."

" There is a but ?"

" Yes ! and indeed a but that reduces all his qualities to nothing. He has never managed to learn to be a useful tool for other people's dirty work."

Then, as always, we fell to discussing what was happening in the country. That was not particularly cheerful.

Everybody agreed that things were in a bad way. Fundamentally, Dragomirov, Tcherevin and Robinson didn't care. After us the deluge. Skobelev was curious to see what happened. He seemed to be indifferent and shared the view of the man who was speaking. Only from time to time his eyes darted a flash which was repressed at once. Voronztov did not see things in a rose-coloured light either, only his view was that there was no doubt that everything would settle down satisfactorily in the end. The Czar knew what he wanted, and knew how to get his own way and the throne was more firmly established than ever.

When they had gone Skobelev burst out laughing. He strode up and down the room. " Everything will settle down ! The throne firmly established ! Sing away, dicky bird. Firmly established ! The show is going phut. There will be nothing left. They will put things to right quite soon ! What do you say, what do you say ?"

" I say," Doshturov stated calmly, " that I am also of the opinion that a catastrophe is to be expected. Only I don't see that this gives cause for rejoicing. Russia will go to hell and we shall all go with it."

" Dynasties collapse and change, and the nations often benefit thereby," said Skobelev. " The Bourbons almost ruined France. Napoleon saved her and made her greater than she had ever been before."

" Things sometimes happen like that and sometimes

they don't. But we are getting away from the question.
Let us suppose that the nation will not collapse and that
only the throne will. We shall collapse with it and I
confess that I have no desire to do so."

" Why should we believe. . . ?

" First of all," Doshturov went on quietly, " I do not
believe that a revolution in Russia could lead to any good
results. If therefore a revolution occurs I shall be hostile
to it. Besides, I am a soldier and I shall carry out my duty
as a soldier. So will you, I suppose ?"

" I," almost shouted Skobelev ; then with a smile he
said, " I understand nothing of politics ; besides, they
bore me. It always makes me cross when people talk
politics, and you know that I cannot control my feelings.
I am not a diplomat. But it is getting late and I must go
home. Besides, you know there's one's duty ! We must
speak of this again. I am dreadfully sleepy to-day."

About a year later Skobelev suddenly died, more popular than ever with the people and more hated than ever
in high circles. " They " pretended that he had been
poisoned, " we " that his excesses had brought about his
premature death. Nobody knew the truth and probably
it will never be known.

The Bolsheviks have destroyed the equestrian statue
erected to Skobelev at Moscow. It seems that they needed
a site for putting up a statue to another hero, the Jew
Silberson. And nobody knows what particular services
that great man rendered to Russia.

A warning to the reader. Those who have not experienced the joys and experiences of fatherhood will do well
not to read this chapter. It will mean nothing to them and
will probably bore them. I myself might have cut it out,

but some feeling which I cannot explain prompts me not to do so. Women will understand this.

Children have always adored me and I was fortunate enough to have three boys, all of them happy, healthy and good looking. I shall not say anything of the elder boys as they are well enough known. One as a commander-in-chief of the Anti-Bolshevik army and the other as a writer.

We loved all three equally, or at least I think we did; for it is impossible to gauge the intensity of feelings which have neither weight nor dimensions; but we loved the youngest quite differently from his elder brothers. It was a morbidly anxious love that was almost a malady.

One day when the child, who was two years old, was out with his mother and nurse an idiot accosted them, and said with a smile to the boy's mother, " Don't be harsh to him. Let him do what he likes. Just let him be happy and run about and play. He will only live nine years."

Reasonable people often believe in the foolish words of an idiot, but only when the idiot passes himself off as a wise man or an authority on politics. This prophet, however, was just a plain idiot, whom all the town knew to be so, and whom no one considered reasonable. One would have had to have been an idiot oneself to have had any faith in him at all.

Neither my wife nor myself were idiots, but the harm was done. Her life had been poisoned. The anticipation of misfortune is often more painful than the misfortune itself. It had never occurred to us that the child might be taken from us. And how, we could think of nothing. As we never mentioned our fear, and in fact tried to make

each other believe we never even thought of it, we increased our sufferings by concealing them.

In due course the boy was nine years old. He was in
perfect health, so that now we thought our fears were
ridiculous and we both said, " I never believed it."

Relieved of this obsession, I returned to two pursuits
of which I was passionately fond of and which I had
hardly thought of for years, collecting and hunting.   It
become quite a mania. When I went into a town where
I might be able to pick up some antiques, I forgot the
friend whom I had come to see and spent all my spare
time in hunting up antique shops and stray people, who
according to those who knew nothing about it, had
wonderful things to sell.

When I wasn't travelling I spent my days hunting.
Was I a real sportsman ? That depends on the meaning
one gives to the word.   If it was simply a matter of
killing game I was not. To kill for the sake of killing has
never appealed to me. The size of my bag has always left
me quite cold. I have often derived greater pleasure from
a day on which I have come back with nothing than
from others, from which I have come back with a heavy
bag.

What a delight it is to live for a day the life of a nomad.
To run up hill and down dale—to sleep under the starry
sky and live in the company of savages, who know nothing
about stock exchange quotations, newspaper scares, the
noise of tramway, telegrams, and the constant importuni-
ties of the telephone. And I had a hunting ground. A
night in the train landed me in the heart of the Caucasus,
an Eldorado for the sportsman.

The Caucausus is Switzerland on a large scale. You

get the same kind of scenery, pasturage, rocks, snow-capped peaks and glaciers. But Switzerland, with the funiculars climbing to the heavens, the railed off precipices with benches for the elderly, the fingerposts, hotels, chalets, cafes, pensions, young German married couples, Cook's absurdities, red-bound Baedekers, stuffed chamois and carved ibexes—Switzerland is banal and commonplace through being too well known. The Caucausus is a poem, and what is more an Oriental poem. It still remains the unknown country where Jason might have gone to search for the golden fleece, where to-day, as long ago, Prometheus remains bound to his rocks. Its people still wear picturesque costumes and golden armlets inlaid with gold and silver.

Falcon hunting is still carried on and a man will still kill his friend to avenge an insult to his great grandfather who has been dead a hundred years. A man will kidnap his own brother's daughters in order to sell them to the Pashas of Teheran or Stamboul. And nobody works. Everything is there to hand. One picks the fruit which grows of its own accord, and shears the sheep which browse around without being looked after. One makes one's wine from vines which don't require training, but climb up the trees and stretch along the branches which hang over one's head. And when the wine is in the cellar one drinks it. And then one sleeps, eats, sings. One drinks again and sleeps off the effect of the wine reclining on wonderfully patterned rugs.

When there is nothing left in a house to eat a great company will set off to help their friends to empty their cellars merrily and to eat their sheep or perhaps to steal from the herds of horses which graze on the mountains.

In times of peace, in order not to let your weapons get rusty and to keep your hand in, you indulge in a little scrapping with relations and friends and old acquaintances or you shoot a stray man in the back. And when Russia is at war you come to her aid and die for the Czar and your country.

When you want to go hunting, you go to a station where you have " kunaks " (friends) ; you get a horse and, accompanied by native Cossacks who act both as escort and as beaters, you start off for the mountains. At your feet lies the plain of Kuban extending as far as the eye can see ; in front of you are the snow-capped peaks of the great Caucasian ranges. You spend the day in beating the forest, in following an animal with a spear, in lying in wait behind a tree, and tasting sometimes the delights of anticipation and sometimes the pain of disappointment. And hours pass like seconds.

Night comes.

The horses are unsaddled, and the camp fire is lit. Lying on your "burka" (cloak) you gaze into the crackling fire and slip gently into a state of calm repose, like some wild animal at rest.

Your whole being relaxes deliciously. You do not sleep ; you are not fully awake. You are conscious. You see and hear without thinking and without any reaction. Just as in a dream one is outside of life, a mere spectator of the things that are happening about one.

The bonfire will suddenly flame up like a brasier and then seem to go out, in a pillar of smoke rising to the sky. Strange beings in long cloaks and furred hats, lit up fantastically by the flames, some red in the blaze and others black silhouettes, roughly outlined, are lying on the ground or come and go round about the fire. A tartar wearing a yellow cloak, with blue stripes, is roasting a lamb spitted on the ramrod of his gun.

He is listening, tall, powerful and supple like a young poplar tree in the midst of its foliage, to an old man with a long white beard, who is telling how, when he was young, they used to go and raid villages, the regular eagles' nests high up among the rocks. Then some Cossack trooper, his cloak in rags but well cut, takes up the tale and tells with graceful, easy gesture of his adventures in Asia and of the battles in which General—— has led them personally into the attack.

One man will vaunt the speed of his horse, another the temper of his dagger, and the keen blade of his sword. And to prove his word the soldier will draw his sword and with one sharp stroke cut off the head of a sheep. The great deeds of ancestors are told and the war songs of generations dead and gone are sung in chorus.

The night comes and more wood is put on the bonfire, and gradually the camp falls asleep. All is silent but for the sound of the horses munching their oats.

The moon rises, bathing earth and sky in a pale silvery transparent light. A young Cossack raises himself on his elbow, and resting his head on his hands remains thus a long time, his eyes looking into the distance. Suddenly, in a low chant he begins a melancholy song which goes straight to your heart ; then a tenor, also in a muffled chant, takes up the tune. And you fall asleep lulled by their song.

One day, while I was hunting we were joined by a young Cossack who said he had been looking for me for some days.

He brought a telegram sent by my wife to the station

L

master where I had left the train. It read, " Ask my husband to come home at once on an urgent matter." I understood. One of the children was ill.

The youngest was dying.

Have you ever seen a child, full of vitality, happy and hungry for life, who knows that it is going to die ?

During long nights which dragged out like nightmares he spoke to us of his childish pleasures, told us how happy he had been, that he did not wish to die yet. That he would be good, so good, would love us even more, if we could prevail upon God to let him live if only for a little, a very little more.

Have you seen a poor little creature, full of terror, beg his father to prevent the terrible old man from coming to fetch him ?

Have you heard a poor little innocent make his last requests, thinking of his old nurse's future, leaving his toys to other children, giving his poor little gun-metal watch to his dear mother, so that she may stop crying.

We saw that.

The day after the funeral, when we went to the cemetery, we saw a man sitting on the child's grave playing with pebbles, and it was the " natural " who nine years before had prophesied the death of the child and whom we had not met since. He smiled at the boy's mother ; " he is happy here, the little darling. No one will make him suffer here. Why do you cry ?"

Soon afterwards we left the South where we had lived for more than fifteen years and went back to St. Petersburg, where the two boys who were left to us were completing their studies.

CHAPTER VI

1895-1904

For twenty-five years, until 1895, I was never at St. Petersburg except as a guest—a frequent one it is true, but nevertheless only a guest. I knew plenty of people there, but, with a few exceptions, the old ties had become loosened. When I went back in 1895 to settle there finally, I felt a little bit out of my element. In many respects the town had altered. Formerly, and even now at times in Moscow and in the country, there had been a certain community of spirit, of feeling, of atavism, among people of the same kind. St. Petersburg, on the other hand, had become merely a rendezvous where people came together who had no interests in common concerning either the past, their religion or their country. Everyone was a stranger. Each man lived for and thought only of himself, loved himself only. Men were no longer valued for their intrinsic worth, but only in as far as they might be useful or not.

What is known as Society no longer existed. One no longer went about as before, simply to amuse oneself, to see people, to talk and pass one's time pleasantly, but rather as one goes to market, not for one's personal pleasure, but to do a little business, to sell one's wares and to use one's knowledge, talents, convictions, and often, alas, one's honour, to the best advantage.

In this market were to be met men who wielded power, great lords, rich people, men who would be useful, but very rarely any real gentlemen. Gentlemen by birth, of course, were to be found there, but the spirit was changed.

The real gentlemen (there were still some left in Russia) retired into their shells—some stayed at home, others lived in Moscow, in the country or abroad.

In this *fin-de-siecle* society it was the fashion to exhibit an unbounded devotion to the Czar, " our adored sovereign." It was a term which stood for a faithful love of one's country, a profound distrust of the Jews, and a marked contempt for all those who were not in the smart set. Of all these high sounding sentiments, only the last one, the contempt for almost the whole of the Russian population was sincere. The rest was merely playing to the gallery.

The " adored sovereign " was all nonsense, and the self-styled faithful servants were merely cringing and obsequious lackeys who abused and ridiculed their master among themselves.

The talk about the beloved country was all nonsense too, only one did not say so. And as for the Jews, they were secretly sought after in the hope that something might be wormed out of them—a well-paid post on a board of directors, or a useful tip on the Stock Exchange.

The women—that is to say the younger women—did little to recall the great ladies that I used to see in the old days. It was not that the latter were wiser, cleverer or more intelligent than the women of to-day ; nor were they better wives or more faithful mistresses—but they were ladies. They knew how to talk and to make themselves agreeable, how to appear to listen when they were spoken to and to smile at the right moment, and how to win the respect of their menfolk, even of their lovers. The standard of women in society was, indeed, sadly lowered. Formerly they conversed, now they chattered ; they used to know how to appreciate good books, now they read nothing but novels and scandalous memoirs. They used to go to the opera, and to see good plays at the theatre, now they preferred to admire the muscles of the wrestlers at the circus, or to go to the ballet to see their fathers', husbands' and brothers' mistresses. In the old days people gave amusing supper parties in their own houses, now they went and drank cheap champagne at cabarets.

In Alexander II's time St. Petersburg society still had the reputation of being one of the most exclusive centres of fashion in Europe. Now it was just like that to be met with at any smart casino, consisting of rather ill-bred women inadequately clothed by well-known dress-makers and covered with diamonds, and ill-bred clean-shaven men in white ties.

The circles of the Intelligentzia were all the same funda-mentally, only the outward form differed. High-sounding phrases which had been repeated for thirty years were indulged in, theories and extreme opinions were blindly acquiesced in by everyone, in order to appear suitably " enlightened people." In a word, it was a rather dirty business, very much of the same unsavoury nature as that indulged in by our own set. The only difference was that we gambled on the continuance of the autocracy, while they banked on the future, and put their money on the downfall of the present régime and the revolution which was bound to come. As for pleasure, one set were as boring as the other, and like all sensible men I stopped going anywhere. Anyway, I had no time to waste.

I was always busy until about four o'clock ; after that I used to go round visiting the dealers, while I spent my evenings very pleasantly either reading or conversing with people who had not yet lost the habit. They were rare, but they were to be found.

Since I have referred to antique shops I must make mention of the passion for bric-a-brac which raged throughout the world and soon degenerated into positive madness; a fashion calculated to disgust the genuine collector. Everyone claimed to be a collector, and these collectors would buy daubs—especially those which were passed off as authentic masterpieces by great masters. That was essential.

One day I saw a rather shabby carriage, drawn by two horses that must once have been magnificent animals, stop at my door. An immaculate and impressive footman handed me a card. Madame——, I did not know the name, wished to see me.

An old lady came in, a lady whom I recognised at the first glance as " authentic " ; and I flatter myself as knowing something about " antiques." She may not have been signed or catalogued, but she was certainly a lady.

She apologised for disturbing me.

" But your niece promised me to let you know that I was coming. It is about a most important matter. I am making my will and wish to be absolutely fair to all my heirs. They are all to share equally. Now I possess a picture which I believe to be a genuine Raphael. All the critics say it is, and I should like to know its true value.

Icannot trust the experts. You know those people Perhaps you would be so very kind as to come and look at it ?"

I replied that I was at her disposal, but that she was asking me to do something very difficult. To put a price on a Raphael ! A master who was not to be found in the market.

" I know that," she replied ; " but I only want to know the approximate price. A hundred thousand roubles more or less is of no consequence."

I promised to go and see the Raphael, and if possible to tell her how many millions it might be worth.

The lady's drawing-room breathed an eighteenth century atmosphere. It made my mouth water. I endeavoured discreetly to ascertain whether these treasures were for sale. No ; she did not attach any importance to them, but these " old things " had come to her from her grandmother. Besides she herself was a collector. And she shewed me the masterpieces which she had bought.

I pitied the survivals from her grandmother. They were in bad company indeed.

She was so delightful to talk to that in spite of her masterpieces I almost forgot why I had come.

" What about the picture ? Would you let me see it, Madame ?"

She rang. " Bring me the Raphael, you know, the one which. . ."

" Certainly, Madame." Four men brought a chest, a real safe, which itself was worth a small fortune. So I remarked.

" Yes," she replied, " I ordered it at . . ." She mentioned the cabinet maker who was fashionable at the moment.

" I am always afraid of the picture being stolen or destroyed ; so you understand. . ."

She turned the safety key and then another key, and revealed the Raphael.

It was a wretched reproduction of a mediocre Madonna by an unimportant Italian painter. A daub that might have been worth ten francs.

But I praised it extravagantly.

The lady was delighted. " How much do you think it would fetch ?" she asked.

" Ah ! that's hard to say," I said.

In the end I advised her to show the picture to the people at the Hermitage Museum. They would be more competent to value it than I, and it would give them pleasure to do so. I don't know how they dealt with the situation.

The horrors which people took in good faith for masterpieces, and with which they cluttered up their drawing-rooms, was enough to make one shudder. The worst of it was that this mania spoilt the market. Thanks to the competition, those rogues of dealers were now asking for any old thing prices for which you could once have bought the whole shop and the dealer as well.

Alas, in this respect, too, the good times were over.

In the eighteenth century, in the time of the Empresses, Russia had been inundated with beautiful things— furniture, bronzes, porcelain and pictures. Neither they nor their courtiers were collectors, but, as is well known, enlightenment was then supposed to come from the North, and in order to maintain one's reputation one had to be a Maecenas. And money was plentiful. The treasury was there to be dipped into.

After the emancipation of the serfs, many old places were sold. The purchasers, who were generally ignorant tradespeople, converted the manor houses into factories, and failing to appreciate the value of their contents, threw them out. There were neither collectors nor dealers at that time, and priceless objects were taken off to the booths where old iron, old boots, and all sorts of rubbish was sold. I knew a worthy fellow who bought old gilt bronzes, took the gold off and sold the bronze by weight to be melted down. He would get twenty francs for an object which to-day would be worth a hundred thousand, yet he made enough by this trade to buy three five-storied houses.

The gentry themselves pretty well equalled the purchasers of their houses in vandalism. They too used to throw away their old pieces, not to turn them into cash, but simply to be rid of them. The old was out of fashion ; it was modern stuff that was wanted. A lady of my acquaintance, having bought some hideous modern furniture at St. Petersburg for her country house, and not knowing where to put the delightful furniture she had, made a bonfire of it. One day at one of my neighbours in the country I saw a hay stack covered with a cloth that attracted my attention. It was a particularly fine old piece of Gobelin tapestry. Prince Golitzin-Osterman-Tolstoi having inherited an eighteenth century town house and wishing to refurnish it, sold a large drawing-room with its bronzes, chandeliers and pictures for the inclusive sum of a hundred roubles. Amongst the canvasses were one by Tocqué and four by Levitsky—our greatest portrait painter.

There were miniatures going for a few pence, and

Louis XVI clocks for a couple of pounds. I bought two pieces of Gubbio and Urbino pottery for a franc, and some genuine Sèvres cups at the same price. And they were the real thing.

There was a booth at the market where bronzes were sold by weight, and pictures by the cartload. A cartful was sold for seventy-five roubles. Portraits were sold at a fixed price—ladies, five roubles, gentlemen, three roubles a piece. If you bought several a discount of twenty-five per cent. was allowed.

I bought some pretty good pictures at that time, including a Tintoretto which is reproduced in the Brussels publication, " Pictures in the Palaces and Collections of St. Petersburg."

After I had fled from Russia I came across it in the house of a collector abroad. He showed me a letter from an American offering a million dollars for it.

Once I bought the portrait of an unknown person who turned out to be an ancestor of mine. A grandfather is hardly dear at ten francs, though it is true he had a slight squint.

My friend, Prince Golitzin, secured a whole line of ancestors for fifty roubles. One day he asked me to take him to the market.

" What are you after ? Bronzes or. . . ."

" My fool of a father has sold my land with everything on it. All my family portraits are lost, and I need some for my dining-room. Some grand-parents and some aunts, even if they be only maternal ones. I know that ancestors are out of fashion nowadays. Raw meat and dead game is the rage, but I have a horror of dead things, and besides

I value family traditions. Those old powdered heads warm my heart."

" But, my dear fellow, you can't just pick those things up.

" What about your grandfather ?"

" That was a stroke of luck."

" I am sure to find a few pretty aunts whom I can if necessary adopt before buying them."

" Why don't you have copies made of your genuine ancestors ? There are some in the History Museum."

" Copies ?   What a dreadful idea !   I detest new antiques—as for their being genuine, I didn't know my ancestors, and I don't care about their effigies. Besides, as I am telling you, I intend to adopt them. When I have done so they will belong to the family. Look at that old fellow there. Why, he was made to be my grandfather. And the lady—a most respectable grandmother ; or rather no, she is my maternal aunt. Grandfather and the three aunts, I'll take the lot."

I was dining with him shortly afterwards. A lady asked him who was the original of a certain portrait.

" My grandmother," he replied.

" Your son is remarkably like her."

" And that one is my maternal great aunt," he continued. " I am said to be the very image of her."

" There is a strange family likeness running through them."

" It would certainly be strange if a Golitzin did not take after his ancestors," said the Prince. " Chips of the old block. Heredity. It's quite natural."

In the financial world I only knew a few people with

whom I did business, and that was the world with which
I had to be in touch. The all powerful finance minister,
Witte, an old and valued acquaintance of mine, introduced me to Monsieur Rothstein, who was also a leading
man of the day, and I was soon on excellent terms with
him. Thanks to him, I was soon in touch with things.

Witte, Witte.   The name was on everybody's lips.
People talked of no one else. The popular belief was that
Witte did everything ; and even if that was an exaggera-
tion it is an undoubted fact that nothing could be done
without Witte.

" Witte is a rogue," some people declared. Others said,
" Witte is a great statesman."

Both were mistaken. A rogue he certainly was not.
He was absolutely straight, at any rate in money matters.
He never turned his power to pecuniary advantage, as
did many of those who accused him of doing so. But
neither was he a statesman in the European sense of the
word.

It is essential that a statesman should have a definite
aim in view and a settled plan of action. He may change
his methods to suit circumstances, and to that extent
become an opportunist ;   but he must know definitely
what he is getting at.

Witte did not know. His one aim was to achieve power,
and having achieved it, he was satisfied.

The result was that he was not a statesman, but an
ambitious man of great intelligence and ability, with a
remarkable capacity for work, and especially for intrigue.
He had unbounded confidence in himself and never
troubled about methods. One way was as good as another
to him.   He knew that in Russia, in the words of an old

proverb, " he who seizes the stick is master," and seeing
the stick in feeble hands he got possession of it. But he
navigated the ship of empire without compass or chart,
guided solely by instinct, and did not know what to do
except when in smooth water. When the storm broke he
was at a loss.

As long as he was in power men bowed down before him.
He knew how to reward his admirers, and little dogs
beg prettily for a bone.

After his fall he was covered with obloquy, in accordance
with the universal rule that asses will always kick the
lion when he is dead.

I had a great deal to do with him. Sometimes he was
not up in the topic of conversation, but he was quick in
the uptake and in grasping a point. Besides, if he was in
the dark he was not ashamed of asking questions.

His colleagues were just the opposite type. They
thought themselves to be infallible, knew everything,
but never succeeded both in knowing and understanding.

I said " colleagues "—" lackeys " would be more
appropriate. Almost all the ministers—in fact the word
almost is redundant—crawled to him ; they even lacked
the necessary dignity and intelligence to keep up appearances.

I once found Witte in a state of great indignation against
the Council of Ministers or the Privy Council—I cannot
quite remember which ; they were, he said, always trying
to put spokes in his wheel. The very day before, the con-
struction of an indispensable railway had been opposed
on the ground of lack of funds.

" That's the result," I said, " of trying to get everything built by the State. If, as before, you had had

recourse to concessions, your railway would be built by now."

" No, there is no money in the market to-day."

" When there is none, there is always a little more."

" If you are so certain about it, find some and I shall give you the concession. Certainly I shall. I want to have the line ; and on this occasion I will make an exception to my rule."

I mentioned the matter to Rothstein, who was chairman of the International Bank. He set the telegraph wires humming and the money was found.

I went back to Witte.

" You go to the Minister of Ways and Communications," he said. " You have to go to him first ; ask for the concession. If he jibs, you may tell him that you are acting in agreement with me ; and indeed that I wish it to be done."

I wrote a formal application and sent it in to the Minister. By a fortunate coincidence I knew him well. We belonged to the same club. He read it, smiled superciliously, and handed it back.

" My dear Baron, I don't want you to lose the forty-eight copeks for the stamp, or to turn down an application of yours. So take it back and let us talk of other matters. Your scheme—excuse my saying so—is quite impracticable."

" Impracticable ?"

" Yes, of course. I am absolutely opposed to granting any concessions, and as long as I am in the Government none shall be granted. You should have known that. Anyhow, you may take it as absolutely definite."

" I understand. But all the same I demand an

official refusal. As you will readily understand, I am not the only person interested in this matter; there are others who have financed it. I don't want them to think that I have treated them casually. Give me an official refusal and they will see that I have done what I can."

" Very well, you shall have it."

A little later he observed : " You are taking it very calmly. I am glad, because I should not have liked to refuse anything on which you set your heart."

" Not at all, my dear sir. As a matter of fact I have not set my heart on it in the least. I was only anxious to do a friend a good turn ; in fact he's hardly a friend, a familiar acquaintance I should rather call him."

" Your friend must be a simpleton to expect such a thing."

" Hardly a simpleton. Witte's the man I mean."

" Which Witte ? The baron ?"

" No, the Finance Minister."

" Oh, I see."

He minuted my application, for the guidance of the head of the department, I suppose—" Reply that he should obtain the sanction of President of the Imperial Council and of the Minister of Finance. In the opinion of the Minister of Ways and Communications the proposal is sound."

Witte rendered conspicuous services to Russian industry, and the enormous advance which it has made of recent years is largely due to his efforts. But in many respects he did more harm than good. He was almost always concerned only with the interests of the revenue and not with those of the country as a whole, and of the general population. For him as for the rest of the Government the people were a more or less negligible quantity. And as for his methods, since he was not over scrupulous, many people derived benefit from them.

I will mention one example. The matter itself is not of great importance, since it affected the interests only of a limited number of persons, but it gives a picture of the times.

One of the over numerous Grand Dukes had ventured his private fortune in a disastrous enterprise. At considerable cost he had bought claims for extracting non-existent iron ore; he had built blast furnaces and put in machinery for manufacturing steel—in fine the young man had lost all his millions. The whole family were very much upset.

"The poor young man; it's dreadful! Witte must save him. Now or never is the time for him to prove his devotion to the dynasty."

In the ordinary way Witte would not have said no. It cost him nothing and gained him friends in high quarters whom he needed.

He was not much liked in those circles. In the ordinary way the procedure was very simple. The money was taken from the State till, and given to the young person who needed it. But not as a present. Oh, no—that would have been illegal. It was lent to him, but without interest or any fixed date for repayment. Thus the amount did not have to be carried to the debit side, but remained a perpetual asset—though not a liquid one, but merely as an item in sundry debtors' account. It was just a loan, and the statement of the income and expenditure of the State demonstrated that all was for the best in the best of all possible empires.

But it was now becoming more and more difficult to have recourse to this harmless kind of generosity. Those " dirty journalists " and others were rummaging about everywhere, poking their nose into other people's business, and in spite of the muzzle of the censorship they were arousing popular feeling.

So this time a different course of action was taken. Witte summoned his friend and counsellor Rothstein and asked him to form a company—to be called, say, Steel Limited—and by this means to buy the claims and factories belonging to the young man at the price which he had paid.

" In other words," observed Rothstein, who liked to call a spade a spade, and did not hesitate to do so, " you are asking me to conduct a fictitious sale ; to get a fool out of the mud and fall into it myself. No, your Excellency, I've had enough of that. The bank has no money to lose."

" But it won't lose money. To make a business succeed all you want is good management. And if the business goes wrong in spite of your skill it won't be the bank but the fools of subscribers who will pay. You will make a profit. You know how to take advantage of a rise. Only don't let the rise be too sudden. That's bad for the Bourse."

" After all," said Rothstein, " why not ? God made the shareholder to be gulled and ministers to be served by bankers."

And the young man got his money back with a slight margin of profit, which is always comforting. And the business succeeded marvellously. Witte acquired friends, the revenue lost nothing, the bank made a profit and the

M

shareholders suffered the inevitable fate of shareholders
—they were plucked.

But these little affairs of the gilded youth did not always
end so happily. Thus the matter of the Zalon forests ended
in a war with Japan, and the war in Russia's defeat. And
it was the people who paid with their blood and money
for the broken pieces.

I am sorry that Count Witte—he was created a Count
after Washington—should have published his Memoirs.
In their writings, as a rule, authors try to appear better
than they really are. Witte did the opposite. He dis-
paraged himself. His Memoirs depict him as a smaller
and more cunning man, more of a parvenu and less of a
man of taste than he really was. In reading them one
cannot help wondering that a man of that stamp should
have played such a remarkable rôle.

As I have just referred to Rothstein I must say a few
words about him. He was the most intelligent, most
original, most impossible and most amusing of men. He
was not in the least like the traditional banker who looks
as if he had just stepped out of a bandbox and is cold,
polite, affable and always ready to say pleasant things,
and to lighten your pocket. Rothstein was short, ugly,
untidy and badly dressed; he looked rather like a
Bohemian gorilla. He was good-hearted, though he
affected ferocity, and would lay out his man with a word;
he had a delightful humour and saw your drift before he
had heard what you said, and almost without troubling to
think he arrived at the solution of the most complicated
questions. Most men approached him with fear and
trembling. I was fond of him. I don't know whether he
was fond of me, but we got on excellently together.

The big dinners he gave almost every Thursday were miraculous affairs. The gourmets would lick their fingers. The wines were unique, and the cooking was worthy of Lucullus.

As for the people one met, they were a marvellous collection. Ambassadors and dago schemers from impossible countries, mummers and ministers, eminent artists and nobodies and old friends of our host, who had started life as an office boy in Berlin. He always forgot to introduce people, a habit which occasioned some very amusing misunderstandings.

I was once sitting next to a man in black wearing a coloured tie. He had fuzzy hair like a native of Borneo. But on reflexion I decided that he must come from Paraguay or Uruguay, countries which are now members of the League of Nations, but were then only known by geographers. I had heard him utter some words in bad French to the wife of a Secretary at the French Embassy, and we started a conversation in that language, although it was hardly a conversation, for I did all the talking. He was in difficulties with his vocabulary. As I had heard him say to his neighbour that he was going to Moscow, and as I did not know what to talk to him about, I thought I might as well tell him something about the city he was going to see, and at the same time I gave him a brief account of the history of Muscovy in the condensed form suitable for a person quite ignorant on the subject. He seemed most interested in what I was saying ; then, when I hazarded a date he observed, " No, that did not happen in the fifteenth century, but in 1549."

" Are you certain ?" I asked.

" Absolutely," he replied. "You will find it in . . ." and he mentioned the authoritative document.

" Do you read Russian ?"

" Of course I do. I am Russian ; in fact I am professor of history at Moscow University."

" Well, why aren't we speaking our own language ?" I said to him in Russian.

" What, do you know Russian ?" he asked with surprise.

" Of course, I am Russian."

We laughed. I told him that I had mistaken him for a foreigner. He said he had made a similar mistake, and when I asked him what he had imagined my nationality to be he replied South American.

" Brazil, Paraguay or Uruguay ?" I suggested.

" Yes, something of the kind."

I felt sorry for the wretched Rothstein at the dinners, and amused at him too ; he looked so thoroughly bored. He did his best to make himself pleasant, but he was suggestive of the lively grimaces of a corpse before it is taken off the gibbet. I got bored with these dinners too after a time, but I could not stop going. He would never have forgiven me. And he was too amusing and useful to me for me to quarrel with him.

" You'll come to-morrow, won't you ?" he said to me the day before one of these banquets. " Don't fail. I am always glad to see someone else, especially a friend, being as bored as I am. My dinners are amusing, aren't they ? And they cost me a pretty penny. Do you know what my last effort cost ? Five hundred roubles a head, and in the old days when I was a Bohemian outsider we had feasts for five marks at which we revelled like young gods. These wretched dinners will be the ruin of me. And one day I shall collapse with boredom."

"Would you like to do a good piece of business?"
said I.

"Of course I would; that's my job. Quick. Out with
it."

"I dine at your house about forty times a year. Let us
assume that in spite of the dreadful things you sometimes
do to me we remain friends for the next five years. I would
cost you altogether, at five hundred roubles a dinner,
more than a hundred thousand roubles. Pay me cash—
say fifty thousand roubles, and don't ask me to another
dinner. You and I would both gain."

He laughed. "It's not a bad idea," he said, "but
impossible to carry out. The others would imitate you,
and being less honest than you, would come and dine
again after pocketing the money, and I would be out of
pocket on the deal. Besides, you don't get value out of
beasts unless you feed them. They must be fattened for
the table. And I need most of the beasts. I invite the
intelligent people in order not to feel lonely. It's very sad
always to be alone. Life is no joke."

One day Witte told him that he was going to receive a
decoration.

"What an honour. Might I ask what order?"

"The order of Saint Anne."

"Oh, dear! Your Excellency, do try and make it a
different one. A saint's order! For me, a Jew! Why
don't you get me the order of the Redeemer? For a Jew
that would have been so much more appropriate."

At one of the dinners a guest observed that there was
no such thing as unalloyed happiness.

"My experience does not confirm that," said Rothstein.
"When I was thirteen, and an office boy, I lived in an un-

heated attic and I only had a wretched blanket that was too short for me. If I covered my feet my body froze, and if I pulled it up my feet froze. I was dead tired and could not sleep ; I suffered in a way which you, who have been born rich, cannot understand. Then one day I had a blanket to suit my size. My happiness was unqualified. I have never known such happiness since."

For many years I had been chairman and managing director of various limited companies, and I often had to see the Minister of Finance on these matters.

One day Rothstein said to me, " That fellow, Witte, is plaguing me to form a company for developing the natural resources to the West of the Caucasus. All the high personages have acquired lands there, and that devil wants to make himself pleasant to them. For the last few weeks he has constantly been bringing up the matter. I have made enquiries and sent a man to inspect. But the country is sparsely populated and there are no means of communication. It is a beautiful desert in which there is nothing to be done for the moment. You will quite understand that I cannot give a blank refusal and run the risk of a quarrel. In Russia a lad like that can ruin you with the greatest ease ; and when his whims are opposed Witte is just the man to do so. But I hope that he will leave me alone now and try elsewhere. I have evaded him with some skill."

" How ?"

" I told him that I didn't know the country, that such a scheme should be launched not by a foreigner—that alone would cause an outcry—but by a Russian, and that

I knew a man who had already launched two big ventures in the Caucasus. I mentioned your name ; so be on your guard. He'll tackle you next."

" Thanks ; that was awfully kind of you."

" Not at all ; friends must do each other a good turn."

" But I too am anxious to remain on good terms with him, my kind friend."

" Yes, you had better see that you do. He is revengeful. Anyhow there is always a way out. As you see, I've managed to get out of my little difficulty. Try to follow my example. Conduct a preliminary investigation ; send engineers. I will defray half the expenses—you see I am generous in my dealings. In a word procrastinate. Besides, who knows ? Maybe you will find something there."

At my very next interview with him, instead of discussing the business I had come to see him about, Witte began to hold forth about the shores of the Black Sea and the immeasurable riches to be won there.

" We have already built a road," he said, " along the whole shore. Communications are an essential preliminary ; I have given four millions to the Prince of Oldenbourg to build a health resort at Gagry and five millions for a road to the town of Romanovsk."

" Romanovsk ? Where is Romanovsk ?"

" Don't you know Romanovsk ?"

" No, I know the coast, but I have never heard of that town."

" How odd. When were you last in that part of the country ?"

" About ten years ago."

" That explains it. Do you know the Beau Plateau, otherwise called the Krasnaya Poliana ?"

"Yes, by name. But I have never been there. It's hard to get at from the sea."

"That's true. Well, a town has recently been built there. It has grown up with a rapidity that is quite American. And according to Abaza it is growing in the most amazing way. It has a prodigious future. And in honour of our august dynasty Abaza has christened it the town of the Romanovs. It makes quite an interesting story. Unfortunately I cannot tell it you to-day, because as you see I have still a crowd of people to see. It's four o'clock already and there are more than thirty people waiting. So let's get down to brass tacks. As you know, the State has done pretty well by the country already. But it cannot do everything alone. Private enterprise must take a hand. Found a big company, something really important, a venture that can pay good dividends. Others will then follow your example. You understand?"

"Perfectly. But what do you want? A mining enterprise or. . . ."

"That's your business; it's all the same to me. But it must be a sound enterprise of the kind that gets itself talked about. It's a splendid country; more beautiful than the Riviera. As sunny as Nice. The roses bloom in midwinter. It has everything. Go and see Kovalevsky; he will tell you more about it. That's settled then. When you have been there we shall discuss the matter further. See you again soon. But don't be too long. His Majesty is personally interested in the country. Above all, don't forget to discuss it with Abaza."

He rang for the usher. "Show in the next caller."

"But, your Excellency, I had come to talk to you about our. . . ."

" That's quite impossible to-day. Come another time. I've got a crowd of people waiting and I must be at the Council at six. Good-bye ; go and see Kovalevsky."

I knew Kovalevsky well. He was an important person in the business world, director of the Department of Commerce and Industry, and Witte's evil genius. A very able and intelligent schemer ; though very superficial, he was the typical high official of the time.

A characteristic and perhaps genuine heartiness made him popular with everybody. He would promise anything, and having done so, considered that he had done his duty. That was well known, but none bore him ill will on that account. It was the general practice.

But who on earth was this Abaza whom Witte talked about ? One Abaza had been a minister, but he was dead, another was a naval officer, a third. . . I had not heard of a third.

" I was expecting you," said Kovalevsky when I went to see him. " The Minister told me you were coming. What a marvellous man he is ! It's astounding. He always manages to seize the psychological moment. The coast of the Caucasus, you know, is very much on the tapis just now. His Majesty and all St. Petersburg are interested in it. Abaza has made it fashionable. He is a very clever fellow, Abaza ! Why, with a gesture he has founded and brought to prosperity the town of Romanovsk. After the final pacification of the Caucasus in 1864 most of the native Mahomedans emigrated to Turkey, and the coast became practically a desert. In order to revive the country the Government is offering land there dirt cheap. Abaza is in charge of the business. The whole of St. Petersburg has brought land, but nobody is venturing to start anything.

And they are certainly right. I have land there, too, and am leaving it fallow myself. Prices will soon go up and then I shall sell. Abaza assures me. . .''

" Who is this Abaza that everyone's talking about, your Excellency ?''

" What ? Don't you know Abaza ? Where have you been all this time ? Abaza ! Why he's the man of the hour.''

" I thought the man just now in favour with His Majesty was Philip the mesmerist.''

" Philip foretells the future for His Majesty, and interprets his destiny. He is the man of the hour in matters spiritual. A pure charlatan ; and anyhow, I believe that his reign is over. Abaza is a serious person. He will bring to the surface the vast riches of the coast and heap gold upon all of us.''

He proceeded to tell me a long yarn, which I just accepted as a fable of the Arabian Nights. I did not yet know that the period of charlatans and of favourites for a day had come.

I learnt that Abaza, who but yesterday was quite unknown, had just been appointed a member of the Imperial Council and sent to the coast armed with full power. In a word he was a power in the land.

He had managed to attach numerous supporters to himself. Instead of giving the State lands to colonists who would have cultivated them, he distributed them amongst the powerful, who seized upon them simply speculating on an early rise in value.

" But let us get back to the point,'' said Kovalevsky. " What have you decided to do ?''

" Nothing as yet. I am trying to get my bearings, but have not succeeded. I hope that you . . ."

" Come, come, my dear Baron. I like that. The country's rolling in riches. It has everything. Nice sunshine. Roses blooming in midwinter."

" Quite ! The minister, too, spoke about the sun and the roses. But I wonder whether your Excellency would grant me authority to issue a few million shares on the Course for the exploitation of the sun and flowers."

He began to laugh. " Why not, if the minister wishes it ?"

" The minister wants a sound business, paying good dividends. Something different from the Steel Company of painful memory."

" Oh, hang it ! That's certainly not easy and is another matter. Of course, Abaza says there are considerable deposits of coal, petrol and vast other natural riches. Of course, the public must not be deceived . . . but between ourselves . . . if Witte's made up his mind that the business shall pay good dividends. I'll tell you what. Why not talk to Abaza ?"

" By all means."

"I have to go to Batum. On my way back I can stop at Sotcky, where Abaza lives. Meet me there. The journey to a successful conclusion whatever happens. I'll tell Abaza to-day to expect you. Is that all right ?"

" Agreed."

In the evening I paid a rare visit to my club. I ascertained that Witte had certainly seized the psychological moment. The coast was the one topic of conversation. " Land would go up in value." Abaza said, " Witte had promised." Abaza was certainly a sly dog and an expert advertiser.

Some days afterwards Kovalevsky told me that he was starting for Batum. I went to Odessa, where I took ship for Sotcky.

After all I had heard in St. Petersburg I expected to find the coast quite changed from when I had known it. But except for a new road which nobody used, and on which the weeds were encroaching, everything was as of old. It was an uninhabited paradise, stifled by the excessive luxuriance of its vegetation.

The only hotel in the little town was crowded out. His Excellency's whole suite of engineers, surveyors and officials of every kind were staying there. Fortunately he had been good enough to keep a room for me ; but for which I should have been reduced to spend the night under the stars.

When I had changed I went to see Abaza, who lived outside the town.

Monsieur Abaza was very prosperous. He was tall and spare, had a fine presence ; the heavy lead playing the benevolent prince. In every gesture he seemed to be saying : " You see how kindly I am condescending to you, but don't forget that I am a most important person.

" My august master," " my adored sovereign," " my faithful duty as a subject," "my devotion to His Majesty," all these phrases, much abused by rascals at the time, were always on the tip of his tongue. And as he uttered them he threw out his chest and threw back his head with the expression of a love-sick tenor and oozed servility.

But these elaborate tricks were a little too obvious. With us in the capital such folk were less blatant.

" You have been warmly commended to me by my friend, the Minister of Finance," said Abaza, " and I am ready to do anything I can to help you, provided, of course, that your wishes are in harmony with the interests of the country. My august master has made me the guardian of it and my first consideration must be the success of the task with which I have been entrusted and not the interests of individuals. That is my duty as a faithful subject of my adored Sovereign and as a patriot."

" I personally want nothing, Your Excellency. M. Witte asked me to see if I could start anything here, and, if possible, to float a public company. He must be unaware that capital is pouring in here in such quantities. He wanted somebody to start the ball rolling. As this has already been done there is no point in my interfering."

I took up my hat and prepared to leave.

" But, my dear Baron, you have misunderstood me It is true that everybody wants to do business here because they know that there are enormous profits to be made and it is not capital that we want, anything but, but I am cautious, perhaps over cautious, and so I asked M. Witte to find a man whom I could thoroughly rely upon. Won't you sit down. I see that you are the man we want. I am sure we shall get on together."

And he got down to the job like a cool commercial traveller. " Here are iron ore, copper, silver, coal, zinc, petroleum."

In fine, there was everything in the world. It was quite a laboratory of minerals. In fact, there was too much to be convincing, and if I asked him if any particular deposit were rich he invariably replied, "Thousands of millions of tons." An hour of this was enough. I felt it was useless to speak to this man, and decided to wait for Kovalevsky. In order not to break off the conversation too abruptly, I turned to a topic which I thought should be congenial— the town of Romanovsk. " I gather that is going to be a very beautiful city ? One hears marvellous things about it." He made a deprecating gesture.

" It will be a beautiful city ; but there is still much that wants to be done. You know, St. Petersburg people always exaggerate somewhat. Things are moving, but not as quickly as I could wish. I will show you the plans of the town. His Majesty has deigned to approve them. That is the town hall."

" Well, that's charming."

" That's the casino. What do you think of it?"

" Delightful."

" These are the baths, but I am not satisfied with them. They are perfect inside. But the front. . ."

" As long as they are comfortable, that is the main thing."

" That is the cathedral."

" Magnificent."

" Yes, but it's not finished yet. His Majesty has given me reason to hope that he will be present at the opening ceremony."

I was dazzled. These buildings were really beautiful.

" I must go and see them. How long does it take to get to Romanovsk ?"

" Yes, I wish you would go, but it takes some time. The plateau is almost inaccessible from this side. There is a path where you risk breaking your neck, and after that you have to cross the terrible Black Forest described by Tolstoi in his " Prisoner of the Caucasus." You cannot

escape catching fever. Wait until the road is built. Just
now it can only be reached from the other side of the
mountains. It's not really so far away. It takes three or
four days to get there and as many to come back, and then
you want three or four days to spend there. If you have a
free fortnight, that would be enough. It is a journey
which is certainly well worth while."

"Unfortunately I must wait for Kovalevsky here, then
return to St. Petersburg. I can't manage a fortnight."

"That's a pity. I should have liked you to have seen it.
To speak without false modesty, it's well worth while.
While we are about it, do you want to buy some land?
Prices are going up. They are already rising every day."

"No, thank you."

Next day Abaza came to ask me to dine with him.
As I was on the way to his house I met Count Sergius
Cheremetieff, who was a friend of the Emperor.

"You here?"

"Yes, I landed yesterday," said the Count. "I bought
some land here and am going to build. Where are you
going?"

"I am dining with Abaza."

"So am I."

On our way we talked about the country and also, of
course, about the beautiful city of Romanovsk. I asked
the Count whether he had been there.

"No. Abaza is going there to-morrow, and I wanted to
go with him, but he said so much against the journey
that I've given up the idea. I am absolutely terrified of
malaria. And then there is the long journey on horseback. . ."

"Why is Abaza going?"

" It seems that he has got to build a tunnel not provided for in the original plan of the road, and an official from the Imperial Board of Control has arrived to investigate on the spot how far this is essential. As you know, control of expenditure is now very thorough and very strict. And as these gentry are very efficient, Abaza is making a point of showing his things himself. I think he is going to unnecessary trouble, because a man in Abaza's position need not fear."

" I should very much like to ask him to take me with him."

" I certainly should ; you are not afraid of fever and the fag of the journey as I am."

I spoke about it to Abaza at dinner.

" I should have been more than delighted," he said, " but I could never take the responsibility."

He proceeded to give a long catalogue of all the misfortunes that could assail me. It amounted to a definite refusal of my request.

It would have been indiscreet to press the point, but Cheremetieff came to my assistance. As I had seen and noted when we arrived, Abaza ate out of the Count's hand, as he knew him to be the favourite of his adored Sovereign, so, whether he liked it or not, he had to give way in the end. But it seemed to me that he did not like doing so at all ; he returned to the topic several times and always on the same note.

" I ask you to bear me witness, Count, that I have made every effort to dissuade the Baron from coming with me. If he falls ill I shan't feel responsible ; I have warned him and have only yielded at your request."

He pleaded so successfully that as we were on our way home Cheremetieff told me not to go.

" These wretched Causasus fevers are the very devil when you're not accustomed to the climate."

He buttonholed the proprietor of the hotel.

" Do you know the way leading to Krasnaya Poliana?"

" Which way, Count ?"

" Through the Black Forest."

" A terrible place. I nearly lost my life there."

" You see what he says," said Cheremetieff. " Take my advice and don't go. Wait until the road is finished. If you were to catch fever I should never forgive myself for having helped you to go on this foolish adventure."

But next day we were in a carriage driving along the road towards Adler through the most beautiful country in the world.

When we came to a certain rather narrow valley we got out of the carriage. The horses, mules laden with provisions, engineers, and Cossacks—a whole caravan—was waiting for us. We needed about eight hours to reach Krasnaya Poliana on horseback ; the plateau which was the site of Romanovsk.

I shall never forget that ride. All went well at first. We went up a gentle incline through a delightful valley covered with flowers, and then through smiling pastures. Suddenly we entered the forest ; a forest such as I had never seen. It was a nightmare ; a tomb covered with a roof of leaves—black, impenetrable and dismal—it was absolutely impervious to the sun's rays ; fantastic scenery, such as might have been the product of a diseased imagination. Grey, sickly trees stretched to an enormous height—they looked like dried-up skeletons ; monstrous

N

abortions, huge and gigantic. No blade of grass or foliage—not a living creature. The fever had destroyed all life. The air was stifling, the sweat rolled in torrents, my head seemed to be in a vice, I felt as though I were going mad ; I thought I would die.

I got off my horse and wanted to walk, but after a few steps I felt faint.

" Go back," said Abaza, " you will never get there. I will give you two Cossacks to take you home."

" No, I shall stick it out."

" It will take us five or six hours to get through this horrible forest. Take my advice and go home."

After another hour he came back to the charge. I was quite ready to do as he wished, but his importunity prevented me.

He had become intensely antipathetic to me ; and as he seemed to set so much store by it I would not yield.

We continued on our way, I scarcely know how. I had lost the power of reflection and went on like an automaton. If, instead of talking to me, Abaza had simply ordered somebody to take my horse by the bridle and turn it about I should have acquiesced.

We were revived by a breath of fresh air. A dim light shone through the tree trunks. Our horses spontaneously raised their heads and broke into a trot. A magnificent picture was spread before our eyes. We were on a delightful plateau, dotted here and there with ancient chestnuts and surrounded by huge rocks which were illuminated by the setting sun. At our feet the sea stretched to the horizon, covered with long streaks of gold and silver.

" How lovely it is," I said.

" Yes," said an old Cossack, who was walking next to

me, who had also halted his horse. "There is only one country in the world that is as beautiful, our Caucasus. And there is only one plateau like this one, our Krasnaya Poliana."

"It is a pity that in order to get here from the coast it should be necessary to pass through that horrible Black Forest."

"But you can get here from another road, from Adler," said the old man.

"Well, why didn't we come that way?"

"I'm afraid I don't know, your Honour. The escort originally had orders to meet near Adler and then, yesterday, we got different orders to meet here. We were told that we should go through the Black Forest. We were quite surprised."

While we were stopping to admire the marvellous view our companions had gone on ahead.

We saw them stop and genuflect in front of a small wooden shed with a cross on top of it.

"We built that chapel with a few boards of wood to sing a Te deum in 1864," said my Cossack. "It was here we heard the news of the final pacification of the country."

Instead of getting on their horses again and continuing the journey, our companions, with Abaza leading, went leading their horses, towards a group of three small huts in front of which some mountain folk had gathered.

I asked my Cossack how far we were from Romanovsk. He gazed at me with astonishment.

"From Romanovsk? Why, your Honour, we are there. Krasnaya Poliana is to be known by that name in future."

"Yes, I know. But what about the town? Is it far away?"

" It is here, your Honour, that the town is to be built,"
and, as with St. Paul on the way to Damascus, a great
light fell upon me. This was the beautiful city, with its
Renaissance casino, its magnificent hotel, its well-fitted
baths, whose façade only was incomplete. This was the
town about which everybody was talking at St. Petersburg—these three wretched log cabins were Romanovsk.
And the little shed with the cross on top was the cathedral—not finished, it is true, but soon to be so.

Next day, when we got back to Sotchy, by Adler this
time—for the Black Forest had served its purpose—the
hotel porter told me that His Excellency General Kovalevsky with his wife and suite had arrived and had asked
for me and that they would call on me next day.

So he had come at last ! It was six days later than the
date which he had fixed.

I was still in bed next morning when Kovalevsky
without knocking, burst into my room.

" Have you any cigarettes ? I've run out."

" Well, you're here at last," I replied. " I had almost
lost hope of seeing you."

" I'm so sorry. What's the time ? My watch has
stopped."

" Half-past ten."

" Oh ! Good heavens ! I promised to see Cheremetieff
at nine o'clock precisely. I'm off."

" But I've got some things to talk to you about."

" Later on."

" Only a few words."

" Impossible. I make a point of being punctual.
Punctuality is the politeness of kings."

" Wait a moment."

" Impossible. Let's lunch at one, if that suits you. We shall be able to talk at our leisure then."

" Very well."

" Please be punctual. Time is money. I have an appointment with Abaza at three o'clock."

At one o'clock precisely I was waiting in the hotel dining-room. He came at half-past two, and he was not alone, but with " his wife " as the hotel porter called her. I knew " his wife " by sight. She was his mistress—a fat and elderly chorus girl from a small theatre.

" I hope I am not late," said Kovalevsky. " Let's sit down. And now we can talk at our leisure about your business."

He had forgotten his wife. She did the talking. When once she was started it was impossible to stop her.

The clock struck four.

Kovalevsky jumped up.

" The clock's mad. What time is it by your watch ?"

" Exactly twenty past four."

" Good heavens ! And I had an appointment with Abaza at three o'clock precisely. By the way, do you know that he's furious with you ? I'll tell you about that later. Now I must be off."

" No, no, Vladimir Ivanovitch. We've got some things to talk over. As you're late already, half-an-hour more or less. . ."

" Oh, no, no. Punctuality is. . ."

I interrupted him.

" Anyhow, I can't stay here for an indefinite time."

" Let's see." He took out his pocket-book.. " I am dining with Abaza. Then I have to go and see the mayor ; but to-morrow morning I am entirely at your disposal.

At eight o'clock precisely, if that suits you ? See that nobody interrupts. That's all right. Eight o'clock precisely ; try to be ready, I'm always punctual. Good-bye."

And he was off.

Next day I waited for him till eleven. Then, as he still had not arrived, I sent to ask whether he was up. The porter himself came to tell me that His Excellency General Kovalevsky, with " wife and suite," had left for Odessa with the six o'clock boat and had told him to give me a note. This said that Kovalevsky had had a telegram the previous evening, which made it necessary for him to return to St. Petersburg. He added in a postscript: " Try to come back as soon as possible, and come and see me at once, as soon as you do." He had omitted to add : Time is money.

The same evening I went away, too, without saying good-bye to Abaza.

I had seen Witte and Kovalevsky several times, but we never mentioned the coast again or the proposed company. The psychological moment was passed. Witte had other worries. A storm was brewing in the Far East.

I have never since heard Abaza or the beautiful city of Romanovsk mentioned. Does it really exist or is Krasnaya Poliana still the beautiful desert that it was ? I do not know. Anyway, to-day, when people are wondering whether Russia herself exists or not, it is not a matter of any importance.

As I have referred to Abaza I ought to mention some of the others—I don't quite know what to call them. " Scum " is coarse and also somewhat vague ; " favourites " is not the right word—shall we say " passades." As we know, that was the name given to those ladies who, without becoming established mistresses of King Louis XV, provided his more casual pleasures, and established a temporary hold upon him. This word seems to be equally fitted to the men who, although not officially in power, succeeded for the time being in establishing their ascendancy over the vacillating will of the poor innocent who, under the name of Nicholas II, occupying the throne of the most extensive Empire in the world, led the country to destruction.

I shall confine myself to one or two—to those whose names have become known to the general public. Otherwise the list would be too long. I cannot even mention all of these, but only those who were particularly notorious and contributed in large measure to discredit their Sovereign in the eyes of his people.

I have already referred to his fancy for Philippe. If I am not mistaken, Philippe was a Frenchman of Lyon, who professed the power of miraculous healing and used to foretell the future to simple women. He had been convicted of several frauds and was closely watched by the police. But, somehow or other, two ladies belonging to high society in Russia, whose names I know, though I refrain from mentioning them, introduced him to our Sovereign when they came to France. He succeeded in imposing on them and he was summoned to Czarskoe-Selo.

For the sake of appearances—for at that time the Court had still a sense of shame—they approached the French Government with a view to having a medical degree conferred upon the charlatan. As they were not successful in this, they did without it, and his degree was conferred upon him by the medical authorities in Russia.

He was also made a Councillor of State, which gave him the right to the title of Excellency.

He wore a special uniform ad hoc, lived in a villa attached to the Imperial Palace, foretold the future for the Czar, gave him advice on men and affairs, grew rich and did himself well. Probably he would have succeeded in becoming all powerful as Rasputin, another fugitive from justice, did soon afterwards, if he had not queered his own pitch just at the moment when, with a little luck, he could have carried everything before him.

Their Majesties had four daughters, and their most fervent prayer was to have a son to inherit the throne. Philippe persuaded them that he possessed the secret of controlling the gender and conception, and succeeded in hypnotising the Empress into the belief that she was with child. There was great rejoicing ; this time they were to have an heir to the throne ! They were so certain about it that they almost shouted it from the housetops.

And then, one fine day, in the eighth month of pregnancy, it turned out that Her Majesty could not be expecting either a son or a daughter. Her pregnancy was merely the effect of a morbid imagination.

Philippe was sent back to France.

He was succeeded by a group of priests. They said that if a holy man called Serafime, who had died at Sarov, a convent in the interior of Russia, were canonized and if the Empress would bathe in the well from which the holy man drew his water, she would have a son.

Serafime was canonized by order of the Emperor. Her Majesty took the prescribed bath and, marvellous to relate, she gave birth to an heir. After this the poor

woman became a mystic in truly mediæval fashion. And
the Emperor, who always did what he was told, became
one too.

His fancy for Achinov is a very amusing story. It is
rather a long one, but I shall tell it and pass over others
which are less funny.

I must go back rather a long time. A young officer,
called Leontiev, was obliged to leave the service after
having run through his money ; he went to Abyssinia and
offered Menelik, " the king of kings and the lion of Abyssinia "—that was his official title—his services, a musical
box which he had bought at Odessa and a double-barrelled
gun, saying that the most powerful monarch in the world,
the Emperor of Russia, had decided to send him gifts.
Menelik was touched. Leontiev remained in his service,
succeeded in winning his regard and was soon created
Count of Abyssinia and Governor-General of the Provinces
of the Equator.

In the meantime Menelik had attracted attention, and
France and England had entered into relations with him.

Leontiev thought it his duty to convey this information
to our Government, and then came to St. Petersburg and
proposed that the Foreign Office should make use of his
services.

There was some excitement at the Pont-aux-Chantres.
We could not let the other Powers get in first; but it was
impossible to employ as our agent a gentleman whom
nobody knew. Leontiev was turned down.

One fine day the man suited for this delicate mission
was discovered.

His name was Achinov ; he was headman of the inde-

pendent Cossacks, " Volyne Kasaky." None ever discovered who these independent Cossacks were or where
they lived ; indeed, nobody ever tried. His Majesty himself had discovered this treasure and had instructed his
ministers to arrange matters with him. After that it was
naturally superfluous to take up references.

I once had the good fortune of meeting him and received the signal honour of a long conversation with him.
He was a rustic of the worst type, who could neither read
nor write, nor even blow his nose, for which purpose he
used his fingers ; completely ignorant but shameless and
insolent ; a regular rascal and a drunkard.

He left on a secret mission to the country of the "king
of kings." A few weeks later (it was surprising how he
had succeeded in doing the long journey in so short a time)
he returned and brought with him a young leopard and a
young African girl, the great king's own daughter. The
leopard was a present from Menelik to the Emperor and
the girl was entrusted by the king as a mark of friendship
to the care of Her Imperial Majesty.

The leopard was sent to the Zoological Gardens and the
coloured princess to the institute for the daughters of the
nobility, to be educated there in a manner suitable to a
girl of royal descent.

Then the headman of the independent Cossacks left
for Abyssinia, generously supplied with gold, on a steam-
ship chartered by the Government, with a whole troop
of his Cossacks, who were armed and equipped at the
expense of the State. Under the influence of drink he
besieged the town of Obok, where the French flag was
already flying. We had the very greatest difficulty in
hushing up this incident. Achinov was disclaimed by his

Government. " Russia has never heard of this individual
and does not even know where he comes from. Russia
has never had any independent Cossacks."

Thanks to the goodwill of the French Government, the
affair had no consequences.

When enquiries were made (better late than never),
it was discovered that the headman of the independent
Cossacks was a Saratov cobbler who had never been to
Abyssinia. The daughter of the great king was a young
creature whom he had picked up at Constantinople, and
the leopard came from a Warsaw menagerie.

His Majesty made himself ridiculous over his fancies,
Philippe and Achinov, but they did not have such bloody
and disastrous consequences as his fancy Bezobrazov.
This gentleman, or rather this fellow, a former officer of
the Guard, and a person of no qualifications whatever, was
the moving spirit of a group of ne'r-do-wells belonging to
the best society of the capital who, with the support
of his Majesty himself, had launched the unsavoury
enterprise of the Yalou Forest, an enterprise which,
as is now generally known, resulted in the Japanese
war.

The whole of this unpleasant business was floated
by Bezobrazov and the Emperor personally and carried
on behind the backs of the Ministers and of our Ambassador in Japan, although they may have known something
of it (they had had wind of the affair). The poor Emperor
thought that he was carrying out a magnificent work and
did not realise that, without his suspecting it, he was
being made to play a most dishonourable part. Bezobrazov was appointed Secretary of State and actually
became Prime Minister. When at last the unfortunate

Sovereign saw that he had been fooled it was too late. The harm had been done. Instead of being hanged, as he deserved, Bezobrazov was ordered to live abroad. It was characteristic of Nicholas II to show leniency to the undeserving.

CHAPTER VII

1904-1914

On the 26th January, 1904, Japan attacked the Russian fleet without warning and sunk three of our ships. Next day war was declared.

I do not believe that a war has ever been less popular. The Russian people had never heard of Japan, and there was therefore no reason for any additional hostility, as there was in the case of Turkey, Poland or England. Those who were in a position to judge, those, in fact, who were more or less civilised, realised that the results of the conflict, whatever they might be, were bound to be harmful to Russia.

If Russia were victorious, the Czar, by which I mean his Government (for the Czar himself was known to be only a shadow), would make use of the opportunity to strengthen absolutism and to treat Russia more than ever before as a conquered country. If, on the other hand, the campaign were lost, revolution would result and, as any man of common sense knew, revolution in Russia would not be a revolution in the European sense of the word—that is, a mere change in the form of government—but would result in massacres, in rivers of blood and in the complete ruin of every vestige of civilisation, as indeed happened a few years later.

But nobody admitted the possibility of a defeat.

" How could Japan, that little race of people, more like monkeys than men, hope to fight against people like ourselves !"

Give the cheeky little fellows a punch on the nose and the war would be over. These absurd little pygmies were a great joke.

I only met three Russians who anticipated that the war might end in disaster. They were Witte, General Drago-mirov and my greatest friend, General Doshturov. When Kuropatkin was made commander-in-chief, the latter prophesied that defeat was inevitable. He said to me :

" I know Kuropatkin through and through. He is as true as steel, knows his job, he is a good strategist and an excellent administrator. He is an ideal chief of Staff, but hopeless as a commander-in-chief. He will poke his nose into every detail, want to do everything himself and command each regiment, each battalion, and each platoon personally ; in fact, he will make it impossible for the individual commanders to do their duty. He will never ask himself whether a thing is necessary, but he will always be wondering whether it will give satisfaction in high quarters. He is not a soldier, but a lackey ; and through his desire to please his chief and his fear of com-promising himself at Court, he will turn tail at the critical moment and everything will be lost.

Alas ! Everything happened just as he had foretold.

I had been told much the same thing, though in other words, by Skobelev, whose Chief of Staff Kuropatkin had been. When I asked him whether he had been pleased with Count Keller, a friend of mine, who had done duty for Kuro-patkin temporarily while the latter was wounded, he replied :

" One of the best. A good worker, intelligent and courageous. He was a most exceptional man ; but I myself preferred Kuropatkin."

" Why ?" I asked.

" Keller was Keller and Kuropatkin was simply my man."

As a matter of fact, on this occasion I must say that it was not the Emperor who had shewn his usual bad judgment, but public opinion that had been misled. When a man was wanted who could bring about a victory everybody shouted with one voice " Kuropatkin."

" And why not he as well as another ?" Dragomirov asked with an innocent expression.

" But, your Excellency, you forget that he was Chief of Staff to Skobelev."

" Yes, and don't you know who has been nominated to succeed Skobelev ?"

The future chief of the army had in one respect at least turned the principles and example of Skobelev to account. Like Skobelev, he got every kind of puff he could. Then he left for the war, taking with him a whole truck-load of holy images which he had had offered to him.

" He has got too many saints," said Dragomirov. " You'll find that soon he won't know which is his particular patron saint."

My eldest son, too, had left for Manchuria. After having got his degree as an engineer, he had done his compulsory service with the Horse Guards ; then, having been accepted for the examinations at the military college, he passed and became an officer. But as we were very far from thinking about a war, and as the life of a soldier in peace time did not appeal to his energetic nature, he soon sent in his resignation. On the very day of the declaration of war he rejoined the army and, at his request, was attached to a Cossack regiment, part of the advance guard which, under the command of General Rennenkampf, was intended to be the first to come into action against the Japanese army.

The war was disastrous from the very start. In March the Japanese sank the ship carrying the Admiral commanding the Russian squadron ; in April there was the defeat at Turentchen and the Japanese attack at Eidsyvo ; in August there was the heavy defeat at Liayan, which, as we learned after the war from the Japanese themselves, would have been a decisive victory for the Russians if Kuropatkin had not turned tail at the last moment. Then, finally, there was the disastrous retreat to Mukden.

But at St. Petersburg people were still saying that everything was all right. A new fleet was to sail for the Far East, Port Arthur was still holding out, and when the fleet arrived a very little fighting would settle the matter.

There were rejoicings in high quarters. The trivial disappointment in Manchuria was of small account compared with the auspicious event which had just taken place. O n the 30th July an heir to the throne had been born. The future of the throne was assured and therefore that of Russia also.

Port Arthur capitulated on the 22nd December.

We were uneasy at home. We had had fairly frequent news of our son at the beginning of the war. We heard that he had been decorated. Then we read a distressing account in a paper of a man who got sunstroke during the fighting. The correspondent had seen with his own eyes the Cossack lieutenant, Baron Wrangel, former officer in the Horse Guards, being carried away dead on a stretcher. Later we had a telegram from him himself, reading: " Health good, have just been promoted full lieutenant for services rendered on the battle-field." And then for some months we heard nothing.

At last he suddenly turned up one day. He had already reached the rank of captain, but his condition was deplorable. He had been invalided home to recuperate.

He was hardly out of bed before he started pulling every wire he could to be passed fit to rejoin his regiment. Fortunately they laughed at him and told him to go and look at himself in the glass and go back to bed.

My friend Doshturov told me that he had been told at the War Office that my son was considered to be an officer with a brilliant future before him. Doshturov was delighted, as he had said so too.

What our son told us was not particularly reassuring. He said that the army in the field, both men and regimental officers were admirable, that the men were well-disciplined, would endure any hardships and were steady under fire, but they were short of many things, and the Staff were for the most part deplorable. Those who had capability were generally turned on to jobs for which they were unfit. For instance, General Mistshenko, an unrivalled artillery expert, had been placed in command of a cavalry corps of the advance guard, although he had never been on a horse, while General Rennenkampf, a cavalry general if ever there was one, had been given the command of an infantry division. The state of affairs in the lines of communication was deplorable, and the worst of it was that revolutionary propagandists were at work,

o

not only behind the lines but at the front. The Intelligentzia rivalled the Japanese agents in their zeal for spreading disaffection amongst the troops. My son could not say enough in praise of the Japanese army. They were admirable in every way ; but all the same we must persevere. We should get them in the end. Only he wondered what would happen afterwards. Whether we won or were beaten we should have civil war.

It should not have been necessary to point this out as it was obvious to everyone except to the ruling clique who ought to have known better than anybody else ; but they remained blind to all the evidence ; indeed, it looked as though they had made up their minds to bring about the civil war as speedily as possible.

Disturbances had occurred in Moscow as well as in some other towns. In the country districts mansions were being burned down and the owners were being molested. At St. Petersburg itself disturbances were a regular occurrence and numerous attacks were made upon prominent persons. The Government replied by repressive measures which were harsh rather than effective, and refused to go to the root of the matter.

After a time the Emperor issued a manifesto, conceived, apparently, with the object of allaying public excitement, but nobody understood what it meant. It made promises, but nobody could see how they could be interpreted ; they implied everything and nothing. It was maliciously nicknamed " The Muir and Meerrilies prospectus," that being the name of a large shop at Moscow which dealt largely in cheap goods. When they met, people used to ask each other whether they had read it. The reply always was : " Yes, but I don't understand it. Do you ? "

" Neither do I."

Two Ministers asked me the question, and my reply was the same on each occasion. An " izvoztshik " (that is, a country coachman) asked me the question too. As I did not want to discredit my Sovereign with him, I replied that I hadn't yet had time to read the Imperial decree.

" Have you read it ?" I said to him.

" I can't read, but they read it out at the eating-place I go to."

" What is it about ?"

" The Czar has said we shall have to pay new taxes."

I think the good fellow was as near the truth of the matter as any of us.

One day the principal works manager of Siemens & Halscke, of which company I was the chairman, telephoned asking me to come to the factory at once. He said the workmen were putting forward ridiculous demands, were threatening to strike, and refused to come to an agreement with him or to negotiate with anybody excepting one of the directors. I was considerably surprised, for up to that time our relations with our workmen had been perfect. In Russia, where industries have only quite recently been introduced, the workman is not, as he is in Europe, a man belonging to a working-class, that is to say, a man whose father has been a workman like himself. He is generally a young peasant who has but lately come from the land, a young savage thrown out of gear by contact with the town and liable to be influenced to any course of action by the first person he meets.

In fact, the men working in our factories were on the whole better educated than the general average of the Russian proletariat ; they were men who had been employed by us for many years, from father to son. They were better paid than any other workmen and their lot was preferable to that of others. I don't want to suggest that their lot was an enviable one. It certainly was not. But our workmen knew as well as we did that the management were not to blame, and that their troubles were due to the police, who worried them in every kind of way ; the police regarded every workman as a revolutionary and used to arrest them and imprison them without any regard to reason.

I went to the factory at once. The adjoining street was full of workmen. The crowd grew more and more unruly the further I went, soon they were openly hostile. "There's one of the rich who trample everybody under their feet," was the kind of thing one heard.

Somebody threw a stone at me. I sent my coachman home and went on on foot.

The engineer informed me of their complaints. There were four pages of them ; some of them were so unreasonable that our men could not possibly have been responsible for them. Before discussing the matter with them we secretly summoned some old workmen whom we could trust.

" Tell us what's the matter," we said. " Frankly, we don't understand."

" Neither do we. It's a lot of nonsense. Raise the wages a little ; everything else is nonsense. They must be mad to make stupid complaints of that kind."

" But, then, why have you, who are reasonable men

signed this petition as well as the others, whom you regard as mad ?"

" The committee insisted that we should, sir."

" What committee ?"

" We don't know."

" What ! You are told to do something ridiculous by people you don't know, and without making any further enquiries you do as you are told ?"

" We have to, sir. At the Nobel factories some of the men kicked and the same night eight men were killed in their homes. The same thing happened at Lessler's. If we all lived in the same district we could defend ourselves, but we are scattered about all over the place. It is impossible to do anything but obey."

" Who handed you the order of the committee which you are talking about ?"

" Some gentlemen who were very well dressed. In fact, one of them was wearing a top hat ; another looked like a student and wore uniform. Whoever they were, they weren't workmen and they were good talkers. They understood nothing about our business and they used words which we could not understand."

" Yes," said another man, laughing, " some very funny words they did use too !" and he gesticulated comically. " ' Dictatorship,' ' proletariat,' ' international,' words which nobody understood. I told my mother about it ; she said she was sure they were Japanese spies. My wife thinks so too, but my son is certain that they were Jews."

Our discussion ended without result and the strike broke out. Then, three days later, without a word of warning, work was resumed. We were more and more puzzled and had a further secret interview with our friends.

" Why and how did it happen ?" we asked.

" Gapon, the priest, arranged it. You know Gapon? Well, it was he."

Gapon was a rather suspicious character. Some people said that he was a terrorist and others said that he was an *agent provocateur*. It has since been proved that he received considerable sums from the police department. He was sometimes pursued by the authorities and disappeared ; at other times he would be going about the town quite openly to everybody's knowledge.

" So the priest Gapon has turned up again ?" I asked.

" Yes. People are signing on with him to take part in the visit to the Czar."

" A visit to the Czar ?"

" Yes. The Czar has invited all the workmen to come and see him. Some fair-minded men who are well disposed to us have informed him that the authorities are oppressing us and he wants to hear our own account of the matter."

" My poor fellow, Gapon is deceiving you. You will land yourselves in a mess. The Czar will never receive you. The priest is leading you into a trap from which you will find it difficult to get out."

He looked at me superciliously.

" It is obvious," he said, " that the rich do not like the idea of the workers getting into touch with our father, the Czar. The Czar has invited us and we shall go, whatever you say."

" If that is your attitude, I won't say any more. Go to him. It's your own business ; but if one of you happens

to be a ruffian who has wormed his way in amongst you
and. . .''

" Oh, no, sir ! Gapon is going to talk to them all first
and tell them that they're not to carry any arms ; and he
is instructing everybody to wear their Sunday clothes.
When you call on the Czar you must look your best.''

Work had started again, not only with us, but in all the
factories ; this was very odd. At this period one works
or another was always on strike. Everybody in the town
knew that a demonstration by the workers had been
fixed for the 9th January.

The morning of the 9th I went to our factory ; but after
crossing the Neva I came back. A police officer told me
that I could continue on my way, but that in all prob-
ability nobody would be allowed to come back from Vasi-
lievsky Ostrov. Serious disorders were expected, and if
they occurred, as they obviously would, communications
would be cut.

An enormous crowd of workmen were in fact massed
on the quay ; but, as far as I could ascertain, they were
just holiday-making and seemed to be perfectly peaceful.
A large number of troops were on duty on the square of
the Winter Palace, where the Emperor was in residence.
It was only through the good offices of a colonel whom I
knew, who was guarding the quadrant leading to the
Morskaia with his regiment, that I was able to continue
on my way. He told me that the soldiers had been supplied
with ammunition.

" Why ?" I asked. " Everything will go off perfectly
all right ; the Emperor will receive a deputation or show
himself to the people from the balcony.''

" My dear fellow,'' he replied, " where have you been

all this time ? Don't you know that His Majesty has left
St. Petersburg ?"

" Left St. Petersburg ! When ?"

" I'm not quite sure when he went away. Some people
said he went yesterday ; others assure me that it was
several days ago."

I was struck by his saying that the Emperor had been
gone some days, for in that case I had been a witness of
his ignominious departure.

One evening, at about seven, I was with a dealer who
kept a shop in the Voznesenskaia, just opposite the big
store. It was just before closing time and the street was
full of people. Suddenly at racing speed a closed carriage
drove up, rushing along like a fire engine. I thought at
first that the horses had bolted ; but it was obvious that
the coachman was deliberately driving them at that
speed, although it was against the regulations. Then I
recognised the Emperor sitting right in the back of the
carriage ; and the crowd in the street had recognised
him too. Urchins were whistling and shouting " Hallo,
Hallo ! Stop him ! Stop thief !" The public were laughing,
whistling and cheering. " The old boy has got the wind
up," they were saying. And the carriage tore on at a
furious pace towards the station. An old soldier, who was
wearing the Cross of St. George was looking utterly dis-
mayed.

" What a disgrace ! What a disgrace !" he cried.
" And it's the Czar. I saw his grandfather ; he was really
the Lord's Annointed !"

The whole world has heard of the massacre of the 9th
January. The workers were formed up in perfect order.
Singing psalms and the national anthem, " God save the

Czar," they crossed the Neva and proceeded quietlv towards the Emperor's residence. The priest Gapon, wearing priest's robes, marched at their head, carrying a cross. After him were men carrying holy images and the Emperor's portrait. When they had reached the palace the police ordered the procession to retire. The men halted. The order was given to disperse.

The crowd did not move and continued to sing their litanies.

The order was repeated three times and then . . . the massacre began.

The number of victims was never known.

The Intelligentzia said they numbered tens of thousands, the official authorities said they numbered about ten. In his Memoirs, Witte says, " There were more than two hundred," which is also rather a vague figure.

Why were such violent measures taken ?

Two friends of mine who were generals on the Staff, and who were both men of the same type and men of judgment, had seen what happened from the same window, but their answers were quite different.

The one said : " It was impossible not to open fire ; otherwise they would certainly have come into conflict with the troops. I am opposed to violent methods, but I should have given the order to fire myself."

" It was quite unnecessary," said the other. " During the Odessa riots I gave the order to fire too ; but now nothing would induce me to do so."

It is impossible after this kind of thing to retain any faith in the views of eye-witnesses.

What I am certain about is that if His Majesty had

shewn himself to the people, nothing would have happened, except that the Czar might have gained prestige But the wretched man never knew how to make use of the opportunities that came his way.

This lamentable episode did much to ruin the last traces of Imperial prestige, and the people said :

" We, the Czar's children, used to tremble before our father; now our father, the Czar, trembles before his children and massacres them in terror."

Some days afterwards, as I was walking along the quays, I met a group of sailors. They were staggering along, half-drunk, arm-in-arm, and shouting for all they were worth. A policeman was looking at them with a benevolent smile.

I asked him what they were shouting.

" Always the same things; the old catch ' Down with the aristocracy.' "

It was the first time I had heard this " old catch," as he called it, at any rate in the streets. I had heard it in drawing-rooms all right, only rather differently phrased.

In February we were completely defeated at Mukden. It was an absolute catastrophe.

At last it was realised in high quarters that the Commander-in-Chief was no use. Kuropatkin was dismissed from his command and recalled. His place was taken by General Linevitch, a man who had nothing to recommend him except that he was old. He was a good fellow, but, according to report, an absolute nonentity.

Kuropatkin as usual behaved like a lackey. He understood his world; instead of coming home he bombarded his Sovereign with obsequious telegrams and was appointed Commander of the Second Army in Manchuria.

My friend Doshturov rang me up to say that he had just been put in command of the First Army. I went to see him at once.

He told me that he had been commanded to an audience with the Emperor, who had a long discussion with him about Manchurian affairs and ended by saying : " What a pity, General, that you weren't there."

" Sire, at the beginning of the war I begged Your Majesty to give me any command there, even if it were only a brigade."

" A brigade ! Surely you realise that that was impossible. You were Commander-in-Chief of the Volunteer Army in Servia after Tcherniaiev ; you were my father's Quartermaster-General for the war in the East, and then you commanded an army corps ; you have been chief of a military district and you are a full General and a member of the Army Council."

Then, after a short silence, he said :

" What are we to do now ?"

" Continue the struggle, Sire. If we are to make an honourable peace we must first gain at least one victory."

" You mean, we must win the war ?"

" No, Sire. I said we must win at least one victory."

" One victory ! That's not enough. We must finish Japan and destroy her."

The Emperor dismissed him.

An hour later he received his appointment without in the least expecting it.

He said to me :

" I always hoped to die on the field of battle. I shall fulfil my vow."

My poor friend ! A few days later he died of an attack of apoplexy.

My son, who was more or less recovered, set off again for the theatre of war.

In early May we heard that the fleet, which had been entrusted to Admiral Rojestvensky, had reached its destination in safety, a fact which the authorities at the Admiralty considered to be nothing short of a miracle, since the fleet consisted of old sardine-boxes which were absolutely useless and which an unscrupulous fellow, a certain skipper called Klado, had passed off on the Czar as battleships. And there were actually rejoicings !

" That settles it," they were saying. " Japan is done for now."

Alas ! It was our fleet that was going to be done for. On the 14th-15th May it was annihilated.

Such a complete disaster had never happened before.

But the war went on. We must do for Japan and " annihilate " her.

In Russia itself the revolutionaries were carrying on with their plans and the Government were remaining inactive. It is true that, after the Gapon incident, General Trepov had been given powers equivalent to those of a dictator, but that did not affect things in the least.

Dozens of Government agents were assassinated daily in Russia, in the Caucasus, the Baltic Provinces and especially in Warsaw. The Grand Duke Sergius, Governor-General of Moscow, Ploehve, Minister of the Interior, and several others whom I have forgotten had been murdered. And now, not only those who had always been opposed to the authorities, but men of the most level judgment, men who had no politics and the most devoted subjects of their Sovereign, everybody, indeed, except the ruling clique had become hostile to the Government and were saying : " It can't go on like this. Things must change."

But the authorities always said : " The autocracy must be saved."

At Moscow, men who were known and respected by everybody, even by His Majesty himself, almost openly worked at a draft constitution.

There was great wrath in high quarters, but these people were so well-known and so respected that it was impossible to take action against them.

In June a deputation from the towns and from the " Zemstvo," with Prince Sergius Trubetzskoi as their leader, waited upon the Emperor and gave him to understand that a change in the method of government had become imperative. The marshals of the nobility in the two capitals and twenty-six other provinces took similar action.

The Emperor only gave an evasive reply. But as Count Witte definitely states in his Memoirs[1] a few weeks later the Emperor at last understood that the state of affairs was such that extreme measures must be taken without delay in order to prevent a final collapse. Just like his subjects, he too was now saying : " Things cannot go on like this ; there must be a change."

And then nothing was done.

Everything went on as before, and the Czar and his men remained inert and—what was worse—were definitely

[1] Vol. I, page 351, Russian text.

hostile to everything that had to do with " them " and not with " us."

On 6th August a new manifesto appeared. It contained more vague promises, but nothing tangible.

In the autumn life became very gloomy.

The news from friends and relations in the country was bad ; one had been robbed by the peasants, another followed by the police, others had had their houses burnt and their cattle slaughtered.

In Manchuria everything was going from bad to worse. Industry was in difficulties. There were strikes everywhere and incendiarism was general. We felt very depressed.

There were crowds of workmen about the capital who had not got any work or did not want to be given work. They invaded the side-walks and pavements and prevented the carriages from passing.

From morning till evening one heard the mournful notes of the " Internationale " and the " Marseillaise " sung by people who did not understand them.

In the evening shop windows were boarded up ; there was a funereal note about the hammer strokes. Now it was the water supply that was cut off, now the electricity ; it was impossible to get candles or petrol ; they were in such demand that the supplies were exhausted. Nerves were on edge. Popular outbreaks were feared, though the fears were groundless at this stage, because, for the time being, nobody excepting the police molested individuals. There was no ill-feeling against anybody except the Government. But the public, having lost confidence, did not realise this, and trembled.

Everybody who could went abroad. The Czar had taken

refuge at Peterhof, though in the ordinary way he never went there at that time of year. The Grand Dukes no longer drove in carriages with the Imperial arms but in humble hackney coaches. The Dowager Empress alone, calm and smiling as usual, would drive in her open carriage, known by the whole town, with her footman, a Cossack in gold braid uniform, conspicuous on the box. She did not fear, indeed she thought it her duty, to appear everywhere amongst the crowd of malcontents. Nobody ever failed to show her due respect. And more than once I heard a passer-by say :

" She is a true Empress. She has courage."

The Revolutionary Committee was in permanent session. The police knew this, but did not dare to take action. Pamphlets were circulated by the million in the streets and nobody dared to interfere.

The infantry, who were ready for marching orders, were confined to barracks. The cavalry regiments had for some weeks been bivouacking first in one place, where the trouble was bound to start, according to the authorities, and then in another ; they were ready for all eventualities.

The mysterious name " Nossar " was whispered about. He was supposed to be all-powerful and to be giving the word of command.

Then on the 8th October the railway from Moscow stopped running and on the 12th not a single train ran in the whole of Russia. Work ceased in the telegraphs, telephone and post office, in factories, banks and offices ; schools were deserted, shops large and small were closed, the tramways weren't running and the electricity was cut off.

On the 15th October life at St. Petersburg too was

brought to a standstill. The whole of Russia, a hundred and fifty million people, was on strike.

It was a terrifying spectacle, but magnificent !

On the evening of the 16th, a motor-car pushing through the streets of the capital at top speed. A man was standing up in it and waving his hands, shouting : " The constitution has been granted !"

I saw a police officer take off his helmet and make the sign of the cross.

" Surely that doesn't please you ?" I asked him.

" I should think it does !" he exclaimed. " At last we'll be able to get a quiet night's sleep. I haven't had one for months."

On the 17th the great news appeared in the official Gazette.

The town was decked with flags, the streets were gayer than usual, and life had started again. The special constable had disappeared.

An enormous crowd was standing at the approach to the town hall and there was unfolded a curious scene which a short time before would have been impossible in Russia, where everything was severely controlled by the police.

The first landing of the great staircase outside the Hotel de Ville had been converted into a platform, which was decorated with flags. Speakers got up and harangued the people from it ; it wasn't very easy to hear what they said, but the words " liberty," " rights," " citizen " constantly recurred, and they were always shouted in a specially loud voice. The crowd, who were obviously unmoved, remained indifferent. It seemed as if there were no reason why they should be there.

" What curious people you are !" a French friend of

mind said to me. " In my country if you go into the street you know at once which way the wind is blowing ; whilst you are always the same, whatever happens, whether it be good or bad. Is that because you are indifferent or because you conceal your feelings ?"

" It's perfectly natural. We have not been able to give free expression to our thoughts for centuries. We are trained to be silent."

Suddenly, when a new man got on to the platform, the crowd, who had hitherto been so indifferent, grew lively. There were shouts of " Hear ! Hear !" and applause.

Without even opening his mouth the man had established contact with the crowd ; he had made their souls vibrate and had managed to fascinate them.

He was a drunkard and could hardly stand straight. He wanted to speak, but only inarticulate noises and hiccoughs proceeded from his mouth. The crowd roared with laughter.

" Disgusting ! On a great day like this," said the Frenchman. " In France the dirty brute would have got a thick ear."

After a few vain attempts, the tribune of the people made a gesture of desperation, as much as to say, " Leave me in peace," and then, stumbling, to the accompaniment of hurrahs and cat-calls from the audience, he left the platform. Then a thin and shrill-voiced urchin of about fifteen years old, who was wearing a schoolboy's shirt, took his place and declaimed like a hoarse young cock crowing : " Citizens, at last we are free men."

The crowd laughed.

" A fine specimen of a free man : Hurrah."

" He's a funny lad."

P

" Your father'll spank you. Get down, impudence !"

And they laughed more than ever.

Other speakers waited their turn, but we had had enough. We went on our way.

A procession was coming out of the " Gostinny Dvor," the big bazaar of the Perspective. They started a hymn ; the national flag was being born before them and men wearing white scarves were carrying the Czar's portrait.

Another procession, singing the horrible " Internationale," and preceded by the red flag, came out of the street opposite.

The two processions came into collision. Fierce blows were exchanged. The public remained unmoved.

" It's incredible," said my friend.

" Why ? That happens with you too."

" Yes, of course it does, but the crowd takes one side or the other."

At the corner of the Liteïnaia a free fight was in progress. The window panes of the large fruit shop belonging to Soloviev were smashed and the " free " men proceeded to plunder the shop window.

At the Liteïnaia, opposite the Yusupoff Palace, there was fighting too ; but, as we gathered from a lady who had been present when the trouble began, politics had nothing to do with it. It had not been started by " citizens," but by some drunks.

" It's disgusting," said the lady, " that the police should let them fight like that."

" The police !" said an indignant passer-by. " I should have liked to have seen them try to interfere. There are no police now. We are free men now, we have the constitution and the right to do as we please. This, for instance," and he proceeded to shout obscene oaths.

Poor liberty ! That's what many people understood by it. With the majority, " liberty " is synonymous with license.

In the capital the new era opened badly.

In the provinces it started off better. The massacres there were on a larger scale. It is stated, and there is no reason to doubt it, that the *agents provocateurs* were not idle.

There were naval mutinies at Nicolaevsk, Sevastopol and at Kronstadt. At Moscow and Omsk hundreds of men killed each other. Everywhere else more or less the same kind of thing was happening. " Black Leagues " who were extreme conservatives, maintained by Government secret funds, considered that the liberties which had been granted were useless. The Intelligentzia declared that it was essential to continue the struggle, since the rights granted to the citizens were not sufficiently " democratic."

All these remarks were mere pretexts. The Government, seized with panic, had allowed its hand to be forced and was now trying to recover itself, while the Intelligentzia for whom the Revolution was not a means but an end in itself and an ideal, was loth to be parted from its idol.

Witté, who had been appointed Prime Minister, hedged between the parties and played a double game.

With a little firmness it would have been quite easy to have induced both the " Black Leagues " and the committees of which Nossar was dictator, to see reason and to have put them on to right lines. The army was sound and the demobilised troops from Manchuria had not yet returned. But they ought to have begun at once. Witté failed to do so, and it was only on the 26th November, six weeks later, when he heard that Nossar was going to have him arrested, that he put a stop to him and his committees. The order to imprison Nossar and his associates was issued and carried out ; but the poison had got into the blood of the people ; they had realised that the country was frightened of them.

The moujik, or peasant, that is three-quarters of the Russian nation, was entirely indifferent to political questions. As long as he had his land and the police did not interfere with him, anything else was " not his business." Let the gentry, the " gospoda," squabble amongst themselves ; it had nothing to do with them. But the peasants had learned that the Government did not count ; that the Czar was an ikon who must be worshipped like any other ikon, that this ikon was not be to feared and that the power was now with them, the moujiks. The dregs of the population had also realised this and generally took advantage of it to do as they pleased.

In the Baltic provinces the agrarian troubles had been degenerating for some months past into peasant risings. Hundreds of landowners had their throats cut ; more than four hundred mansions were burnt and the properties plundered. The Government let things take their course. Fortunately the mansion of one who was very popular at Court was burnt. The owner raised the alarm without consulting the Prime Minister, who was still trying to run with the hare and hunt with the hounds, the War Office sent General Orloff to the scene with two regiments of Guards, and in two months complete order was restored.

In Russia proper, burning and plundering was pretty general too, but the landowner was rarely assassinated, in fact only when he made it unavoidable. Everything went off smoothly and without ill-feeling, as a rule, in quite a friendly way as is right between neighbours who like and respect one another, and it was very rare indeed for a peasant to rob or fire his " own landlord's " property.

" Good heavens, no ! He was far too attached to him to do anything of the kind. Fathers and sons, they had always lived together."

The peasants did not rob their own landlord, but his neighbour. And the neighbour's peasantry robbed the landlord who had been spared by his own tenants. Nobody was the loser ; the moujiks had simply divided up their spheres of interest just like the Great Powers.

Things were generally managed quite pleasantly and in the following manner : Peasants, a whole village of them, would arrive in carts, bringing their wives and children to help with the work. Their ambassador, the most respected man of the community, a venerable old gentleman with a white beard, would go to the lord's house and, holding his hat in both hands as a mark of respect, would humbly ask for an interview. Then he would sigh and say :

" We're here now, batiushka ! We must get away as quickly as possible. That will be much better. The ' rebiata '[1] might give you a bad time. They might really. Ah, yes ! To the young men of to-day nothing is sacred. They're absolute criminals. And whatever you do, don't forget to give us the keys to the barns. It would be a

[1] Rebiata—young roughs.

great pity to have to spoil those fine new doors. We have already told your coachman to harness the horses and to take you to the station or to the town, whichever you prefer. Only see that you are well covered, the cold is fearful, and I shouldn't advise you to go by the open fields ; that road is very bad. And you'd better avoid the bridge, it's rotten and you might have an accident."

When the carriage was brought out the landlord was helped in, with his luggage, and his feet were covered with a travelling rug. " Good-bye. The Lord keep you in good health, batiushka. We love you like a father. Oh, dear, we don't want to leave you."

" One can always come to an understanding if one is well disposed."

But sometimes the poor moujiks weren't well treated, through the base ingratitude of those to whom they had been so kind.

The young Princess B—— who almost always lived in the country, and devoted a portion of her income to philanthropic work, happened to be in St. Petersburg when a riot broke out in the province where her estate was. She returned to it at once and summoned the moujiks.

" My friends," she said, " I must come to an understanding with you. Will you accept my word ?"

" Accept your word, matushka ?[1] Could we believe in anything if we didn't believe in what you say ? Your word! Why, you're talking nonsense ! As though it would be possible for us not to trust it. It's like the Gospel to us."

" Thank you. When do you intend to come and raid me ?"

" Raid you, you ! What a dreadful idea ! You, our

[1]Generally translated " little mother."

dear treasure ! Raid you ! Only a man who was damned by God could think of such a thing. Raid you, our angel, our white pigeon ! If anyone should dare to touch the tip of your finger. . ."

" That's enough. Listen to me and remember carefully what I'm going to say to you. If anyone—you or anybody else, it doesn't matter—touches anything here whatever or sets fire even to a haycock, your whole village will be reduced to ashes. Down to the last hut. I give you my word and swear to God that it shall be done. Though I lose my name, my honour, my fortune, though I go to the galleys for it, it shall be done. Look ! I swear to it and I kiss the image of the Holy Virgin and I take God to witness. Good-bye, my friends ; I have nothing more to say to you. Wait ! One word more. As I realise that you might start by assassinating me, I made my brother, whom you know, swear to keep the promise which I have just made. Now I have warned you. Good-bye."

Almost all the neighbouring estates were pillaged ; on that of the Princess nothing was touched. The little woman knew the people she was dealing with.

They didn't go in for fires in the towns, especially in St. Petersburg. The houses were built, not of wood, but of stone, and the Russian firemen are excellent. Besides, it was not the modern method, it was not up-to-date. They did not rob in the towns either, they " expropriated." The newspapers had made the word fashionable and the Intelligentzia were at pains to explain to the ignorant the difference between armed robbery and expropriation. " Robbery " was a crime, provided for by the penal code, whereas " expropriation " was a political act, a right, granted by nature to the poor man to protect himself against the abuses of the strong. Suddenly, all the robbers and burglars gave up their profession and disappeared completely. It is true that occasionally a young scamp who had appropriated a trifle was caught and at once confessed himself guilty of theft. But serious burglars no longer did this, and the judges nearly died of boredom. It was expected that they would soon not be needed any more. It should be explained that expropriators, when accused of political offences, are not handed over to the magistrate or to the assizes, but are dealt with by an *ad hoc* tribunal.

For instance, a motor-car full of bullion chests for the State bank, is driving along in broad daylight. A bomb is thrown ; and the car is stopped, the employees of the bank are done in and the gold is transferred to another car, which goes off at top speed. That is not highway robbery, but a political crime—an " expropriation."

A few men enter a bank or a large shop, draw their revolvers, shout " Hands up," and get away after emptying the till and robbing all the employees—expropriation, a political misdemeanour. I could quote examples for a whole day. It was always the same story. But I must mention one of these political misdemeanours. The story fully justifies it.

More than four hundred students, fine healthy young fellows, were holding a " meeting." This word had become fashionable ; they were attending a meeting, an amusement as popular at that time as political murders, riots and expropriations. A few men came in and shouted " Hands up !" and the four hundred young fellows raised their eight hundred strong arms like one man and quietly surrendered their watches and purses. Next day, if anybody asked them how they had been robbed, they were indignant. " We robbed ? Nothing of the kind ! We wouldn't give in to robbers. We were expropriated by Socialists."

They were quite proud of having had to do with such respectable people.

Riots, murders of Government officials and expropriations went on in spite of the Constitution drafted in October, while the " cadets " in the Duma, who prided themselves on being a moderate party, " His Majesty's Opposition," refused to express any disapproval of these political misdemeanours.

It was fortunate that Stolypin, who was Prime Minister at the time, was less advanced and more courageous and paid no attention to their harangues.

He had hundreds of murderers and expropriators court-martialled—and hanged—and the so-called political misdemeanours ceased, but Stolypin had to pay for his good work and was assassinated. Not by one of his political enemies but by a secret agent of the police.

As a matter of fact, if revolution means a change in the Government régime brought about by force, and not simply disturbances or riots without any real result, the Revolution had come to an end on the 17th October, 1905. The disturbances and the riots, sometimes on an enormous scale, as at Moscow, in the South and in Siberia, which took place since, were only a ground swell, the inevitable result of a storm.

The date for the elections to the Lower House of the Duma had been fixed and, excepting the moujik, all

Russia, which had hitherto been so silent, waxed rhetorical. Words devoid of all meaning were poured out in streams. In a single day one would hear more platitudes than in the whole of one's previous lifetime. Rhetoric and words for the sake of words had become a craving. For centuries silence had been compulsory; there were a lot of arrears to be made up. Young and old, children and nurses, " meetinged," buttonholed the passer-by to teach him their political principles, roused you suddenly in the middle of the night to convert you to their side, or rather to discharge the overflow, not of their souls, but of their tongues.

It was terrifying, but sometimes amusing. Two bright, chubby little schoolboys were walking in front of me one day.

" What's wrong with you, Pete ?" one of them said " Have you got a sore throat ?"

" No. I had to make a long speech at the meeting yesterday. I couldn't get out of it. It's made me quite hoarse."

Poor little Pete ! He was exhausted ; he would much rather have played or gone to bed, but he had " had to " speak. Without him, the " free men " would not have known what to do and the country would have been ruined. It was fortunate that Peter was there to protect his country's interests.

I got numerous letters from Rostov, a town where I had lived for about twenty years. I had been a municipal councillor, an honorary justice of the peace, president of the finance committee and president of the board for examining recruits. I was very well-known there, they had seen me at work and, putting aside false modesty, I may say that I was appreciated and popular. They now invited me to come down as their candidate for the Duma, and being a simpleton like Pete, I thought it my duty to do so. . . I dreamed of serving my country as I had done in my youth.

I went to Rostov. Instead of the town, almost all the inhabitants of which I knew, I found an enormous lunatic asylum.

Men of the most sober judgment had lost their heads. Some had become incendiaries, others wanted to get back, if not to the times before the flood, at any rate to the reign of Ivan the Terrible. They thought me impossible. My politics were too " left " for the one lot and too " right " for the other. In short, I was ignominiously turned down ; bearded Petes obtained a crushing majority.

I won't conceal the fact that though it was what I expected, I was disappointed.

Now I am not sorry that it should have been so. I should have been sad to have been amongst those whose ineptitude contributed to the final disaster.

The Duma opened. On the first day of the session the Emperor received the deputies at the Winter Palace, where all the high dignitaries of the Empire were assembled. Not being one of them myself, I was not present at the reception, so I can only repeat what I have heard from those who were.

It seems to have been a curious scene. On one side were the Ministers and Government officials, festooned with ribbons and decorations and covered with gold lace. On the other side were the newly elected ; a menagerie such as had never yet been seen in those high quarters.

The two groups eyed each other suspiciously. The old inmates of the Palace seemed to be afraid that the intruders might leap at their throats and devour them. The newcomers affected a profound contempt for them and for all the splendours of the Court which they saw for the first time, but in spite of their assumption of supercilious indifference they conveyed the impression of being nervous.

The Czar handled the situation very well. He said that he was " happy to see the elected of the nation, the best men that Russia could produce, and that he was confident that they would all march together harmoniously towards the same goal, their country's happiness." He smiled benevolently.

As I have already said, at a first meeting he was charming, but, although it had never happened before, on this occasion his charm was wasted. It did not come off, and they went away suspicious and dissatisfied.

I did, as a matter of fact, see "the elected of the nation " on their way from the Palace to the Duma. As they passed the " Cross,'' that is the centre gaol, where those found guilty of offences against the common law were imprisoned, but no political prisoners, they waved their handkerchiefs and their hats and shouted wildly at the prisoners, who were staring through the bars. The prisoners answered them like brothers and colleagues.

When they got to the Duma they forthwith demanded a general and complete amnesty for all prisoners.

I am ready to believe that the Petes who arrived from every quarter, from the North Pole, from Central Asia, from Poland, from Lithuania and from a hundred other places, were really the best that Russia could provide ;

but to look at these men with their bewildered expressions, one would hardly have thought so. It was more like an anthropological museum than a parliament.

There were Poles with long moustaches, wearing "kuntushes" and "chapskas," picturesque Cossacks carrying daggers ; there were even Turks and Sarmatians, wearing large turbans and Oriental robes ; there were occasional lawyers and doctrinaires who were more or less well known ; there were men from the depths of Siberia, Tartars and Letts, whole squadrons of sickly priests, fat and oily, their hair floating in the breeze or hanging in pigtails like little girls' ; eccentric priests, either survivals from the Middle Ages or ultra-modern decadents, very different from the town priests. Then there were moujiks, moujiks and still more moujiks, some of them looking uncomfortable in town clothes which were either too loose or too tight, too long or too short ; others were still wearing their caftans and tall boots. Most of them were not true moujiks—I mean the honest moujik who cultivates his land, loves his cattle, devotes himself to his home and has a say in the affairs of his commune—but sham moujiks, schoolmasters, public scribes, village shopkeepers and surveyors, a medley of that semi-Intelligentzia who, having somehow or other managed to learn to read, use their knowledge only for the purpose of swallowing a mass of Socialist pamphlets and poisoning their minds with the rubbish.

Having been treated as inferiors, almost as pariahs, all their lives, and suddenly finding themselves great personages and "legislators," these poor *déclassé* wretches had lost their moral balance, and such was the force of circumstances that they either would not or could not see things as they really were, but saw them through a prism darkened by their former sufferings and by the hatred and envy with which their minds were warped.

Never having been out of their burrows before, they were bewildered by the noise and magnificence of the capital ; intoxicated by everything they saw and by the reception they were given, they thought themselves all-powerful, and burned with the urge to avenge the sufferings of the past and the desire to change the whole face of things at a stroke. The new Duma could not help being, as it in fact became, " the Duma of the Wrath of the People," a name given to it, not by its enemies, but by its apologists.

The Government, like the Duma, was unequal to the task before it. It had learned nothing and forgotten nothing, and, moreover, was dishonest. Mad with fear, it had promised everything in a moment of panic, but it was firmly determined not to keep any of its promises, and was not even clever enough to hide its intentions. Such was its overcoming self-confidence, that it believed that " those savages " had not the sense to see through its treachery, even after the words uttered by the Emperor shortly afterwards to a deputation of the extreme right :

" Nothing is changed, everything shall remain as it was. Autocrat I am and Autocrat I shall remain."

Instead of being a sanctuary where the future well-being of the country could be developed and the needs of the people could be considered, the Duma degenerated into an arena in which the elected representatives of the nation delivered high-sounding discourses for the benefit of the gallery, abused one another, tried to discredit those in power and to sow dissension.

It soon lost prestige. The Duma still counted in St. Petersburg, Moscow and a few other centres ; but in the country outside it did not count at all. It was just an ornament for the capital, something to throw dust in the eyes of Europe.

In fact, everything, or almost everything, in the country, to use the Emperor's words, " remained as it was."

The landlords regained possession of their ruined estates, the workmen returned to their factories, the provinces relapsed into apathy, and the Government into insolent inertia. The Intelligentzia went back to its books and to the intoxication of extreme theories, impossible to apply in a country which was not yet ripe to carry them into practice.

And the tottering autocracy, whose foundations had been undermined so that it was ready to crash, although it still presented a bold front to the world, continued to be the *Bastille* of the spirit and genius of the nation. Poor Russia !

Seven long, monotonous, anxious years followed. We knew we were sitting on a volcano, but we tried to forget it and to live as far as possible from day to day without thinking of the morrow. The Government fell more and more into contempt ; the people,forgot their ancient gods, and had not yet created new ones. The Czar was no longer mentioned, for people almost forgot that there was one. He lived modestly at Csarskoye-Selo, only seeing those whom he absolutely had to see ; he avoided direct contact with men and affairs, shunned new faces, and absolutely refused to recognise that we were heading for disaster.

The reports which reached him were sometimes disastrous. But, as a rule, the reports were returned to the sender with a marginal note by the Czar, which was laughed at and soon became famous : " uteshitelno," " that's very consoling." Naturally people more and more avoided telling him the sad truth, tried to present things in a rosy hue, and only to let him see what appeared to be " consoling." For, barefaced lying apart, there was nothing truly consoling to say.

And then one day people began talking again about the Czar and what was happening within the Imperial Palace. A fugitive from justice, who was a horsedealer and had been found guilty of seducing minors, a moujik, who hardly knew how to read, was laying down the law there. He was no mere passing fancy, like Philippe and the others. His power increased daily ; he would soon be all-powerful ; the Master.

Alas ! It was only too true.

But what was at first whispered and later shouted from the house-tops was generally speaking a baseless slander. The Empress was and always remained an honest woman, devoted to her husband and her children. But the hysteria to which she had been subject for a long time had turned into mental insanity. The desire to bear a son had been an obsession with her, an obsession which Philippe had contrived to exploit in order to get close to the throne. Then, when it became obvious that all his assertions were idle inventions, his credit fell.

She had since borne the son whom she had so much wanted ; in fact he had been granted to her miraculously, thanks to the prayers of the saint who had been canonized at Sarov. But alas ! her son suffered from a complaint

she knew only too well, for it was hereditary in her
family, and unless another miracle intervened he was
doomed to die. Who was the saint who should save
him ?

Rasputin contrived to persuade her that the saint was
none other than himself, the fugitive from justice, and
that he, the man chosen of God, would save not only her
son but her husband, herself, the whole Imperial family,
and therefore the Empire. For the well-being of the
Empire depended upon, was in fact but the natural consequence of, the well-being of the Czar.

When an ordinary citizen shows signs of insanity he is
put into the hands of a mental specialist, and, if it is
necessary for his health, shut up, but the wife of an
autocrat and a demi-god cannot go mad ; that would be
contrary to nature.

If, in defiance of laws human and divine, it should happen, the fact must be concealed. The doctors dare not
admit it, the Court dare not see it, the general public
must not understand it, and the husband, at any rate
in the case of Nicholas II, must obey the sick woman's
orders, though it cost him his dignity and his Empire.

The private letters of the Empress have been published.
I quote a few passages :

" Our friend (Rasputin) says that we must appoint
so-and-so as a Minister. Do this, for he loves the holy
man.—Dismiss so-and-so ; he refuses to carry out the
wishes of our friend who is watching over us.—He says
that the troops must be ordered to advance in this or
that direction. Don't listen to what the General Staff
says, but do as ' he ' says.—Touch the wand which our
friend has held more often, it brings good luck.—Before

Q

going to the Council of Ministers comb your hair with the holy man's comb." I am quoting from memory, but you will find all this in effect, even if the words are not quite accurate. And the Czar did as he was told.

Rasputin's creatures recommended by the Empress were nearly always contemptible scoundrels, despised by honest people and not only by them but by the whole country ; so that it was no longer only the people but the immediate entourage of the sovereign, in fact, the whole of Russia, that was saying : " Things can't go on like this any longer," only " they " had different views as to what should be done.

The Terrorists said : " We must destroy everything " ; the leaders of the Duma : " You must let us form a ministry," while the greater part of the country merely sighed and said nothing.

The faithful adherents of absolutism alone were quite certain what had to be done. In order to preserve the principle (we may deduce that the principle was their personal interests), what was wanted was a Palace revolution. The Emperor must be dethroned and his heir proclaimed in his place. This was absolutely essential.

That would have been a possible course of action and it would certainly have been preferable—especially during the war—to a revolution. The difficulty was that those who said so were all waiting for somebody else to act. Nobody thought of risking his own skin.

One of the principal dignitaries of the Empire once spoke to me about the " adjustment " in question.

" You have access to the Emperor," I replied. " Your son is his aide-de-camp, nearly all the people about him are relations or friends of yours ; you could do it more easily than anybody else. If that is your opinion, why don't you act ?"

He nearly jumped out of his skin.

" Me ? Are you mad ? Supposing it didn't come off. I've got a family ; dash it all !"

And in spite of everybody saying : " Things can't go on like that," they went on ; not " like that," it is true, but from bad to worse ; and there was no need to be a soothsayer to see that soon things would not go on at all.

It is amusing to try and solve a riddle when one thinks one is on the right track. I have often been asked : " How do you explain the fact that Rasputin, an illiterate moujik of evil reputation and a coarse, vulgar scoundrel, should have succeeded in imposing upon a civilized and sensitive woman, the daughter of an English Princess and an Empress ?" My answer is : " Just on account of the qualities mentioned." During the whole of her life Her Majesty had seen nothing but correct and elegant, well-bred gentlemen, who smiled pleasantly and rounded off their phrases. She was accustomed to that, and a man belonging to the world she knew was necessarily more or less like all the others. Besides, has God ever chosen his elect from amongst courtiers and officers wearing spurs and swords ? Never. It was inconceivable. The saints of every age had been, not monocled gentlemen, but simple, straightforward men who said right out what God bade them say, without seeking to embroider their words as simple mortals did, without trying to please or to be agreeable. Nobody had ever spoken to his Sovereign in the way that Rasputin did ; certainly no ordinary mortal would have dared. He was therefore a being apart, the elect of heaven, and he must be believed.

What one is accustomed to see seems banal in the end. Only the unusual impresses the imagination, especially of a woman.

Once he had produced his first and decisive impression, the saint had managed to make allies of everybody who could, in one way or another, assist him to attain his ends.

You may wonder how he managed it. He simply applied the time-honoured principle of intimidating one set and giving the other an interest in his success. The principle always works.

Intelligence comes in useful too, especially if it is applied without too much scruple as to method. The rogue was certainly intelligent and he stuck at nothing.

CHAPTER VIII

1914-1918

When Austria's ultimatum to Servia was published I was at Vichy, in bed with a violent attack of gout.

Durnovo, former Minister of the Interior, was taking the waters there too. He telegraphed to Sazonov for news as to the position. The answer was reassuring : " There is no danger. Go on with your cure."

But the next day, when I sent to the bank for money, they would not give me any. Payment on letters of credit was suspended. On the same day our mobilisation was announced and I left for Paris.

On our arrival there we heard the news that war had been declared. There was not a porter, a cab or a taxi at the station ; it was pouring with rain ; and my foot was so swollen that I had not been able to put on my boot and was only wearing a stocking. Luckily I was not alone. My friend, General Bibikov, and his family were with me, and somehow or other they managed to get me to the hotel.

I had also been in Paris when war was declared in 1870. The difference was remarkable. The feeling then was one of the most frenzied excitement. On this occasion the attitude was admirable. The war was regarded as a disaster, but it was a disaster that everybody was resolved to meet calmly, in a spirit worthy of a great nation, and everybody was quite sincerely preoccupied with one idea only—to do their duty to their country.

We asked anxiously what was happening in Russia. The last letters from St. Petersburg were scarcely reassuring. For some time strikes had been a regular occurrence and disorders had occurred lately in both capitals.

In spite of our wish to get home as quickly as possible, we had to remain in Paris for more than a fortnight

There were no trains to Marseilles nor to the Channel ports, and, besides, we had no money. It was some days before the banks resumed payment.

I wonder whether the Parisians, who were certainly kept busier than we were, for we could do nothing but stand by patiently and look on, realised how completely Paris was changing from one day to another. For some time after the declaration of war, it was like a simple provincial town. The rue de la Paix was almost deserted, and in the morning staid citizens wearing skull caps and slippers took their coffee and read their newspapers in the doorways. All men in the prime of life had disappeared ; there were only old men and children ; every man who was fit was under arms.

I was particularly amused by a group of loafers who hung about certain stations from morning till evening. At first I thought that they were just travellers, waiting for tickets ; but to my great astonishment I discovered that they were expecting nothing more nor less than the arrival of the Cossacks. Where they were to come from, and how, nobody knew, but everybody was certain that they might turn up at any moment.

An old dame told me that a regiment of them had already arrived. She had seen them with her own eyes.

It is curious how prevalent was the myth of the Cossacks, not only in France but in England too. People used to talk to me about it in London, Newcastle and Edinburgh.

In Edinburgh, an officer—I believe he was a major—in spite of my assertions that it was impossible, assured me that a squadron had disembarked that very morning. He had seen them " with his own eyes."

" What did they look like ?"

" They have long, gaily-coloured coats and big fur caps. But they carry bows and arrows instead of rifles, just like the Zulus."

" They won't get far with those arms."

" We shall equip them. They are said to be very brave and good horsemen. That's the chief thing."

" What are their horses like ?"

" Rather like Scottish ponies, only bonier."

He had seen all this—probably in the illustrated papers of 1815. At first I thought he was trying to pull my leg, but no, he was perfectly serious.

When our troops invaded Prussia the Russians became the heroes of the day. One was constantly being asked :

" When do you think they'll be in Berlin ?"

" Berlin is still a long way off."

" Oh, I know, but approximately ? Three, four, five days, a week ?"

At last we got our tickets for Cherbourg. Just as we were leaving I saw a telegram in my paper mentioning the battle of Kauschen. A brilliant cavalry charge was mentioned. The third squadron of Horse Guards had captured a Prussian battery. The paper added : " The pick of the regiment fell on the field."

My son was in command of the regiment. So you may imagine my joy and my anxiety.

When we got to London we found the papers full of the affair. There were no details to be had at the Russian Embassy, except that the Ambassador, Count Benckendorf, had just had a telegram, telling him that his son, an officer in the Horse Guards, had been severely wounded. Then I heard from another of my countrymen that his two nephews, who were in my son's squadron, had been killed.

During the night somebody knocked me up and the whole family of my friend Bibikov embraced me. A telegram had come in saying that my son was unhurt and had been decorated with the Order of St. George, the highest reward for a soldier.

This marked the beginning of his career. Three months later he was Colonel and Aide-de-camp to the Emperor, then in the course of the war he became Brigadier-General, Divisional General and Commander of a Cavalry Corps. When the lawyer Kerensky became Commander-in-Chief of the Russian armies, he was recalled. After the collapse he was arrested and condemned to death by the Bolsheviks, and it was only through the courage of his wife that he escaped. Then he joined the anti-Bolshevist army and was first in command of a big detachment, later of a division consisting of the Volunteer Army of the Caucasus, and finally he was made Commander-in-Chief.

In the end, after numerous vicissitudes, we got back to Russia.

The war had brought about a reconciliation between the Czar and his people. The strikes had ceased and the disturbances were over. The Sovereign and his people were henceforth united. The Grand Duke Nicholas, who up to then had been little liked, was suddenly become popular. To everybody's astonishment, the mobilisation had proceeded without a hitch. The Opposition in the Duma gave its full support to the Government. A declaration regarding the autonomy of Poland was greeted with acclamation both by the Poles and by the Russians.

For some months everything ran perfectly. At St. Petersburg there was hardly a sign that we were at war. In contrast to what I had seen in Paris and London, the streets were full of young men, fit for military service, yet nearly six million men were already mobilised. There was no restriction on the sale of any kind of goods. Only a number of halls and large private houses had been converted into provisional hospitals and many ladies were wearing Red Cross uniform or mourning ; their number increased day by day.

Our second son, who was medically exempt from military service, had left for the theatre of war, too, with the Red Cross. In the spring he came home for a few days, deeply impressed by what he had seen and full of plans for the future. New horizons had opened out before him. Up till then he had applied himself entirely to the history of the arts ; he was now planning out a great historical work which should trace the whole progress of humanitarian ideas. He would start on it when the war was over.

Poor boy ! A few days later we had a telegram saying he was dead.

The war of movement soon degenerated into trench warfare. We lacked arms and ammunition, and having nothing to fight with, the army rotted in the trenches. The Duma got indignant ; members asked questions. The Government denied the evidence, and, as usual, took refuge in lies ; it gave the Chamber clearly to understand that it was meddling in matters with which it had nothing to do. Relations between the Government and the nation were again strained and became if possible worse than before. The popularity of the Grand Duke Nicholas alone survived. He had succeeded in winning the affection of the troops, and in times of crisis the people look for someone about whom they can rally, and are prepared to make a popular idol of anybody, whether he deserves it or not.

In spite of the past, the Intelligentzia and the Government proved once again that they had learnt nothing and forgotten nothing.

In spite of the war, the Intelligentzia continued, as before, to see in the revolution the universal panacea for all ills, whilst we others (for there had been no real Government for some time) sought the remedy in absolutism. The conflict of views resulted in complete confusion, leading inevitably to disaster. In such circumstances it became impossible to bring the war to a successful conclusion. The Allies understood this and became agitated. The French Ambassador, Monsieur Paléologue, tried to make His Majesty see the real state of affairs. The Czar smiled at him in his charming way, agreed to everything, promised everything and did nothing.

When at last we had arms and ammunition for fighting the supreme effort was made. Galicia was invaded and Lvov fell. Then, instead of sending out what was necessary to consolidate our gains—troops and ammunition—they sent out whole convoys of priests to introduce Orthodoxy into Galicia, and of tshinovniks, to Russianise the country.

This strange strategy had certainly not been recommended by the Grand Duke or by his General Staff.

The conduct of the war was no longer dependent upon the Grand Duke Nicholas. His views were coming to be regarded as " advanced," that is to say, he was one of those whom those in authority considered harmful and pernicious. Rasputin was hostile to him ; it followed that the Empress became hostile to him, too, and, as a natural consequence, the Emperor also.

It was known in the town that Rasputin, whose influence increased daily, had expressed a wish to visit the theatre of war. But the Grand Duke did not want him, and he let this be known quietly. The Empress, who was very obstinate, especially where the holy man was concerned, wanted to force the Grand Duke's hand, and sent him a telegram asking him to receive Rasputin. He replied : " Am eagerly awaiting him. The order to hang him, as soon as he arrives, has been given."

I don't know whether the story is true, but whether it be true or not, the Grand Duke was shortly afterwards relieved of his command and the Emperor himself took his place and left to join the army.

Three years had passed since the beginning of the war and the most bloody butchery that humanity has ever seen still went on. Hundreds of thousands of men had been slain, and hundreds of thousands had been mutilated ; but the fallen were replaced by others and those by others again.

For lack of labour the fields remained uncultivated

Industry had suffered a severe blow through the emptying of factories as the result of an order stupidly issued and still more stupidly carried into effect, so that hundreds of thousands of workmen were thrown out of employment. In the frontier provinces millions of inhabitants who were non-Russians and not of the Orthodox religion were treated as enemy aliens, carried off from their homes and exiled to other provinces, where they had to beg their bread and became a charge on the native population. Vast quantities of horses and cattle, which had been unnecessarily requisitioned, were collected into dumps, where they perished from hunger and neglect. Enormous stocks of food-stuffs destined for the army were left to rot for lack of means of transport. Millions of men, who had been unnecessarily and hurriedly mobilised, filled the cities and the capitals. Badly clothed, badly housed and badly fed, without officers to look after them, they swarmed in their barracks with nothing to do, died of boredom and got demoralised. In short, confusion and disorganisation were universal.

But the country bore its afflictions without a murmur. Faithful to its duty and to its Allies, the army held its ground. It believed in victory to the end, and that if munitions and arms were lacking to-day there would be plenty to-morrow ; and that then we should be victorious.

Nicholas II was still on the throne. He had taken over the supreme command of the armies, but in fact he was neither ruler nor commander. Rasputin was the master. He whispered his wishes to the Empress, and she imposed them upon the Czar ; the autocrat of all the Russias blindly obeyed and imposed upon his peoples and upon his armies the wishes of the fugitive from justice.

The ministers and chiefs whom Rasputin did not like were deposed and replaced by his creatures. Hated and despised by the nation, those who had contrived by money and by foul means to win his favour, trafficked with his influence. The Czar was unable to disassociate himself from these intrigues, and shared in the resulting discredit.

Treated by the Government with hostile contempt, the Duma had become a platform for sedition. Even the extreme right, which in spite of everything always extolled absolutism, now loudly denounced the Empress and her mentor.

Rasputin was assassinated by a deputy of the extreme right. But his creatures remained in power.

And suddenly, without any apparent cause, the edifice of absolutism, which even yesterday had appeared to be inviolable, tottered on its foundations and fell. It was not overthrown by human hands. It collapsed of its own accord, for it was rotten, and sooner or later it was bound to crash.

As I have already said, I am not writing history. I am simply telling what I have seen and experienced. Others shall have the glory of presenting a complete and brilliant picture of that nameless thing, suggesting both the celebrations of slaves freed from fear of the whip and a barbarous dance of death, which we call to-day " the great Russian Revolution." The episodes which I saw were deplorable rather than grandiose, and calculated rather to arouse disgust than to provoke admiration. I shall confine myself to recounting what I actually saw, without seeking to compose a complete picture or attempting to impose my conclusions upon anybody.

For some months the " disturbances "—that is what the police called them—had again been part of the daily routine. They no longer frightened anybody, either the Government or the public. We were used to them, and besides, they were not very terrifying. The workmen and students—or rather young idlers who were supposed to be studying, but were not—strolled about the principal streets of the capital, yelling their eternal " Internationale " and singing the " Marseillaise " in the wrong key. They took up their position in front of the church of Kazan, and sometimes, when they were specially exhilarated, they smashed a few windows and got a touch of the Cossacks' whips. Then, proud of having fulfilled their duty as citizens, they would go quietly home and start the same game again a few days later.

One morning I was lunching at the Hotel de l'Europe with an American journalist. He spoke Russian fairly fluently, but very oddly. He used phrases that are only found in a dictionary and spoke like a character in a book. He knew our literature and our history and was well posted in his facts, but understood neither the soul nor the mentality of the Russians. He had come to Russia specially in order to be present at the great Russian Revolution, which he was certain was coming, and he was watching for it. He seemed to think that the Revolution must change for the better, not only the face of Russia, but all Europe. The programme was alluring. There was only one drawback : the American thought that the Russians were a civilised people—indeed, that they were more civilised than any other nation. He had come to this conclusion after reading the writings of our Intelligentzia.

" Otherwise," he said, " your writers would not have written as they did. You can only preach doctrines suited to the circumstances. It would be stupid to speak in the way they do to people who are half savage."

" That is actually what they have done in Russia. We do, in fact, inculcate ideas which are beyond the range of the people's understanding."

He shrugged his shoulders.

" Then you would have me believe that your men of letters are fools ?"

" Not fools ; but they don't know what they are doing."

We were lunching by the window and saw a troop of Cossacks cantering past. We were told that disturbances had taken place at the *Perspective*. My American seized his kodak and rushed into the street. He was anxious to see the beginning of the great Russian Revolution ; I followed him. Everything went on peacefully, just as usual. The people marched, shouted and took up their positions on the Kazan square. The American button-holed a passer-by.

" What is the aim of the movement ?" he asked.

" Excuse me, I don't understand what you mean."

" I want to know what is the object of the demonstration. What are the aspirations of the Russian people ?"

" I beg your pardon. Did you say aspirations ?"

" I should like to know what they want to seize—the Imperial Palace, the seat of the autocracy ? The Ministry ? The Government offices ? The arsenal, where the arms are stored ?"

" They don't want to seize anything, sir. It's just a disturbance."

" A disturbance ?   Sensible people don't make a disturbance without some definite object. They must know
what they want."

The other man was still looking at him with a bewildered expression.

" I should like to know what are the aims of the Russian
people."

" The aims ? Why, it's a demonstration."

The American got angry.

" A demonstration ? This a demonstration ? A demonstration, sir, is a reasoned, organised action, the object of
which is to impress one's opponent. A demonstration, sir,
is a reasonable action with a definite aim. That, a demonstration ? It's nonsense, a moral insanity . . !"

Then he turned to me and said : " It's not interesting.
Let's go and lunch."

But our Intelligentzia thought otherwise, and conduced
to the view that these disorders, which the American
qualified as " nonsense," as " moral insanity," were more
than a civic demonstration. And the proletariat, ignorant
as the students who had left their books, were intoxicated
with their words and thought themselves heroes.

Towards the end of January the disturbances became
more frequent. No great importance would have been
attached to them, for they were now in the nature of
things, if the new Minister of the Interior, Protopopov,
one of Rasputin's creatures, had not boasted to everybody
he met that he was not a man to be treated lightly. He
would restore order permanently without any trouble.
His Excellency, poor man, as everybody knew, was
threatened with a mental disease, so he was anxious to
prove that the rumour was unfounded and to show the

public that he was not a madman but a great statesman. He gave orders that " these disturbances should be the last of their kind." And the police took measures accordingly.

As the Minister's orders had occasioned several brawls in the town, much larger crowds than usual collected on 26th February. Both demonstrators and ordinary inquisitive citizens were curious to see how the illustrious statesman and candidate for the padded cell would deal with the situation.

The crowd, which was congesting the streets, was not in the least aggressive. Except for a few fierce-looking proletarians and young men who had broken off their studies and who, taking their rôle seriously, posed as conspirators, most of the people were there just to be in the movement and to abuse the Government, not to overthrow it. Proletarians and bourgeois chatted together in a friendly way. To be a bourgeois was not yet a crime ; contempt for the Government was unanimous. The result was that the classes had as yet no reason to hate each other. But, as always happens when people are expecting something extraordinary to happen, they were more nervous and highly strung than usual. When people are like that a mere spark is enough to start a conflagration.

Sentry posts were doubled. The reserves of " pharaohs" as the people called the constables, were called out. They were reinforced by Cossacks, but not the fine, elegant, well-mounted Cossacks of the Guard who knew their job and whom the capital was accustomed to see and the populace feared. These Cossacks, like the rest of the Guard, were at the front. Their place was taken by poor devils from the reserve.

R

These so-called soldiers were pitiable. They had only recently been uprooted from their villages and were dilapidated and comic-looking, either too old or too young, with poor horses ; they looked more like peasants than soldiers.

If these wretched creatures had to fire they would only increase the disturbance instead of suppressing it. Nobody but a madman like Protopopov would have dreamed of relying on them.

A group of students, of the type that works hard and enjoys a joke, burst into roars of laughter at the sight of these strange warriors.

" Hi ! there ! Archangel Gabriel," one of them shouted to an old man. " Beware of the girls, my fine bronzed hero. They'll hug you to death."

A student who must have been quite young and seemed to have come straight from college said : " What ! Is that the famous Imperial Guard that we've heard so much about ?"

" Certainly, old boy. Fine fellows, aren't they ?"

" I call them ragamuffins."

" Like master, like man," said a snub-nosed little urchin who had been thirsting to get a word in. The student gave him a terrific look.

" You wretched little worm ! You're taking up the cudgels against the Government too, are you ? Come and see me. I've got some nice stories to tell you about it."

" Look, sir, look !" shouted a fat old dame. " He'll do some harm."

She was pointing at a strange man who was gesticulating on the pavement. There was no mistake about it —he was mad.

" I tell you he'll do some harm, sir. He ought to be arrested."

" You mustn't suggest such a thing, my dear lady. Impossible. He's the new Minister of the Interior, Protopopov."

They all laughed.

" What, is that him ?"

" Of course it is. Just watch."

The wag went up to a police officer and, touching his hat, said : " Excuse me, I should like to ask you a question."

" I am at your service."

" Is it true that that gentleman "—and he pointed to the madman—" is the Minister Protopopov ?"

The officer smiled.

" Pass on, gentlemen, pass on. Meetings are forbidden."

The public laughed.

" That's a good one, young man."

" Pass on, gentlemen," shouted an urchin at a constable, " Pass on, gentlemen, please ; pass on."

" Dirty pharaoh !"

" Pharaoh ! Be off and be hanged !"

" Pass on, gentlemen."

" Those dirty police have nothing to do but to annoy the public."

Everywhere more or less similar scenes were occurring. But the pharaohs were gradually losing their patience, and here and there the usual " Pass on, please " was reinforced with a truncheon. But nothing serious occurred. The blows were taken in good part and even laughing.

I went up to the Perspective again and walked towards

the Moscow station. The crowd got thicker and thicker ;
it was difficult to make headway.

" Pass on, gentlemen, please."

It was impossible to do so.

New streams of people arrived from every side and
poured into the middle of the road, where lines of Cossacks
on horseback were proceeding at a walk.

The police were trying to press the crowd back. The
crowd were jostling them.

" Trot !" shouted an officer. But the crowd seized the
horses' bridles and tails and held the Cossacks by their
legs. A man was unhorsed, and a horse reared and broke
down. The police used their truncheons. The populace
retaliated. A command was shouted and the Cossacks
unsheathed their swords. Suddenly one of them fired
point-blank at a police officer. The man threw up his
arms and fell dead in the road. A cry of distress, like a
huge sigh, went up from a thousand breasts. Then there
was a deathly silence.

" Hurrah !" shouts a child.

A terrific hurrah rings out like a thunderclap, the
tempest is let loose. Thousands of human animals shout,
yelp and roar. The " hurrahs " ring out like cannon
shots.

It was impossible to understand what is happening to
them. Cossacks fraternised with the crowd, the police
disappeared, men embraced each other, jostled each
other, crushed each other and went mad with excitement.
There was a general movement and I was carried by the
stream into a side street. I walked straight ahead without
knowing where I was going.

I got into another district, where everything was quiet

and normal. It seemed as if nothing had happened. There were few people about. Somebody spoke to me.

" Excuse me, have you come from the Perspective ?"

" Yes, I have."

" I hear that the public are being massacred there."

Some other passers-by stopped and formed into a group.

" There are hundreds of victims already."

" Five hundred," said somebody.

" Only yesterday the Preobrazhenski regiment went over to the people."

" That's not true."

" I heard. . ."

" So has the Volhyniaf regiment."

" Let's hope they've really done it this time."

" I tell you that. . ."

I went on my way home. In the evening the town was quite quiet. Cars were about and tramways were running as usual ; cafés were packed. Only the police had disappeared.

There was some casual discussion of the events of the day, but nobody regarded them as very significant. We had got used to such things, and we never imagined that the reservist's shot was to be the prelude to the stupid and bloody drama that was to be played.

I woke up later than usual next day and was surprised that the streets were so silent. I missed the noise of trams and cars and the thousand sounds of the city, which by this time was generally bustling with activity. I went to a window which looked out on a junction of four roads.

The sight I saw had the ashen-grey quality of nightmare —sad, monotonous and repulsively ugly, but pathetically moving. A vast crowd of beings, strangely clad in long grey cloaks and grey caps, dirty rags of uniform, having served their time, filled the streets. It was like a vast flock of sheep, such as one often sees in the Eastern steppes, grey with dust and caught by the storm. Mad with fear, they stand huddled together motionless, hour after hour, with bowed head, waiting till the storm is over, when their shepherd will drive them where he will. They were the mobilised reserves, who for months had been swarming in their melancholy barracks, demoralised by boredom and idleness. Driven by the wind of license which had been blowing the day before, and without any idea as to what they were about, these wretched men had obviously overpowered the guard, left their barracks and now, trembling at their crime, they were awaiting, just like sheep, the wishes of their master.

Would he drive them to the slaughter-house or would he leave them to graze a little longer ?

I went out into the street ; the human herd was still there. The poor wretches seemed so miserable that it was quite affecting.

Weary and dejected, their dull eyes sunk in vacancy, they shifted about without uttering a word. It was appalling.

Suddenly they shuddered. Firing was heard in the distance.

" They're firing !"

One wretched man looked at me and made as if to speak. A profound sigh escaped him, but he said nothing; he sighed again, stepped back and was merged again in the crowd.

" It's getting warm," said a workman.

" It's on the other side of the Neva," said a passer-by.

I looked around. The old man who had wanted to speak to me had been standing next to me.

" Batiushka," his voice trembled, " there is no point in our being here. We shall be held responsible. What will they do to us ?"

" We only came out of our barracks to see what was going on without intending any harm," said another.

The workman laughed.

"You don't think they are likely to believe that, do you ?" he said.

" Our comrades will bear witness. . ."

" Your comrades ! They'll be shot first. The officers won't wait for your permission ! One knows what they are, the traitors !"

The firing began again, harder than before. It was now coming from the other side.

" It's coming from the side of the Quadrant," somebody said.

The old man crossed himself. " May God watch over us !"

" God !" jeered the workman. " Don't be silly. God doesn't exist."

" Don't blaspheme."

" We are innocent. . ."

The workman laughed.

" Don't be frightened, you old fool ! Don't you see that we're all right ? We've got the upper hand ; we only have to stand firm. Go back, take your rifles and shout ' Long live the people ! ' ''

" But we haven't got any arms."

" Get some from the arsenal. I'll take you. Come on."

He started off. Some men followed him, others went a little way and then stopped.

The flock did not move.

A few hours later the picture had changed. The grey flock of sheep had disappeared. Workmen and students, men difficult to class, alone or in groups, in a squad, armed with rifles and wearing cartridge belts came and went, stopped and went back again. You could see that they weren't quite clear in what direction they should go, what they should do, and that they had no definite aim ; but it was urgent that they should act, and they did so. Armed men became more and more numerous. Motor lorries full of them kept passing backwards and forwards. The trams had stopped running. Hardly any cabs or private carriages were to be seen. A lady drove up in a motor ; they stopped the car, made her get out, and asked her who she was and where she lived. They turned over the cushions, searched under the seats, held a long consultation, and finally the lady got in again and the car was allowed to go on. It was obvious that nobody knew why they were acting in this way, or why it was necessary, but henceforth every carriage was stopped and searched.

Another motor drives up. It is being driven by an officer, He is told to stop, but the officer pays no attention, and speeds up. The revolutionaries scatter and the car passes. When it is some distance off they fire a few shots at it. One of the champions of liberty is wounded by his fellow. He is carried off, and they revile the dirty rich who crush the poor. But that doesn't last long. There are other things to do. Other carriages that must be searched drive up.

A troop of revolutionary cavalry appears. They are mounted on cab-horses, on blood horses, on old draft horses, on ponies and on chargers. Their riders are equally diverse, but they all have sabre and spurs. How on earth did they manage to bestride their mounts ? It's a mystery, but they are quite proud to be there. They pull their wretched nags, make enormous efforts to get them to prance, and when they succeed in doing so they have to hang on to the horse's mane or to the saddle in order not to fall off; they lose their stirrups, and when the horse drops back into a walk they look contemptuously, like conquerors, upon those who are walking on foot.

In the square, urchins with rifles taller than themselves light a bonfire and then, after posting sentinels, lie down by the fire.

The lorries, rushing about at top speed, become more and more numerous. They are full of armed men, workmen, students and girls waving red flags. Everybody is singing, firing into the air and shouting ": Hurrah !" The streets cheer them and the dogs bark ; there are such crowds of them that the window-panes tremble. Dozens, then hundreds, of cars, full of the same kind of people, roll by in one continuous, horrible train.

The people shout and sing and wave red rags. Fierce warriors lie on their stomachs on the side-walk, rifle at the shoulder, ready to fire. That appears to be essential, for it is always done.

Then the cars are no longer to be counted by hundreds, but by tens of thousands. There is no end to them.

One's head begins to whirl. The poor devils have never been in a car before and they are making up for lost time.

And they go on driving past, driving all night until the next morning, still driving, as long as the tyres will hold out. When the car is broken they abandon it. They requisition another and off they go again! To roll along in a car had become a passion a fixed idea which lasted several days—in fact as long as there was petrol to commandeer.

A group of " comrades " enter a neighbouring garage ; they have had a breakdown in the middle of the street. There is still a car left, but it won't go. The careful chauffeur has seen to that.

One of the wenches, disappointed of her joy-ride, has hysterics. In order to help her to recover, her friends smash the window-panes, break up the car and beat the driver. They would certainly have done for him if somebody had not run up to tell them the joyful news that another car had been found. The " bourgeois " had been turned out of it. They are on to it at top speed, and now they are off again, driving along, shouting, firing and waving their red flags.

When I think of the opening scenes of this great revolution, the first things I think of are the grey sheep and the thousands of cars. Indeed, in the early days, to drive about was the great thing to do. But it wasn't everything. As we shall see, it did not prevent a man from carrying out his other civic duties.

Towards evening the Palace of Justice was burnt and the house of the Minister of the Imperial Court and a few others were set on fire. Shots were fired at random, here and there, and after a little shooting, those who hadn't got cars went off to bed.

The next morning the game went on more merrily than ever. The cars kept on driving past with people singing, shouting and waving red flags, but they weren't firing into the air any longer, but just anywhere at random, all over the place. In some places there were even a few small pitched battles between tiny detachments of the regular soldiers (there were hardly any left in the town, for they were all at the front) and whole regiments of the disaffected reservists. But these battles did not last long, the sides being too unequally matched.

The ministers were arrested, and also a few stray men, known and unknown, and were locked up in the Duma, where they had to sleep on tables, chairs and on the ground.

The prisons containing those detained for political offences were thrown open and then for the sake of consistency the prisons for ordinary criminals as well. A flood of convicts in their grey clothes, with the convict's yellow square on the back, streamed out. These excellent fellows plundered the confectionery shops, changed their clothes in the street and, good citizens once more, mingled with the crowd.

I saw this incident myself, and it was not very reassuring. On that day a large number of crimes were committed. Nobody felt safe, especially as the authorities, including the police, had disappeared.

But liberty had been won, and now we were all free men, riding in cars. At any rate, the papers were unanimous in saying so.

The papers even asserted that the "great Russian

Revolution " was the most " splendid, the most magnificent, the most glorious and the most peaceful revolution
that the world had ever seen." Mark the word " peaceful."
The newspapers always know best, and they must be
right. But I must confess that I had not yet noticed the
grand revolution. To drive for nothing in other people's
cars, to let off rifles in the main street, to deafen everybody
with shouting is, no doubt, to acquire some of the rights of
man. Only, as far as I am aware, this is not called " revolution," but something else ; what, I don't know. My
American had used the right terms when he called it
"nonsense" and "moral insanity." And was it "peaceful ?" But I do not lay stress on this term. It is said that
there had been even then thousands of victims, and that
was only the beginning. But everything is relative. Even
if the victims had amounted to a hundred thousand, two
or three hundred thousand, or even a million, it might
have been called peaceful. But was it " splendid,"
" magnificent," or " glorious "? " Splendid " it certainly
was not. It had been frankly ugly and, what is worse,
stupid. " Glorious and magnificent ?" It must be admitted that it will be difficult for the future historian to
prove that this Revolution (a peaceful one, if you like) was
glorious and magnificent. He will have to be helped out
somehow. We shall have to try and whitewash this disgusting Revolution and disguise its worst aspects.

At the beginning the organisers seem to have been
aware of this, and on the second day they discovered
what was necessary to make it " great and glorious."
They started a war of extermination against the police ;
against the unfortunate policeman, who, quite recently a
moujik, had then served three or four years in the army,

and finally, a king of Egypt with twenty roubles a month
as his pay, watched over the security of the citizens and
was occasionally given a small glass of wine by a drunk
who didn't want to be locked up.

To declare war was not a bad notion, even Austria had
done so ; but how were they to start hostilities ? All
the police had disappeared. So that was that ; there was
not a victim to be found for all the gold of the Indies.

Where were those infamous tyrants ? There was the
rub.

It was scarcely probable that, like a well-known character in the Bible, they had been taken up alive into heaven.
The Emperor William had declared that God was the
special deity of the Boches and was looking after their
interests. It was therefore unlikely that such favour
should have been shown to the agents of a Power at war
with Germany.

It was also impossible that they should have escaped
to Belgium, Egypt or America ; the police did not know
of the existence of those countries. They must therefore
be hiding in disguise in the town itself ; and they proceeded to hunt for them. It became an absolute passion.
Shops, stations, dog-kennels, houses, attics, basements
and especially roofs, were searched for these agents of the
bourgeoisie. It seemed that Protopopov was stated to
have posted machine-guns on the roofs, and there could
be no doubt that the ruffians were there, ready to fire at
the word of command on the wretched people. Gangs of
" comrades " (the word was now fashionable) invaded
your house and your rooms, pointed revolvers at you,
rummaged about everywhere, opened cupboards, looked
under the furniture and under the carpets, and while they

were about it pocketed any small objects of value that might be lying about. Then they went off to search elsewhere, while others took their place.

Sometimes a comrade would pull the trigger accidentally and then there would be trouble. There would be shouts of " They are firing on the people !" and the householder would be killed.

A man went into the baker's shop opposite. An urchin shouted : " A policeman in disguise !" The man was killed.

It was the proprietor of the shop himself.

A man was seen walking on the roof. There were shouts of : " A policeman !" The crowd rushed up the staircase ; but a comrade, who just happened to be passing, fired at him, and the man fell dead on to the pavement. It was a mistake ; he was only a chimney sweep.

A police officer's family lived in a wing of our house. The man, of course, had fled. The comrades only found his wife there with three young children. The youngest was only a baby. The wife was seized and dragged off to show where her husband was hidden. The two elder children hung on to her skirts and were killed. The baby started crying. They took it by the feet and dashed its brains out against the wall.

I saw a platoon of soldiers firing at a house. I asked a sergeant, who was a fine specimen of a trooper, why they were doing so. He saluted.

" We are told that some of those rotten policemen are hiding there, your Honour. But rifle fire is certainly no use. Ivanov ! Run off to the gunners and tell them to come and lend a hand."

A little further off a crowd was collecting. A group of

comrades were dragging along a man who was as pale as
death. The crowd was booing him ; those who could get
at him were beating him. One of his escort stopped and
asked me for a light. Some idlers came up.

" Was it you who arrested him ?" one of them asked
him.

" I was one of them. He's a nasty one ! We know
what to do with those blighters. We knocked and knocked
and nobody opened the door. We forced it. There was
nobody there. The dirty brute had hidden under the bed.
Nosov—you know him, he's in the third platoon—
dragged him out by his feet. He had the wind up all
right."

" The filthy beasts ! They are all cowards."

" Yes, that's a fact."

" As timid as rabbits, those bobbies are."

" I've caught. . ."

" Do let him speak."

" He was as limp as a rag. He couldn't even stand up,
he was trembling so."

" You should have given him a few good blows to bring
him round. It's an infallible remedy."

" What do you take me for ? That's just what we did.
We know how to deal with them. We're not such fools
as you think we are. I don't care who knows."

" What did he say ?"

" He told me he was a cleaner."

" That's a good one ! A bobby scrubbing floors ! A bit
thick "

" He's got nerve."

" A nice fellow !"

" What do you think we ought to do ?"

" Do let him speak. If you always interrupt. . ."

" Then of course we started beating him. But Ivanov—you know who I mean, the one in the third, not the one in the fifth—said : ' Stop that. Don't kill him. You must take him to the Duma. If they handle him properly he'll tell us a few things. That lad knows everything. He's one of the chiefs ?''

" A policeman in disguise !" shouted somebody in the street, and everybody dashed off to the new victim.

" They're a fine lot," said our concierge to me. " The poor fellow ! He lives in No. 20. Yes, sir, he's been living there for the last eight years. He's my wife's cousin, and so of course he's a friend of mine. He's a cleaner who works in the best houses. He's got a splendid clientèle. He's an excellent fellow, one of the best."

" Why didn't you say so ?"

" Why, they would have killed me, sir. You see that they have gone raging mad. Besides, it never does to poke your nose into other people's affairs. They're mad, I tell you. Wanting to do without the police ! That'll be a nice thing !"

" Will be !" I thought. It had already happened. And very nice it was too.

The police-hunting mania did not last as long as the motor-car mania. Next day policemen were at a discount. They were murdered when opportunity offered, but people didn't trouble to hunt them out.

Disarming officers was the next popular sport. And that in war-time ! But I shall not speak of that amusement—I don't know what else to call it. It was too distressing. Even to-day, when I think of those disgraceful scenes, I am overcome with nausea.

In spite of the efforts of the Intelligentzia, we did not manage to get up even a fairly decent revolution. The " great and glorious revolution " remained what it had been at the start : a " moral insanity," a brawl of wild savages and apaches, an absurdity.

The word revolution implies a struggle ; but to have a struggle there must be somebody to struggle against. This essential factor was lacking ; there was no enemy. There was no one to show fight. The authorities were in hiding, they had abdicated ; the police, headed by the prefect, had disappeared ; the bourgeois remained inert and trembling with fear. There being no combatants, the fight had become impossible. The military consisted of a few wretched handfuls of regular soldiers, who struggled as long as they possibly could, that is, for a few moments. The remainder consisted of the wretched flock of grey sheep, waiting patiently for their masters. And the master (the first person who turned up) came and said : " Shoo ! Go to the arsenal and get arms." And they did so. " Shoo ! Fire !" and they obeyed. And then, as they got no further orders, they did nothing, for there was nothing to do except to roam about, drive in motor-cars, thrash those who were alleged to be police and deprive of their arms those officers who had been wounded or who were going to leave for the front or had come home on leave, and to take stray people off to the guardroom or murder them.

It was an aimless revolution, in which there was no enemy, and neither conquerors nor conquered ; for everyone was an enemy of the existing régime. Victims there certainly were in plenty, but no conquered, for nobody offered any defence. Everyone submitted, except-

s

ing the few regular soldiers, who fought. In any case, such fights were very uncommon episodes.

It was a revolution in which the only strength of the conqueror lay in the weakness and cowardice of the conquered.

An odd kind of a revolution !

Everyone—the Czar, the Government and the Intelligentzia—shared in the responsibility for the revolution (if revolution be the right word for this stupidity) ; but nobody, excepting the agents of Germany, assisted it in a scientific way. The proletariat had no right to claim the credit for it. It was a monstrosity born of Stupidity and Chance. And it ended, as it was bound to end, in a general mess-up.

Having regard to all the circumstances, a revolution—I mean a genuine one—was inevitable sooner or later, and perhaps even desirable, had there been men capable of guiding and controlling it. Unhappily there were none, either amongst " us " or amongst " them." A swamp can only engender amphibious creatures, without backbone or muscle. It cannot produce men who are stronger and more powerful than the crowd, which is indispensable for carrying out an attack but useless for anything else. As a matter of fact, better men were needed for the attack too, and such strong men as the country still possessed were all at the front.

On the 1st March, when I got up my servant told me that some troops were arriving. I looked out of the window and I thought I was dreaming. The houses were covered from top to bottom with red bunting. A large and orderly crowd, wearing red buttonholes, were lining the pavements. Huge red placards were borne in front of the regiments, the battalions and the platoons. A huge crowd, wearing red ties, stood on the pavement. The reflection of all this red colour, red houses, red scarves, red flags, red placards, made the whole street look red, as though it had been painted in blood.

Eighty thousand men, the whole military strength of the capital, were on their way to swear fidelity to the Revolution, just as, a little while since, they had taken the oath of allegiance to the Emperor, who was still on the throne and did not abdicate until some days later.

At the head of these red troops marched the former marines of the Imperial Guard, now become the Red Militia, " the pride and glory of the Revolution." Under a red scarf, with a red favour on his chest, marched its chief, an admiral, an aide-de-camp to His Majesty, a cousin of the Emperor, His Imperial Highness the Grand Duke Cyrille, who to-day has the audacity to declare himself the legitimate heir to the Czar's throne.

I should add that all these so-called Guards regiments were reserves. The genuine Guards were at the front, fighting the enemy. Those who were marching past under the red flag were simply reserve units attached to the regiments consisting of men who had just been mobilised. The real Guards remained loyal up to the moment when the Emperor himself absolved them from the oath of allegiance which they had taken.

The town knew that the Prime Minister and the President of the Duma had informed His Majesty, who was with the army, what was happening, and had insisted that other ministers should be appointed. That would have been enough to pacify the town. The Grand Duke Alexander, the Emperor's brother-in-law, had also urged this ; but the Czar had replied that he knew best what ought to be done. He had ordered General Ivanov to proceed at once with a battalion of picked men who were all holders of the St. George's Cross, to the capital and to re-establish order at any cost. Other troops would be sent after him.

The General left. Then the order was revoked.

Things got worse. The Czar in the end consented to a change of Ministry.

The reply came : " Too late. You must abdicate in favour of the heir."

That was all that was known in the town.

In the meantime the Duma, like everybody else, was doing its duty. It was in permanent session, and a committee of public safety had been elected or had elected themselves, I am not quite sure. They debated, made statutes, wrote, telegraphed and were enormously busy ; but nobody ever knew what they were doing. It is alleged, though the fact is not absolutely attested, there being no documents to prove it, that the committee was chiefly busy trembling before the workmen and the populace. Personally I don't believe this is true, in view of the fact that Monsieur Rodzianko, who is, I am assured, a man to be believed, telegraphed to the Emperor, assuring him that he was master of the situation. And you cannot be master of a situation if you are in a panic.

In the evening a lady who was weeping bitterly, told us that her husband had not been seen since that morning. She thought he must be under arrest and a prisoner in the Duma. As I have already explained, that is where they deposited all those who were arrested at random, such arrests being very frequent.

I went off to enquire. An enormous crowd was collected in front of the Duma. I managed to elbow my way through and after a struggle to reach the door. I was not allowed in. I applied to a deputy who was a friend of mine and happened to be there. He laughed.

" They won't let me in either."

We applied to a comrade ; he just laughed at us. We offered him a cigarette. He lit it and spoke to another comrade. " Impossible," they said. In the end they let us through. We got inside.

The rooms were full to suffocation. Comrades, soldiers (belonging to the flock of sheep I have told you about), Jews, women, Armenians, students, sailors, more sailors, Semites, Semites and still more Semites—in fine, all those who were soon to become the " Soviet of Soldiers and Workmen," the potentates of Russia. They come and go, pass in and out, sleep on the benches and on the ground, harangue, argue and give and receive instructions, eat sausages and drink beer, smoke and spit on the floor. A lady is weeping in one corner ; in another some comrades are roaring with laughter. The smoke is blinding and makes it difficult to breathe. The heat is stifling.

We are told that Kerensky, the celebrity of to-morrow, who is a deputy now and is making a lot of noise, but who is not yet regarded seriously, has charge of the prisoners. We stop him as he passes. He is tired out and does his best to appear so. He looks as though he were going to faint. He takes out a notebook and turns over the pages, rolls his eyes wearily and mops his brow ; then he tells us to whom we should apply. So we get to work with our elbows again, jostle and get jostled.

At last we get to the man. The fellow sends us to

another one and he sends us on again to a third, who
sends us to a fourth, whom we never find. Exhausted by
the struggle, utterly wearing, panting and half-dead, I
succeed in pushing my way through to the exit and get
back home without being robbed on the way, swearing
though it is rather late in the day, that I shall never let
myself in for such a job again.

Everybody's husband can disappear, I don't care. The
women will find new ones ; there are plenty of fools in
the world.

On the 3rd March Russia was informed by Imperial
manifesto of the abdication of the Emperor Nicholas II
in favour of his brother the Grand Duke Michael, who,
preferring to go on having a good time, declined the
privilege, and handed over his powers to a Provisional
Government.

The curtain had fallen upon " The absolutism of the
Romanovs." It was to be followed by a stupid farce :
" Eunuchs in power," and that by the closing tragedy :
" King Israel," a drama approved by the Governments of
Germany, Britain, Italy and Bulgaria. Absolutism col-
lapsed and died away as any being is bound to die away
that lacks the strength necessary to continue existence.
Nothing unexpected occurred, nothing serious happened to
it, but the hour struck and it was finished. It had fulfilled
its function and it returned to dust.

If a man live too long and die later than he should, his
heirs begin to sigh as soon as he is impotent and a

burden to others, then, glad to be their own masters at last, they enter upon their inheritance, convinced that they will be able to manage things much better than the old man who, according to their statement, was "already quite feeble."

So the Provisional Government went happily to work ; with such success that six months later they were completely bankrupt. Of the enormous wealth acquired during the centuries there was not enough left to pay the chemist's bill. And then they no longer heaved a sigh of relief but of despair.

A dull story, you say. Patience ! It will soon get more exciting and the end will be quite amusing—not only for the Russians.

The fall of absolutism did not arouse much sorrow. Everyone had had pretty well enough of it, except those of "us" who trembled for their skins. In fact many people were delighted ; it was a solution of sorts. Indeed, during the first few days it seemed as though at last everything would run smoothly. The disturbances ceased, and in spite of the absence of police life resumed its normal course. The trams ran, carriages had reappeared and drove in an ordinary way, just as they used to. One almost wondered that such a well-behaved public should need police at all. Only the roads became filthier and filthier, and were soon like sewers ; but that was only natural. Men had not become free, heroes who with their own strong arms had not demolished a throne, to go on sweeping the streets and do dirty work, or indeed to do any kind of work at all. The result was that people

stopped working, and under the pretext of civic demonstrations strolled about the streets.

There were demonstrations from morn till eve. They
were preceded by enormous red banners with inscriptions
such as : " Soldiers, to arms ! Workers, man the barri-
cades !" " We'll fight to a finish !" Then came the schoolboys, whose banner read : " For free men work is a
pleasure." There were hundreds of other slogans, all
equally amusing, for in point of fact they were doing just
the opposite—nobody was working at all. One met
demonstrations of workmen, of grey sheep, of employés,
of civil servants, of public women, of hunchbacks and
cripples and many others too, in fact of everybody
excepting infants in arms. I'm sure there must have been
some of them too, only I hadn't the chance of seeing
them. And there were meetings, meetings, and still more
meetings. People held meetings all over the place. The
speeches were always the same : " Comrades, by a superhuman effort we have overthrown the tyrant ! Now, by
efforts as terrific we shall lay the enemy low."

" Pravilno !"[1]

" Comrades ! The tyrant who has compelled us to cut
our brothers' throats—for all men are our brothers—has
been laid low by your superhuman effort. Let us be mag-
nanimous, as the noble working-man always is. Let us
lay down our arms. There shall be no more war. There
are neither Germans, Russians, Jews nor Christians,
there are only free men. War is a crime, and your
women and children need you."

" Pravilno ! Pravilno !"

[1] Pravilno—hear, hear !

Whatever was said they always agreed and shouted :
" Pravilno ! Pravilno !''

I once heard a cynical jester shouting out with great
enthusiasm : " Comrades ! Now that the bloody tyrant
has been overthrown by your superhuman efforts, now
that his myrmidons are no more, I shout in the streets
in the public squares, on the roofs whence only yesterday
you were being treacherously shot down, ' Pravilno !
Pravilno !' I shout everywhere : ' Comrades, you are
idiots, the greatest idiots that the world has ever seen,
and you will always be so."

" Pravilno ! Pravilno !''

Every day there was a splendid procession preceded
by a band with banners flying, and grey sheep lining the
route, to meet the great heroes of liberty at the station,
who were returning from abroad, whither they had fled to
escape the vengeance of the tyrant, of that sanguinary and
ferocious monster who had just been conquered by the
process of taking joy-rides.

Now it would be the " grandmother of the Revolution,"
Madame Breshko-Breshkovskaya, returning from exile ;
now it would be the " grandfather," Prince Kropotkin ;
now it would be brothers-in-law, uncles or nephews.

The most magnificent of these receptions took place in
the month of April, when " all nature comes to life again,
and the sun gives the fields their fresh array." This fresh
array consisted of the Communists Ulianov-Lenin,
Bronstein-Trotzky, Radomysslsky-Zinoviev, Nakhamkes-
Stenlov and others whom Germany generously presented
to Russia, having given them sixty millions (the fact and
the amount are proved by authentic documents, and
Ludendorff confirms the fact in his Memoirs), to work in

Russia for the glory of the enemy. The mission on which these rays of sunlight had come was a secret to nobody, especially as they were travelling in carriages which were the property of those whose agents they were. But instead of being hanged they were met with great ceremony at the station, where they were acclaimed by members of the Provisional Government and saluted with red flags.

You are puzzled? So am I. For the Provisional Government did not aim at making Germany triumph, but at bringing the war to a successful conclusion. But although we may not understand it, the Intelligentzia, who, it seems, are more intelligent than we are, understood. " A free people (the freest people in the world, as Kerensky declared) has not the moral right to forbid anybody, even the agents of the enemy, to express their opinions freely."

Pravilno !

This surprises you ? It does not surprise me. Nothing could surprise me after what I saw and heard at that time. If anything could still surprise me it would be, certainly not the folly of humanity, but the amazing energy and endurance shewn by the venerable " grandmother of the Revolution," Comrade Breshko-Breshkovskaya. The Minister Kerensky had made the old woman his mascot. She lived with him in the Winter Palace, and he kept her on the run all day. They used to review the red troops together, went together to the theatre of war, to the Soviet and everywhere. And the old woman kept on without turning a hair. It was impossible to exhaust her. I believe, God forgive me, that even now the old woman is still on the move and that she is kept in heaven as a mascot for the second coming of the great eunuch.

I say " great " to distinguish him from the other members of the Provisional Government, who were all eunuchs too ; figuratively, of course. At least I hope so, for their sakes and that of their wives. The Provisional Government consisted of Messrs. Kerensky, Miliukov. . . but there is no point in mentioning their names. These men, these emasculated wretches, rather, are not as interesting as Europeans believe them to be. I have seen more than one of their kind in the East ; at the first glance you would never suspect them of being the kind of creatures they are. It is only when you see them at close quarters that you can see that they are entirely lacking in virility and that they are incredibly flabby creatures, absolutely destitute of will power ; that they are good for nothing and not even competent to look after the ladies of the seraglio, who pay no attention to them and can do what they like with them. Just as in Russia, the members of the " Soviet of Workmen and Soldiers " settled everything not in accordance with the wishes of the eunuchs of the Provisional Government, but as they themselves decided. The wretched creatures were therefore merely ornamental objects who did more harm than good. They were harmful because they brought everything into confusion and chaos and let things take their disastrous course.

But I must say a few words about the Grand Eunuch Kerensky. For some months he was the favourite clown, the principal actor in the farce, the star buffoon who got the show publicity. He played every part : Minister of Justice, tribune, darling child, young premier, grand old man, Prime·Minister, Commander-in-Chief of the armies.

He played all the parts badly and caricatured them.

He had no talent for anything except impudence. His father, a poor Jew called Kirbis or Kirbitz—I'm not quite sure which—died when the boy was about ten years old, and his mother, after being baptized, married a Monsieur Kerensky, a civil servant in the Education Department, who had little Aaron baptized too, adopted him and gave him his name.

When he had passed his examinations, Kerensky, as he was now called, became a provincial lawyer; then he came to St. Petersburg, where for some years he cut a melancholy figure at the Bar.

The following anecdote will give you some idea of the man and of his value as a human being.

An accident had occurred in the mine belonging to the Lena Gold Mines Company Limited, of which I was a director for some years. It is now called the Goldfields Corporation. A police officer, seeing a crowd of miners making for the chief engineer's house, and thinking there might be trouble, ordered his men to fire on them. A number of men who were perfectly innocent were killed. The opposition papers exploited the incident and started a campaign.

The police officer was censured, but the victims' families had no chance of getting compensation either from the Government or from the police officer, who had no private means.

In these circumstances they were advised to take action against the company, which they did.

The action could not possibly succeed, since the company was not responsible for an act committed by a Government agent. The management agreed, however, to make payment, and their lawyer, Monsieur Scheftel, was instructed to come to an arrangement with the lawyers of the other side and to compensate anybody who had a claim. The lawyers of the other side agreed at once, excepting Kerensky, who definitely refused. His colleagues made very effort to persuade him that it was no use taking the thing into court. His answer was: " I realise that, but this case is necessary for me. It will be talked about, and that's what I need in order to get on."

The wretched man had not enough sense or shame simply to say " No " without any explanation.

The case was brought and lost and the unfortunate plaintiffs, who had entrusted their interests to him, got nothing, and Kerensky's name became a joke afterwards.

Then his high-sounding phrases, his hysterical speeches and a lot of mummery with which he struck the workers' imagination got him into the Duma. There he gave forth floods of rhetoric in the rôle of popular tribune. He made himself a laughing-stock, but was always admired " by the fools of the left" (the phrase is not mine but Milyukov's) his reputation increased with the comrades in proportion as he was ignored by everybody else. He was carried into the Provisional Government on the flood-tide of the early days of March. Being more timid than his colleagues, he was not content, as they were, merely to intrigue with the Soviet, which was becoming more powerful every day, but became entirely its slave. The general public did not understand the position, and thought that he was in control.

He always managed to hold the stage, and, like a popular actor, would show himself full face, three-quarter face and in profile, drew in his waist, rolled his eyes, fainted with despair, roared like a lion, bounded like a panther ; in a word, he was always acting a part and always changing his rôle. Only he took himself quite seriously, and genuinely thought himself a great states-man and a great leader of men.

This puppet, dancing to the tune of the Soviet, seemed to be more like a sentimental prostitute than a man, the kind of girl who, while selling herself to the first person she meets, remains faithful to the memory of some Arthur or other, the romantic hero of her reading or of her experience.

I would wager that, whether he was doing the poor devils of the Lena Company out of the money they might have had, or whether he was helping the emissaries of Germany to carry out their dirty work, he was always deeply moved by his ideal. He would be generous, great and noble. Besides, he was a romantic and impotent cad.

The Soviet was the fruit of spontaneous generation ; it owed its life to nobody. There was a desire to belong to such a body, and at least half the people who felt this desire were of non-Russian nationality—either Semites, Georgians, Letts or Armenians. Such Russians as there were, were sailors, deserters from the army, and escaped convicts. Both categories contained a large proportion of German agents. Both Houses, the Duma and the Council of Empire, were *abolished* by it. Soon it was impossible to say where the Provisional Government ended and where the Soviet began. In point of fact the Soviet controlled everything, and the Government, while pretending to have absolute command, merely acquiesced in the require-ments of the Soviet and gave its wishes the force of law.

One of the first acts of the Soviet was to publish the famous General Order No. 1 : the soldier was only to obey his officer when he thought it right to do so, and much more in the same vein. The result is common knowledge. The agonies of our army began then, and with the assistance of the German emissaries it had soon ceased to exist.

As a reward to the grey sheep for the distinguished services rendered to the nation in the early days of February, all the troops who had taken part were promoted " red guard." The Government granted them the privilege that they should never have to leave the capital and never be disbanded. So they could now put up on their placards without any fear at all: " Soldiers, to arms ! Fight to a finish !" That did not commit them to anything. They were not running any danger.

The Red Guards, simple sheep who had been promoted to be Pretorians, having no longer to obey their chiefs or to fear that they might be sent out of the capital, could have plundered the town from end to end with impunity if they had been less inert. The town was at their mercy, and any other soldiery left to itself would certainly have done so.

Thanks to their inertia and their incompetence, they did not do so, and contented themselves with poisoning the lives of the inhabitants.

In the exhilaration of their new dignity, these feeble scourings of the population decided that there was no point in their dressing decently. They went about the streets and public places filthy and unkempt, with their horribly grey rags of uniform hanging from their shoulders.

They took their siesta, and did worse things than that, on the benches in the squares and the public gardens, or snored at full length on the lawns. The sentinels on duty ensconced themselves in armchairs requisitioned from neighbouring houses, put their rifles against the wall and smoked cigarettes. They hailed women as they passed, made offensive remarks to them and compelled them to sit on their knees. They monopolised the trams and the theatres. Of course they never paid, and if there were no empty seats they just drove away the people who had seats. All this was merely a beginning. By the autumn they were robbing people in the streets in broad daylight ; and they would, no doubt, soon be improving on that.

Fortunately the Bolsheviks cleared out the eunuchs shortly afterwards and rid us of that verminous crowd. That was the one good action they did ; though it is true that afterwards they extracted heavy payment for that service.

We have passed through many experiences since. We have seen rivers of blood, mountains of corpses, many scenes more terrible, but none as sickening as that of the sight of degraded brutes flaunting themselves as masters in the capital which they had reduced to a latrine.

The emissaries of Germany, Lenin, Bronstein, Radom-yslsky, Nashamkes, Uritzky, Zederbaum, Dzherjinsky and their consorts had bred a numerous progeny with the fertility typical of their race and, without paying any attention to the Provisional Government, the whole swarm had seized the houses belong to the dancer Kseszinska and to General Durnovo, and from morning to night they preached peace with Germany and war on the bourgeois from the balconies.

The military command had several times proposed that the Jews should be turned out, but Kerensky always opposed the suggestion.

" Our guests, the Communists," he used to say, " must be housed suitably. I have told Pereversev, the Minister of Justice, to find them suitable accommodation and then we'll see what can be done."

It seems that the Minister of Justice was not equal to the duty of carrying out Kerensky's command, for several weeks passed without his succeeding in finding anything suitable. By July, our guests, tired of waiting, tried to overthrow the Government. It would seem that the Winter Palace, where the Grand Eunuch and his mascot lived, appealed to them. Kerensky took it amiss and suddenly had them imprisoned. An enquiry was instituted, and treachery in favour of Germany was proved without the shadow of a doubt. Enough evidence was forthcoming to hang the whole lot more than ten times over.

But they were not hanged. Kerensky personally released the traitors, stopped the proceedings and, when the judge insisted on continuing them, dismissed him. Then all the documents disappeared. Robert and Bertrand had come to an understanding.

When he had disposed of this matter Kerensky returned to the theatre of war to inspire the troops to resume the offensive. But Kornilov, the Commander-in-Chief, told him plainly that this was impossible as long as the Bolsheviks remained in power.

Kerensky and the General decided that Kornilov's troops should occupy the capital and dispose of the Communists. Kerensky would return to St. Petersburg to take such measures as were necessary. When he got back he outlawed General Kornilov, had him arrested and imprisoned.

T

It seems that in the meantime the Bolsheviks had had enough of him too, and as they were not weaklings they had the members of the Government arrested and imprisoned them all except Kerensky, who, disguised as a sailor, had managed to get away.

Thus the farce of " the eunuchs in power " failed and was hissed off the boards; the Intelligentzia, who still hope to see it put on again, alone protesting. " It is true " they say, " that Kerensky sometimes did not play his part very well, but he is such an honest man." It would be interesting to know what their idea of a scoundrel is.

CHAPTER IX

1918-1920

THE sons of Israel had carried out their mission ; and Germany's agents, having become the representatives of Russia, signed peace with their patron at Brest-Litovsk. But their patron made a blunder. Instead of taking over responsibility and dismissing the servants whom they needed no longer, they elected to secure an immediate return on their money. Israel paid them out two hundred million obtained from the State Treasury of Russia and their patron left them in authority with full power to take what they could lay their hands on.

I am sorry, for of two evils I prefer the lesser. Germany is a very good administrator and if, instead of abandoning Russia to the power of the Bolsheviks, she had exploited her herself, we should both have done better out of the arrangement. It would have cost us dear, but infinitely less than the Bolsheviks, who massacred millions of people and who in the end only achieved their own bankruptcy and the enrichment of a few thousand assassins and robbers.

But I must not anticipate.

When the Communists were haranguing the populace from the balconies of Madame Kseszinska's house and behaving like madmen, nobody thought for a moment that these strange figures, ridiculous rather than terrible, would soon be master tyrants such as the country had never seen.

" Who are those madmen, batiushka ?" an old woman asked. " Look how they're going on. The poor fellows look as though they had colic."

" Who knows ? They don't look like Russians. Perhaps they're Frenchmen, or Persians or Englishmen."

" That's it, old dear, they are English," said a passer-by. " Only they are natives of Jerusalem or Berdichev. Look at their ears."

" I hear that Lenin, their chief, is a true Russian; that he's a saint and will perform miracles."

" He's performing them already. He's stolen that house without being put in prison."

The people laughed. When they overthrew the Government they laughed too and, frankly, there was something to laugh about. Unrivalled as executioners they were frankly stupid as legislators. Here are some examples :

" All existing laws are repealed. So too are those which do not exist but which might attack the democratic principles of the people. Anyone committing an offence against this decree will be deprived of his property."

People used to ask as a joke whether, without running the risk of forfeiting their property, they could clean their teeth. Certainly not. The proletariat never did. To do so would therefore be to infringe democratic principles.

The decrees became more and more ridiculous ; but at the start they were fairly harmless and nobody took them seriously. Israel was full of splendid intentions, but there was as yet no administrative machine for carrying them into effect. Then, when the light-fingered gentry began to enroll under their banner, the position became

less humorous.   Nevertheless, for the first few months
one could still carry on ; it was possible to live, and even
to laugh, and one laughed a good deal.

" Let these puppets amuse themselves," we would say.
" We shall soon be sending them to an asylum.   They are
really more comic than harmful."

But they went on issuing decrees.

" The inhabitants of each house shall form a corps
which shall elect a president.   The president is responsible
to the Soviet for everything that happens in the house.
He shall make a daily report to the commissaire for the
district."

And so forth.

" Persons guilty of any offence against this order shall
be deprived of their property."

We formed a corps and unanimously elected our concierge as president.   He naturally objected, for his duties
were certainly not easy ; but he was offered a minister's
salary and in the end he accepted.   After a certain time
his salary was tripled, as the president had to share it with
the commissaire for the district.   Then it was doubled
again as the commissaire of the district had to share it
with the commissaire of the borough.   Then it was doubled
again as the central commissaire also had to have his share.

Our concierge was a very worthy fellow, though perhaps
a little too obsequious.   Now that he'd become president
he felt the responsibility of his position and became
somewhat exacting towards us.   He came every day to
see what we were doing, though he did so, it is true,
without molesting us, treating us as comrades rather
than as subordinates.   He would turn up smiling, con-
descend to shake us by the hand, ensconce himself in an

armchair, light one of my cigars, cross his legs and we would chat. Fortunately his wife suffered from a pituitary gland and so we had a pleasant topic of conversation.

A new decree was issued as follows :

" The tenants in each house (the tenant and his family counting as one) shall, each night in turn, take duty as sentry at the entrance to the house." The offender, of course—but you are familiar with the refrain : confiscation of all his goods.

In the house where I was living there were only four flats ; in an annex to it there was a small flat, inhabited by a master cleaner. It was the master cleaner who, as you may remember, had been arrested as a policeman and by a miracle had got off with the loss of one eye.

One of the larger flats was occupied by a member of the Diplomatic Corps who, being a foreign subject, was exempt from any forced labour. Another was occupied by an old lady who was paralytic, the third by a member of the Imperial Council, who was eighty years old, and the fourth by myself, who was seventy years old and suffering at the time from an attack of gout which made me unable to move. The only person available was the unfortunate cleaner. But the cleaner was no fool ! He had already enrolled in the Communist party and so, as he was now responsible for the safety of the Republic, he was exempted from any duty.

What were we to do ?

The president went for instructions to the commissaire, who was fortunately an acquaintance of mine ; he had been my groom.

His reply was : " One of the members of the family must do duty instead of the head." Anybody failing to—

but you know the refrain, and I shall not repeat it again.

My family consisted only of my wife, who was sixty years old. The member of Council's family consisted of his two grandchildren, one aged twelve and the other five; that of the paralytic lady consisted of a parrot and a cat. Neither the child nor the parrot nor the cat were seriously competent to look after the security of the tenants, so the " comrade " of twelve armed with a tin gun, and my wife, shouldering her umbrella, did sentry duty at night in turn and kept off the robbers, who were terrified by their imposing appearance.

Fortunately one could generally adjust matters. We set our influence to work and M. le Commissaire, for a reasonable consideration, released the nightwatchmen from their duties.

After three nights on duty the Baroness was able to put away her umbrella again and after that the " comrades," freed from their fierce watchdogs, had a great time.

Then all the tenants under sixty years of age were instructed to clear the road of snow and ice.

For the first time we had occasion to thank heaven that we were no longer young, for we were over that age and useless. So this decree delighted me. At last all men were equal; and priests, society ladies (girls and fifty-nine year old matrons), doctors, engineers, professors, artists, high officials (at any rate those who had not been shot or imprisoned), all now carried out their duties as citizens with pick and shovel, though not very efficiently perhaps, for they had not yet acquired the habits of the free man. It must be admitted that the education of the upper classes had been sadly neglected up to that time. But they set gaily to work, glad at last to be of some kind of use. It must have been an absolute holiday for them. I even saw a gentleman wearing a morning-coat and fancy waistcoat to celebrate the occasion. And I was told that a senator put on his best red uniform with gold braid, the red ribbon of the Grand Cordon across his chest. As the uniform and the ribbon were the fashionable colour nobody did him any harm.

It really made a touching picture. I was moved when I saw the poor members of the proletariat at last resting their limbs wearied by honest toil which was beyond their strength—for they of course were released from the obligation of doing any forced labour. As the bourgeoisie had been sucking their blood for centuries (the phrase was now being repeated at every opportunity by all the proletariat) they were no longer capable of manual work and only worked with their brains.

Now, with cigarettes in their mouths and their hands in their pockets, they watched the bourgeoisie working and encouraged them pleasantly with cheery remarks.

" Put a little beef into it, you dirty idlers."

" You've been sucking our blood long enough, you filthy brutes."

" Hi, you there, lassie ! Stop smirking at me. If you think you'll get off with me you're mistaken. You're far too filthy."

And in order to hearten his people by showing himself to them, Israel kept on driving by in armoured cars which had belonged to the Imperial Court. We were happy then !

Alas ! Those good times were soon to be clouded over.

A new decree granted the proletariat the right to go and

live where and with whom they pleased. The bourgeoisie lived like princes ; let them pack themselves tighter and share their rooms with the comrades.

The laugh was over. The farce had taken a definitely tragic turn.

Prodigious efforts were made to find people who were reasonably clean to share one's rooms free. It was disagreeable in any case but not as awful as living with " comrades " and their delightful families and their vermin.

I solved the difficulty fairly well. I moved some of my offices to my house and put the office furniture in some of the rooms. And my noble friend, the commissaire, promised that for a reasonable consideration that would be all right for the present.

But everybody was not so fortunate. Many people, after having tried the comrades, left their flats with everything in them (shortly afterwards it was forbidden to take anything away) to go and live with friends, acquaintances, or even with strangers who appeared to be fairly respectable, but often turned out not to be. Others were simply thrown out of doors.

A new decree was published : " All foodstuffs hereby become the property of the State. The State has the right to sell and buy them. Every citizen has the right to a fixed ration per day on payment." I don't remember what the ration was, but it was sufficient to starve on slowly. As the proletariat complained, the law was modified.

The whole population was divided into three categories. The first category consisted of the Communists and the employees of the Soviet, the privileged class. The second category, the soldiers and the proletariat. The third category were the bourgeois pariahs. The first category was liberally supplied, the second had a sufficient ration, while the bourgeois only had the right to half a pound of bread and a herring. Then, when bread became scarce, to a quarter of a pound.

As the bourgeois was still glutted with the blood of the proletariat with which he had gorged himself to satiety, this ration was more than sufficient.

But the bourgeois, always insatiable in his appetites, thought otherwise and complained, though not too loudly, for it was as much as his life was worth, counter revolution being punishable by death.

Nevertheless we would queue up for hours to receive our miserable ration and often, when it was raining, blowing or freezing (and remember we were not in Nice but in Russia), we would spend the night waiting, as otherwise there was a risk of getting nothing. When everything had been taken by the first comers, the shop was shut.

A little additional food could naturally be obtained by stealth at fantastic prices. The Government agents and the " red " soldiers trafficked in everything, but it was dangerous for the buyer. The administrative machinery was beginning to improve ; you might have your domicile inspected and then, if anything whatever were found, it was the worse for you. You remember the refrain : " Any offence. . ." etc.

This was no idle threat any longer. The administrative machine was being perfected. It is unnecessary to add that the State inspectors, when carrying out their duties, immediately carried off any articles which were inconsistent with the democratic principles of the proletariat. Such articles were numerous. They included any object of value, fur coats and especially boots. If boots were found anywhere excepting on your feet, there was trouble.

You will readily understand that it was not desirable to be in possession of boots. They were hidden, as young women hide their little secret extravagances.

The burning question now was how to solve the food problem. It was the sole topic of conversation and if one's friends heard of any supplies they would ring one up to say where to apply.

Only you had to be careful. It was dangerous to have dealings with unknown persons. When the goods had been delivered and paid for they would denounce you, and the authorities, who were their catspaws, would come and seize your goods. But for about a thousand roubles a day (about three thousand francs) it was still possible to keep alive. Those were happy times ! It cost two millions later. And the curious thing is that there were even then people who failed to die of hunger ; not many, it is true but there were some. One may do what one will but the dirty bourgeois will go on sucking the blood of the poor proletariat.

The decrees kept on being issued ; decrees ordering the surrender of blankets, clothes, flannel waistcoats, etc.

The proletariat stopped at nothing and neither did the commissaires.

Finally there came the knock-out blow : " All land, all houses and immovable property, deposit and current accounts at the bank, belonging to individuals or companies, are hereby confiscated and declared to be the property of the nation. The former owners are allowed to draw three hundred roubles a month on their current accounts.   Shares, debentures, State bonds, and other certificates are hereby cancelled.''

The only right left to the bourgeois was to die of hunger. Fortunately, the legislators had been careless. They had left out movable property. In order to live, people proceeded to sell this.

Notices offering to buy and sell goods appeared everywhere. Everything was for sale and everybody became a seller. Buyers were not lacking either. Members of the proletariat, red soldiers, commissaires, sailors—'' the flower and glory of the Revolution ''—all had to set themselves up completely and to do so on a decent footing suitable to their new station. After all people do not overthrow a throne in order to go living as pariahs, and the women, and especially the sailors, were fond of jewels.

The sailors had an absolute passion for them. They wore double and treble necklaces round their bare necks, and to do their taste justice they chose well. They had bracelets, watches and rings besides.

Dressed like little lords, clean-shaven, scented and perfumed, with manicured hands, they were loathsome. There was certainly every reason to call them '' the price and glory of the Revolution.'' They had travelled and seen all lands and, as is well known, nothing does so much to polish a young man as travel.

The other *nouveaux riches* were equally splendid in their newly acquired wealth, but, although they were fellow countrymen, the truth must come before everything, and they were really rather unsavoury—especially the fine ladies. The rich dirt of their nails, and the lichen growing luxuriously on their teeth, quite outshone the

splendour of their jewels and the magnificence of their
furs. And to hear them talk! It made me blush for my
country.

Money flowed in streams; it was to be had for the
asking. It was a real land of milk and honey. For one
thing, millions of officials had been created, as the State
owned, and had to organise everything, and you will
readily understand that amongst its servants were many
who did not work to make money for Israel but for themselves.

Besides, it was only necessary to make a " naliot," the
modern euphemism for a raid on the bourgeois, to get
anything one wanted in the way of money, jewelry and
furs, and so on. The only point of making purchases in
the shops as well as that one was offered a greater choice
there, whereas in making a " naliot " one had to be satisfied with what one found. That, of course, is trying for a
man of taste and refinement. Besides, one did not exclude
the other, and money did not cost them anything. When
their pockets were empty they filled them again at
once. Fortunately the bourgeois still existed and the
source was not yet exhausted.

One day, before the knock-out blow, I went in to the
most fashionable jeweller's, who had been at school with
me in Switzerland. I found some society ladies there, not
to buy, but to sell the few things that had not yet passed
into the hands of the comrades.

" So you're still buying ?" I said to him.

" Of course. I sell as quickly as I buy. Business has
never been as good as it is now. But I only sell big stones,
not really artistic objects."

" But who on earth are the buyers ?"

" Why, the soldiers, sailors and riff-raff.   No respectable people, of course."

" Aren't you afraid of the ' naliot ' ? "

" No. I've managed to get protection."

" Couldn't you get me protection too ? "

" Quite impossible. It's a professional secret. Besides,
I'm an Israelite and you're a Russian, so you understand."

While we were talking a red soldier and his lady came
into the shop. He was a clod-hopper, straight from the
plough, a simpleton who was quite bewildered by his good
fortune. She was a kitchen-maid who was up to all the
tricks of the game, as she had knocked about the capital.
She was marked with small-pox, had a red complexion
and a shiny skin, dazzling jewels, splendid furs, a gorgeous
frock and an enormous hat. Her nails were black and she
was painted so that you wanted smoked glasses to look at
her. The yokel was quite proud to be seen with such a
great lady. She must be at least a princess. Just think !
Him, a simple ploughboy, and her, a lady with a hat ! He
was beaming with happiness.

" A pearl necklace, and see that they are genuine," the
creature ordered nonchalantly, to impress the poor
wretches who were standing by her.

" Not glass ones, but very expensive ones," said the
booby. " Shining ones like the ' baryni '[1] wear. They're
for her."

So that there couldn't be any mistake he pointed at
her.

A necklace was produced. The beauty looked at it
contemptuously.

" How much ? "

---

[1] Baryni—real ladies of the nobility.

" Forty thousand roubles. (Our money had not yet lost its value. The rouble was still worth about three francs).

" I want more expensive ones ; not dirty things like those."

" She knows," said the yokel. " Oh, yes, she knows all right. You can't fool her. She's a devil, she is."

Another necklace was produced.

" This one is seventy-five thousand."

The woman didn't even look at it ; the price had convinced her that it was inferior.

" I must have something better."

" Certainly," said the soldier. " Something much more expensive. She really couldn't wear that."

" I am sorry, madame, at the moment we haven't got anything better. In a few days perhaps. . ."

" She must have it to-day. We are going to the reception at the Winter Palace this evening. She can't dance without pearls. The bourgeois has been sucking our blood long enough !"

" Let's go to the Gostinoy Dvor," said the beauty, pushing aside the jewel-case. " We are sure to find what I want there. You can get anything there."

The ladies could not refrain from smiling. The stores in question only dealt in imitation jewelry. The beauty blushed with vexation under her paint. She saw that she had made a blunder. She tried to recover herself :

" As I've had all the trouble of coming to your shop I'll take the wretched things. When you have something better I'll buy it too. We can afford it."

" Yes," said the yokel. " We can afford it. I refuse her nothing. We share everything." He burst out laughing. " Yes, everything. Don't I, Melanie ?"

Looking very pleased with himself he paid and handed the jewel-case to his lady.

" Take it with my love."

When they had gone, one of the ladies observed :

"Did you see the clasp on that creature's coat? Perfectly magnificent ! I'm sure it comes from Lalique."

" You are mistaken, madame, it's our work. I made it for the Princess," and he mentioned a well-known name.

The lady sighed : " They've taken all my jewelry too."

" And mine too," said another. " But I managed to save my diamond necklace. When they called I threw it out of the window into the snow. They didn't notice it."

It is unnecessary to add that the yokel was on " naliot " duty.

To carry out " naliots," to be a " naliottshik " as it was called, had become a trade, just like being a carpenter or a confectioner had been.

One day I found our president's wife, an excellent woman, in tears. I asked her whether her pituitary gland was giving her trouble. " No," she said, " it was better, as she was applying hot poultices." She was crying because that rascal Serguey had stolen all her money. To think of it ! A little boy of sixteen, stealing a thousand roubles from his own aunt, his father's sister. If he'd been a little older. But at his age ! Nothing was sacred to-day. God was forgotten.

Three days later the good woman was beaming with pleasure.

" I am glad to see that your pituitary trouble is better," I said.

" Alas, no. Poultices are no use. My neighbour has advised me to try another treatment. I'll give you the prescription. But I've got my money back, and more. Serguey is really a good boy. He's carried out a " naliot " with some friends because, you know, he wants to become a " naliottshik "—he has indeed become one already—and he got twenty thousand roubles from it. Just imagine, a beginner, and twenty thousand roubles in one night ! It's very good and, besides, like the good boy he is, he has given me my money back and a present of three thousand roubles besides."

I have known the woman for fourteen years and she has always been honesty itself, but ideas had changed and men had become different. Three years later, practising Christians who were accustomed to fast on Fridays and Wednesdays, had become cannibals and were eating their own children.

They were not doing that yet, but were fasting, not only on Fridays and Wednesdays, but throughout the week, and we, who hadn't ever fasted at all, also fasted for the whole week.

Nevertheless, we were comparatively fortunate. We still had, at any rate for the time being, a large flat full of numerous objects, valuable pictures, bronzes, antiques and all kind of things. If we were not robbed we had enough to live on for some time.

But what about those who had not all these things ? They were the great majority, even of those who were well off. What they still had disappeared with a terrifying rapidity and soon destitution was general.

Everywhere you saw people staggering along with wan, sallow complexions. And the wretched children ! You could tell by their eyes that the poor little things were dying of hunger. I saw many a drama in the " office for

U

purchases and sales " where I went like everybody else to sell something or other. One day while I was there, a delightful little girl, about five or six years old, came in, huddled in old rags. I had often noticed the little girl driving with her mother, a beautiful young woman, in a carriage drawn by high-stepping horses. The child put a doll and a pair of shoes on the counter.

" Why hasn't your mother come ?"

" Mother can't go out. These shoes are her last pair."

" Have you sold everything ?"

" No, sir. We've still got a kettle and a lot of chairs. Four. There's an armchair and two tables besides. But nobody wants them. And I've still got a doll. But mother says that nobody will pay anything for it. It's nose is broken. It wasn't I that broke its nose but my little brother, who died a few days ago. Mother had no money left to buy him Nestlé. You know the powder that small children eat."

" Where's your father ?"

" Father ? The sailors killed him."

In the street old men, ladies and girls whom I had met in society were selling matches and newspapers, and were badgered by the regular vendors with whom they were competing.

My friend, the old Princess Galitzin, surreptitiously sold little pies which she made ; my cousin sold knitted wear, others sold paper flowers, luxury articles in great demand, slippers made from their old carpets and a thousand things of their own invention. A former gentleman of the bed-chamber to the Emperor had had a brilliant idea, which enabled him to live in style. He had succeeded in becoming concierge of a museum where strange creatures were kept in methylated spirits, strange abortions, embryos and other objects of the kind. Strong drink reached fabulous prices at this period, as it had been prohibited since the war. He substituted pure water for the alcohol in the cases and bottled the methylated spirits. The comrades were delighted with this nectar.

More trying even perhaps than the shortage of food was the cold and lack of light. The flats above, below and on either side were unheated and even those who could make a fire at home shivered and froze. As I have already observed, we were not in the South but in the North, where the cold is intense in winter, sometimes really terrible, and the winters are long.

The electric supply had failed for some weeks ; candles and oil were unobtainable and in St. Petersburg it is dark in the winter at about two or three o'clock in the afternoon until nine o'clock in the morning. One stayed at home, shivering with cold, famished and with nothing to do, expecting at any moment a visit from the victims whose blood one had been sucking. It was no fun, and one's thoughts at the time were far from amusing.

Every day brought bad news. A relation or friend had been shot or assassinated, another had been imprisoned, and a third driven out of his house.

And yet these were still the good times ! The nightmare of the red terror was still to come.

Germany had placed Lenin and Israel in power, but she had not definitely abdicated. Her agents at St. Petersburg and Count Mirbach with his general staff at Moscow saw to the consolidation of the Bolshevist régime and assisted it with their advice and suggestions. Israel knew—perhaps better than his advisers—what he wanted, and was less particular about the means than they were, but he lacked experience of affairs and the Germans were past masters in that respect. Once the necessary experience had been acquired and the power more or less consolidated, Count Mirbach was assassinated by his pupils and the other instructors were sent home.

But to consolidate the power was not an easy matter. The adepts of Bolshevism were comparatively few. There were practically no true converts and the thousands of men who declared themselves adherents of the faith were merely imposters, riff-raff which took it up in order to be able to plunder with impunity. The bourgeoisie were hostile, the working classes and the proletariat were a crowd who might rat at any moment and would certainly do so the moment that they saw that the cake was not for them. But the great danger in the Capital was the garrison, the eighty thousand sheep converted into red guards armed with rifles and machine-guns, who, having overthrown the monarchy, had come to realise their power and could quite easily, without any danger, liquidate Israel as soon as they decided to do so. As for Russia itself, the rural population and the moujik, they did not count yet.

The important thing was to seize power as quickly as possible in the towns. The moujik did not bother about finding out who was boss : provided he was left in possession of the land, of which he had robbed the proprietors, it was all the same to him. Government by the Czar, by eunuchs or by Israel, it was all one to the moujik.

On these *data* it was not difficult to evolve a programme. The most important thing was to disband the red guards and replace them by a soldiery upon which Israel could rely blindly. The next thing was to get rid of the bourgeoisie, with whom it would certainly be impossible ever to come to terms. Then, to make the proletariat harmless and reign supreme.

The red guards were prettily duped. They were foolish enough to think themselves all-powerful. A few regiments of Chinese and Letts were recruited at great expense and stationed in the neighbourhood of the Capital and at the railway stations.

Then the rumour was spread about that the peasants were dividing up the land and that those who were not there when it was being divided would get nothing. The red guards immediately all asked to go on leave to get their share. The Government looked dubious and then consented to let them go ; but they declared that they would take their arms with them. There were further discussions. And in the end the Government yielded again, but on one condition. It was impossible that the Capital should do without them all at once ; the counter-revolution would take advantage of the position. They would have to leave in small detachments.

This was done. When they got to their stations, the Chinese and the Letts disarmed them and they were forbidden to return to the Capital under penalty of death. The heroes, grey sheep once more, cut a sorry figure.

You may have observed that the typical feature of the Russian Revolution—the passivity of its victims—was common to all its phases, whether comic or tragic.

Just a joke—and without the least resistance the

throne crumbled. A handful of knaves were sent by the enemy into Russia to destroy her, and without a protest the Provisional Government let itself be put to bed like an infant.

That Government in its panic had converted the timid sheep into all-powerful Pretorian Guards—and now, of these eighty thousand Pretorians who caused the Government and the Capital to tremble, thanks to a simple trick, not one remained.

The bourgeoisie did even better. Hundreds and thousands of men allowed themselves to be taken to the slaughter-house without any resistance—and to be slaughtered.

And Russia as a whole exceeds even this. She allows Israel to take her by the collar, buffet her, throw her into prison, reduce her to nothing, spit upon her God and lord it over his ashes.

And to-day a hundred odd million of human animals wander scattered throughout the world, rot in prison, or die of hunger in the fields which formerly used to feed Europe, and tremble with terror under the lash of criminals, their jailors. Germany, England and Italy look on and applaud, while they are saying at Moscow: " Patience, gentlemen. Your turn will come. Lloyd George and Heinrich Wirth are doing their best."[1]

Once the pretorian sheep had been disarmed the Chinese and Letts took their place. They were good soldiers, admirable jailors and executioners ; they would be needed. The bourgeois must all be got rid of. It is true there were men for the job but they were only fit for the unskilled work and not for carrying it out artistically.

[1] Written in 1922.

As the whole of Europe has been engaged in mutual slaughter for some years the most humane being can kill a man as coolly as he used to tie his tie. It's all a question of habit.

Before 1914 it was painful to see a dog run over. Then every day one would see tens, hundreds and thousands of men killed and mutilated, and amongst them friends, brothers, one's own children, and one got used to it. It used to be thought horrible to spend the night in the company of a corpse but since then we have slept in barns containing many more than one corpse and sometimes we have taken one of them to serve as a pillow.

That has become a matter of habit, so familiar that it seems to belong to the natural order of things, and to kill or be killed is nothing. The mental attitude of crowds, and often of individuals, depends upon the time and the environment in which they live. That of early man must differ from that of our contemporaries and the mental attitude of the men of 1920 was necessarily different from that of the men of 1913.

I once met the son of one of my friends in Finland. I had known him well before the war. He was an educated young man, of a very gentle nature, and well balanced. He had since been a volunteer in the war, then he had been with Yudenitsh's army, and according to his chief he was a brave and gallant soldier.

In telling me of his experiences he told me that one day he had suddenly come into a district where he had found twelve Bolsheviks torturing a family. They had tied a pot with a rat in it to the mother's stomach and the rat was gnawing her entrails. The hands of the wretched woman were nailed to a table, on which two young children of hers, who were still alive, were tied to a plate with a knife and fork through their bodies. They had already had their eyes gouged out.

"What did you do to those wretches ?" I asked.

"The General, who happened to turn up, ordered them to be hanged," and he began to laugh.

"What are you laughing at ?"

"I remember one of them, a very nice-looking boy, rather fair. I only had volunteers with me, who were almost children, and none of them knew how to set about the job. So I had to hang the whole dozen of them by myself. You know, to hang a man is not so simple as it seems. And when there are twelve of them. . . You understand. . ."

"Is that what you're laughing at ?"

"I'm thinking of the little fair man's head. I couldn't get him to put it through into the noose. He was quite determined not to. He was funny. He looked like a colt which you are trying to put into harness for the first time. When I succeeded and the job was done, he danced about like a puppet. I had to hang on to his legs to stop him. It was just like a swing. It nearly broke my arms."

The Chinese and the Letts were at their posts ; the hour for the bourgeois had struck.

And the dance of death began ; a dance such as the world had never seen. The slaughter-house worked twenty-four hours a day and there were not enough hands for the work.

I will spare you the details. They are too terrible and too repulsive. Men of to-day shrink from the hideous pictures of a Ribera : victims whose skin is being taken off them like a glove, whose eyes are burnt with white-hot metal, martyrs whose entrails are wound on to reels like thread, men being flayed alive. We are too civilised for such revolting scenes. To-day we want themes which are more noble, more amusing, and above all more refined : the negro Siki driving in Carpentier's jaw with his fist, or the King of Italy shaking hands at Genoa with Monsieur Tchitcherin, the tail-coated representative of the Government of the Moscow executioners. Besides, people only half believe in " these Russians who are eternally dying of hunger on their Volga without ever finishing the business, who beg for rations at Constantinople, who clutter up Europe, bother everybody for visas, never stop telling their depressing stories and are always exaggerating."

One day I was rash enough to describe the horrible death of one of my relations who had been assassinated by the red guards to a charming Parisian lady, who was well read and of fastidious taste. I will tell you her reply.

" Your nerves are really getting into a very bad state. You see the dark side of everything."

As my elder son was married and my younger son dead, our flat was too big for us. We two alone felt rather lost in it. But we needed a place for all the odds and ends which we had picked up all over the place during half a century ; we were fond of the things. We couldn't use my offices. My clerks had gone ; they only called occasionally so as not to leave us entirely alone ; then, when the trains stopped running, their visits ceased. Our servants had left us too, excepting a woman and her brother who had been attached to us for years. The big cold rooms (from which every day some beloved object disappeared to be converted into cash) their gloom and emptiness made us feel quite sad.

For a long time we had been thinking of leaving the town, where life had become impossible. But nobody was allowed to leave without a special permit and in spite of all our efforts we had so far failed to get one.

The big mining company, of which I was one of the directors, had not been nationalised yet, but all the members of the board had already left the town excepting one of my colleagues and myself. We thought it our duty to remain at our posts as long as we possibly could.

One day, when we were at work, a son of Israel, a youth of about twenty (we gathered that this comrade had been a locksmith) appeared, followed by two men carrying books, of the same race, and about ten Chinamen. He presented his warrant.

It had come at last ; the Company was declared to be State property. We were instructed to hand over the cash-box, and to submit our accounts to the Commissaire General for all mining enterprises in the Republic. The locksmith was the commissaire in question.

We did so with pleasure, glad to be relieved of our duties which had become somewhat irksome.

The accountants checked the books—they were trained men and knew their job—and then the cash. When that had been done the grand commissaire told them to take it away. Then he proceeded to cross-examine us about the business. At the first word he said it was obvious that he did not understand a thing about it. Probably he realised this himself ; and he went to consult one of the accountants. Then he came back and said :

" Comrades, you will continue to manage the mines as commissaires of the State. The comrade accountant has told me that it is necessary to provide the comrade miners with food. See that this is done at once."

" In order to do so we need money, and you have taken the cash."

" You will get money out of the mines."

" No, the mines aren't working."

" It is up to you, comrades, to see that the comrade miners start work again."

" You know quite well that they won't listen to us."

" That's nothing to do with me. We've talked long enough. If the comrades have to go without food you will both be shot."

" We request you to nominate others to carry out our duties."

" What do you mean ? We shoot anybody who refuses to carry on. Bear that in mind. You've not got to talk but to obey. We know how to make the dirty bourgeoisie work. They've been sucking our blood long enough. I'll come back in a fortnight and then—you'd better take care !"

We decided to flee at once. That very day, my colleague, who had a permit, left for the South. He put me on to a man who would undertake to get me over the frontier without a permit. We decided that my wife could not leave with me but should join our son in the Crimea. A train was to come from the Ukraine to fetch the wife of the Hetman Skoropadsky ; she could take advantage of this and leave without a passport.

While we were waiting we rented two rooms opening on to a little yard, from an old lady who was a friend of ours, so that when I was gone, the Baroness would be able to stay there. She would attract less attention there than in our large flat.

When I got home after making several calls, I found my wife on the staircase carrying up wood with considerable difficulty. She told me that our maid and her brother had both left us, as they'd heard that lands were being divided up in the country and it was essential to be on the spot. The president's wife was suffering from her pituitary trouble and he was too important a person to help us. We were left to our own resources.

At dawn—it was still dark and the rain was coming down in torrents—the Baroness left to queue up at a baker's. I went down to get wood ; but I found I could not get it upstairs. I was over seventy and twisted with rheumatism.

I cleaned the boots, washed the pots, swept the rooms and brushed the clothes. Then I wanted to boil the samovar to make some tea, but I was not able to do it. I was not physically capable even of that.

My wife came back exhausted and soaked to the skin. The oven had gone out. There was no hot water for tea and no light. She had to go down again and bring up wood, she, a weak old woman. And I, who quite lately had thought myself a strong man, was so distressed by my weakness that I sat down on a chair and felt the tears coming to my eyes.

The bell rang. I went to open the door ; a man came in. I couldn't see who he was until I took him to the window—it was still dark. He was a friend of my son's who had come from Moscow on business. When he saw our condition he said nothing, turned on his heel and disappeared. We didn't know what to think. Half an hour later he was back with his trunk. He said he would stay with us and do the heavy work.

The man who was to get me away came to tell me that we should leave on the following Thursday. I was to dress shabbily, have a beard of some days' growth, wear dark glasses and appear to be seriously ill. My only luggage was to be a small trunk. The employees of a hospital train, which was to take invalid Germans to Pskov, a town which was still occupied by the Germans, had consented to take me as contraband if—that was the crux of the matter —if I could manage to get into the train. As my man had colleagues in the station the plan might succeed with luck. Only if by any chance the reds came to inspect the travellers during the journey it would be up to me to get out of the difficulty as well as I could. He would be on the train to help if he could but he would pretend not to know me. The difficulty was to get to the frontier. It would be quite easy to pass it as he had a letter from the German Embassy to the " Kommanditur."

I said good-bye to my wife, and my young friend, who was carrying my trunk, went with me to a baggage shed, from which the train was to start. The shed was over-flowing with German sick and wounded, and women and children. In spite of their strange clothes I recognised amongst them Ditmar, the Colonel of the Guard, and Baron Pilar, an officer in the Horse Guards. They didn't recognise me, as I heard afterwards, owing to my black spectacles.

The train was to start at three o'clock ; but we were still waiting for the inspection at midnight, sitting on the ground, as we had no seats.

At last a group of comrades appeared and sat down at a table. Sentinels guarded the door. The roll-call began. Each person as he was called out went up to the table, his papers were examined to see if his name were on the list and then he passed. At the door leading on to the platform there was another inspection, but this was less strict. The sentry, a stupid-looking youth, simply examined your passport.

Dragging my trunk with great difficulty, I made my way amongst the crowd to the door, without passing in front of the table. I knew that my name was not on the list. The only passport that I had was a document signed by myself covered with a lot of fancy rubber stamps. Rubber stamps always impose upon people who cannot read, and I counted on that.

When the chief inspection was at last over, the door was thrown open and the crowd began to pass through, one at a time. The men at the table, glad to be finished with their job, stretched themselves, began to chat and smoke and to drink tea. Then I went to the sentry and showed him my permit.

" That permit's no good. You want one from the High Commissaire."

I feigned stupidity.

" Commissaire, commissaire. Jawohl."

" Look here, you old fool. . ."

" How dare you insult a German subject !" thundered a man with the Red Cross brassard. " You can see that he can't talk Russian and that he's deaf besides. I will report you."

The sentry was terrified.

" I'm only asking to see his passport."

" You had much better ask whether his name is on the
list. That's much more reliable."

He shouted :

" This tall old man here, is he on the list ?"

" Yes, he is," shouted somebody. " Let him pass."

The man with the brassard seized my trunk and dragged
me with him. There we were on the train. The carriage
was clean and had beds laid out in it. I was laid on one of
them, fully dressed, and covered with a coarse blanket.
It was the compartment for the seriously ill. The train
started.

The man next me was a young man on the point of
death. He was clutching at his blanket with emaciated
hands which were white as chalk, and kept mumbling :
" Ida. . . I'm coming. . . Ida. . . I'm coming. . ."

That went on for some hours.

Then a sigh and he stiffened. He was dead. We came to
a station and stopped. Papers were to be examined
again and luggage. The sick began to moan : " Why
doesn't this torture come to an end ?"

" Opening our trunks again. There'll be nothing left."

" You've sucked our blood long enough, seems to be
the appropriate remark."

But the joke fell flat. Nobody felt like laughing. I
didn't feel like it either.

The moment had come which was to decide my fate ;
my heart beat as though it would burst but, curiously
enough, when the door opened and the crowd came in I
suddenly felt perfectly calm. My courage had returned.

I remained with closed eyes, stretched on my back,
and breathing with difficulty, clutching the blanket with
my hands. I had studied the part from the man next me

" Your keys and passport. Bestir yourself." The rustic pulled at my shoulder. I opened my eyes, looked at him with a glazed look and then shut them again :

" Trinken (water)."

" He is dying," said the man with the brassard. " You will have to take him out with the man who has just died."

" Take him out ? What are you talking about ? We wouldn't dream of it. It's not our business."

" Corpses mayn't be left on the train."

" We've got enough corpses as it is, old boy. We don't need any of yours."

" If you want corpses I'll let you have them at a reduced price, ten for five cigarettes."

" Even for three," said the first. " Quite fresh and warm from the incinerator. We've just been roasting them, they're still smoking."

" We can't keep dead men in the train."

" You don't like them ?"

" You ought to. . ."

" Enough said. Let's go and get out tea."

" Good evening, niemetz (Boche). Kind regards to William."

" Give him your two corpses from me. We'll send him the others by post."

And they went out roaring with laughter. The man with the brassard leant over me.

" Do you really want something to drink ?" he asked.

" No, thank you." I pressed his hand, and asked him whether it was over.

" They'll come again at Torochino. It won't be so easy to get rid of them there."

" When shall we get there ? "

" Not before eight in the morning. I'll bring you coffee at seven."

" Thank you."

I had a good sleep and woke up very hungry. When the coffee was brought I got out of my trunk the provisions which my wife had packed up and proceeded to have my breakfast. I had a whole hour to spare.

The door suddenly opened. A whole pack of them were there. The ruffians had got on to the train at the last station. It was impossible to pretend to be dead.

They consisted of two commissaires and some soldiers. One was a coarse brute who laughed all the time in an idiotic way. The other was an old card sharper; I recognised him at once. Before the Revolution he was always hanging about Witte's house.

" Your papers, please."

" Ha, ha, ha ! A hundred millions ? "

He looked at me with a bewildered expression.

The man with the brassard whispered to him. The commissaire burst out laughing.

" That's a good one ! So you are the famous Rothschild ? "

" Ha, ha, ha."

" We know the Rothschilds," said the card sharper. Get along, you. Stop pretending you're mad. It's no use pretending. Anyhow I've seen you before. Who are you ? "

" Baron Rothschild."

" I've had enough of this," and turning to the big commissaire, he said :

" I advise you to make him get off at Torochino and

v

put him in gaol. I've got other business but I'll be back in a few hours. We'll make this bourgeois talk."

The other man laughed.

" That's it ! We'll make him talk, we'll make him talk all right."

They left two soldiers behind and went off. Alas ! The man with the brassard had disappeared.

At Torochina a German train, full of soldiers, was standing on the line parallel to ours. I was told to get out. I saw the man who was looking after me getting back into the train. He did not even look at me and I was taken off. At the entrance to the station, a Prussian officer was speaking to the commissaire. As we passed he shouted :

" Halt !" My escort halted.

The officer looked me up and down and knocked my glasses off with his hand.

" So it's you, is it ? I recognised you by your figure. Don't say a word. You can make your explanations to the court martial. I know you : Müller, the escaped convict."

" It's false."

" Shut up."

Then he turned to the commissaire : " As this man is a prisoner of ours I'll take him back."

" Very well."

I was pushed into a truck with barred windows on the German train.

When the train had started the door opened and the Lieutenant came in.

" Your name ?" he asked.

I told him my name. The officer saluted.

" You have been recommended to us by our Embassy. I must apologise for having had to be so rough. It was the only way of getting you out of their clutches. Luckily that man was a fool. If the other man had been there you would have been done for. Will you kindly go to the Kommandatur at Pleskau."

Pleskau, Pskov as we used to call it, had already been given a German name. A lump came into my throat. The station was decked out in the German colours and the band played a Prussian military tune ; I was amongst men—and not amongst those animals.

I will now close. But I want this story, like all stories, to end with a moral. It's old-fashioned and it doesn't lead to anything—but I hold to it.

Besides, I don't want to be misunderstood.

I can imagine everybody saying : " Israel must pay for this with their blood. The day of vengeance will come."

The day of vengeance has already come. Israel has extorted capital and interest on the sufferings endured during centuries and, as always happens in these cases, it is not the really guilty but those who had nothing to do with it, who have had to pay. We have paid for our fathers and reaped what our predecessors have sown. The account is squared.

Let us forget nothing, let us pardon nothing, but let us be just. Let us have no mass judgment, no revenge and no reprisals. Punish the guilty, Jews or Christians— whichever they may be, but do not make the innocent suffer. Let us cease to be wild animals and become human beings again. It is high time we did so. Let force be guided by right.

And then, as in the old fairy tales, we shall live happily hereafter and have many children.

THE END